26⁹⁵

God in Proof

*The publisher gratefully acknowledges the generous
support of the General Endowment Fund
of the University of California Press Foundation.*

God in Proof

THE STORY OF A SEARCH
FROM THE ANCIENTS TO THE INTERNET

Nathan Schneider

UNIVERSITY OF CALIFORNIA PRESS

BERKELEY LOS ANGELES LONDON

University of California Press, one of the most distinguished university presses in the United States, enriches lives around the world by advancing scholarship in the humanities, social sciences, and natural sciences. Its activities are supported by the UC Press Foundation and by philanthropic contributions from individuals and institutions. For more information, visit www.ucpress.edu.

University of California Press
Berkeley and Los Angeles, California

Library of Congress Cataloging-in-Publication Data

Schneider, Nathan, 1984–.
  God in proof : the story of a search from the ancients to the Internet / Nathan Schneider.
    p.   cm.
  Includes bibliographical references and tabular index.
  ISBN 978–0–520–26907–1 (cloth : alk. paper)
  1. God—Proof.   I. Title.
  BL473.S36   2013
  212'.1—dc23   2012033541

Manufactured in the United States of America
22   21   20   19   18   17   16   15   14   13
10   9   8   7   6   5   4   3   2   1

In keeping with a commitment to support environmentally responsible and sustainable printing practices, UC Press has printed this book on Rolland Enviro100, a 100% post-consumer fiber paper that is FSC certified, deinked, processed chlorine-free, and manufactured with renewable biogas energy. It is acid-free and EcoLogo certified.

After all, everything is a consequence of inconsistent premises.

JON BARWISE AND JOHN ETCHEMENDY,
Language, Proof and Logic

CONTENTS

SKETCHES OF BABEL

One almost-gone afternoon in November, as I stepped out into what sun remained in the day, a proof for the existence of God took hold of me. I was a freshman in college and had just finished a meeting with a teaching assistant. The department house's heavy wooden door thudded shut behind me. Light; truth. A sensation flooded me with the semblance of logic, without the words to describe it or instructions to complete it. I still couldn't even say if I believed in a God or not. Yet there it was: a promissory note, at least, for propositions and definitions and conclusions to come, with the vowel-y echo in my ear of the word *proof.*

Hurrying down the steps and across campus, past the buildings standing at attention all around, I had no idea how to write my discovery down. Over the days and weeks that followed, sitting at a desk in my dorm room or under a winsome tree, I would start to think through its steps in words and sequence but then get stuck. Stuck—that's what I was, in more ways than one. The idea of a proof had caught me, or caught up to me. There was no turning back. After just a few months, I would be baptized a believer.

I didn't tell anyone about this strange, problematic, unsatisfying thought then, nor would I know what to say if I had. But the germ of a proof was in me, somewhere, treasurelike—a blueprint for my own Tower of Babel. Dissatisfaction urged me on. Every once in a while I'd try again to spell it out and get a little bit further, and then get frustrated. Did it make sense, or not? Was it

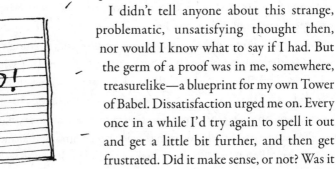

valid as logic, or even as a description of experience? I still can't say. Perhaps this book, a decade later, is one more attempt to be done with it.

The premise of Laurence Cossé's novel *A Corner of the Veil* is that someone discovers a proof of God's existence—a real proof, finally. A priest who has just seen it walks through the streets of Paris and looks at the people around him, imagining what it will be like when they, too, see what he has seen.

> Probably, for a time, everything would come to a halt. People wouldn't go to the office anymore. The children would be sent to school, but they'd stop along the way, caught up by great circles of orators in tears.
>
> People would talk on sidewalks, in the Métro, at church doors. Ah, the priests wouldn't know where to start! People would talk for hours in the rain. Neighbors who had always eyed each other with suspicion would be talking to each other. Couples ten years separated would phone each other from distant places.
>
> The post office would stay closed. There would be a notice on the gate: HALLELUJAH. On the other hand, the museums would never close again, nor the Métro, nor the public parks. The guards would never figure out where their caps had disappeared to.
>
> For days it would feel like a kind of general strike, a huge drunken spree.[1]

Isn't this what we should rightfully expect of a proof? To claim, as a proof of God does, such certainty and finality about so exalted a thing should warrant nothing less than ecstasy. And some people do say there is proof. So why does this scene only come in a daydream, in a work of fiction?

Some will object to talking about proof at all. They'll say that any absolute or mathematical proof for God sets the bar too high, or too low. Instead, call it argument, or demonstration—or call it faith. But *proof* fits the story I'm trying to tell like no other word.

The Latin root is *probare,* which has to do with testing something to see if it's any good. It used to be more common to speak about proving as a kind of experience, something one has to go through or even suffer—as in, to prove oneself. Proving meant becoming, or growing. A thing proved might be a trip that turned out well, or well enough, or even just with you intact and unsullied. That's why we call a jacket waterproof when water can't get through. And that's part of what a proof for God promises to offer: a seal on every seam, an answer to every question, a rampart for every flank.

The remnants of these meanings have spread among the trades. Proofing dough is making it rise. Printers, engravers, and photographers all have their proofs, just as armies have their proving grounds. Lawyers look for proof in evidence. And distillers speak of proof as a mixture whose volume is 0.5727 pure alcohol—which would be an experience in itself.

So, yes, primarily what I mean by *proof* is the 1933 *Oxford English Dictionary*'s definition I.1:

> That which makes good or proves a statement; evidence sufficient (or contributing) to establish a fact or produce belief in the certainty of something.

And more. With every "that which makes good" comes a story, a test, a sojourn. Like a baker's proof, it forces one to grow a little, and, like a printer's, it won't always come out right the first time. Like the distiller's, it can be exhilarating. We can only hope that our proofs, like a good jacket, will hold up on rainy days.

The search for proofs of God's existence is its own genre, winding through history and sprouting capricious branches. Like any genre, from impressionist painting to romance novels, proof has never spoken for any whole society. It's rarely anyone's sole occupation, but still it has occupied some of history's most brilliant men.

I do mean *men*. As it happens, the genre comes to us through history as almost entirely an undertaking of men, making this story, by implication, a study of masculinity. It's a story of what a communion mostly of male minds has fashioned through this ongoing conversation over thousands of years, with their arguments speaking to each other more than to those around them, but more to those around them than they realize. It's also about what ideas they, thanks to whom they exclude, leave out.

These men have had big ambitions for their proofs. Plato thought that proofs of the gods might finally set his society right, that he could reform criminals just by reciting them. Ibn Tufayl, a Muslim in medieval Spain, imagined a proof powerful enough to soothe away the will to live. The Jewish heretic Spinoza turned a venerable proof for God into one for an apparently godless universe. Descartes and Leibniz intended their proofs to heal the rift that the Reformation had driven through Europe. And the genre continues today, as much as ever, if

not more. In Turkey, I met a man trying to bring peace to the Middle East through proofs of divine beauty in nature. I've spent weeks driving around the suburbs of Southern California, from storefront to storefront, visiting organizations that promulgate one proof or another. I've attended classes by William Lane Craig, God's most fearsome advocate on today's debating circuit, and sat down with his archnemesis, Richard Dawkins. They're all out to rejigger the world and themselves and us in the process.

So how exactly is it that some people think that they can prove God exists, or doesn't, and why do others fall short? How did ancient arguments transform into an outgrowth of the culture wars? Why is it that for some of us everything depends on these proofs, while for others they're completely beside the point? These questions of *we* then throw themselves back on *me* again. I've had to think about abstractions and my own very real life in tandem.

The proofs show up in textbook after textbook, torn away from the flesh from which they came.[2] They're taught, argued about, and forgotten, sometimes saving a person's particular faith, sometimes eroding it, and usually neither. There's no surer way of knowing than proof, by definition, and it's hard to imagine any more enticing knowledge than that of a God. Still, the world goes on in disagreement, in belief and unbelieving, with so many forms of each. Some few keep up the search for proof of a God, and for the hallelujahs that would surely come from finding one. While tracing their steps, though, I keep getting stuck trying to figure what God we're talking about, what existence might mean, and what, exactly, we expect from a proof. My own proof has never become much more than a possibility and an expectation, but that hasn't kept it from commandeering my life.

First Causes

ANCIENT TIMES AND REASONABLE MEASURES

The first time I remember thinking about proofs for the existence of God was when I was seventeen, thanks to a book I came across at my friend Corinne's house. It was muddy green and fairly large—an encyclopedic, spirited compendium of things about which one should know. The proofs took up no more than a couple of pages, and they weren't cast in an especially favorable light. They were more like a centuries-old joke, actually, a joke that one should be prepared for just in case anyone ever tries passing them off as anything other than that. One should be ready for the punch line.

The book listed and summarized three proofs, each hiding behind impressive names: *ontological, cosmological, teleological*—having to do with being, world, and purpose. I instantly became attached to it and went about dropping hints to Corinne that it would the perfect present for my upcoming birthday. But the message didn't seem to get through. Why would it? How could she guess what effect it was having on me? How could she know what those proofs felt like in my head?

I had spent my childhood watching my parents as they did their own experiments with, if not proof, truth. As they went about the business of seeking, I followed, tiptoeing through rooms full of meditators and testing my aptitude—low, it turns out—for extrasensory perception. My mother, especially, sought out teachers and books, and there was an ongoing procession of diet regimes. These experiments could involve some reference to God, but it was a God of the vaguest sort, whose name my parents were sure to pass over quickly so as not to confuse it with the Jewish and Christian deities that they had learned, and disavowed, before I was born.

The premise from the start was that I should choose what to believe about religious things, since they were still choosing for themselves. For an only child this was bound to be a lonely task, but I took to it early on. I would ask to go to synagogue with friends, and deploy parables of the Buddha during fights on the playground. One can only experiment so much though. "There are years that ask questions," Zora Neale Hurston wrote in passing, "and years that answer."[1] By the time Corinne's book came around, a need was gnawing in me for answers, and no answer seemed more satisfying than a proof.

Philosophy, when it takes hold of a teenager, means taking oneself very seriously on matters of gross incompetence. There are no minor leagues, no lower gears; one goes straight from zero to everything in no time, and the most alluring stuff is exactly the most fundamental and the most lofty, just when one is least prepared to take any of it with a grain of salt. Even so, and consequently, there's no better time than adolescence to fall in love with philosophy, or to develop an intellectual dependency on it. Neither love nor addiction occurs when one is being sensible. They thrive on heroic feats of self-delusion and clever rationalization, and so does philosophy.

Causes, though, can be a trickster. What causes what? How and why? What really caused me to care about these proofs so much, and where did the proofs come from in the first place? Talking about the cause of anything is harder than you might think.

It's conventional, in this case, to start with the Greeks. I wish I could do otherwise, for originality's sake. But while those -ological terms I came across were a later invention, their etymology is Greek, and for good reason. Without exactly meaning to, the ancient Greeks were the ones who caused the whole story of proofs to happen, or at least to happen the way it did.

The kind of Greek religion I had been briefly obsessed with in fifth grade had no place for proofs—the myths, the temples, the heroes, the cavorting. People had reasons for believing in the gods of Mount Olympus other than proofs. Homer's verses of deities and warrior-kings uniting in the siege against Troy reminded the disparate Greek city-states of what they had in common. Hesiod's tales told lessons about morality and economy, together with answers to questions about the universe, and one could repeat them to seduce a lover or to scold a misbehaving child. The public sacrifices made to these gods were carefully orchestrated affairs, and the role one played in them reflected one's position in society.[2] The gods were real—or else. And while public ritual served politics and epic myths made for literature, so-called mystery cults allowed people to go deeper. There were illustrations in the books I read as a kid of people gathered in caves or dark rooms, conducting rituals and repeating secret doctrines said to have been conferred by a patron god. These mystery cults provided transformative experiences. Through them, ancient Greeks knew that esoteric knowledge can have spiritual power.

Then, around the middle of the first millennium B.C.E., a new batch of sages, students, and charlatans appeared, many from the Greek colonies across the Mediterranean. They converged at Athens, calling themselves philosophers—lovers of wisdom. Rather than ritual, voice, and memory, their tools were prose, writing, and reason. Instead of glorifying the human body, as Olympian religion did, the body became a prison for the thinking soul to escape. Their method was *logos,* a term with meanings as diverse as those who used it: word, reason, logic, mind. They departed from the capricious gods and the rituals of popular religion, but they shared the mystery cults' appetite for powerful knowledge and the poets' willingness to dream up stories about invisible things. They made myths of their own out of proofs.

∴

One of the first proofs most of us encounter in school is that for the Pythagorean theorem, which deals with the lengths of the sides on a right triangle. It is as good a place to start as any; proofs of a God will come soon enough. Pythagoras of Samos probably didn't discover the theorem that bears his name, though he and his followers certainly studied it. The legend goes that after fleeing his home island of Samos in the Aegean, Pythagoras had a restless youth, studying with Egyptian masters and being taken as a prisoner to Babylon. Both civilizations had sophisticated mathematics to support their architectural ambitions, so young Pythagoras learned from the best. He encountered ideas from as far away as South and East Asia. Then he

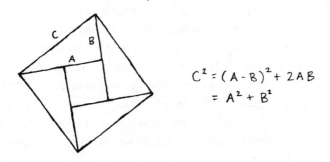

$$C^2 = (A - B)^2 + 2AB$$
$$= A^2 + B^2$$

finally settled in the Greek colonies of southern Italy and gained a following. The ancient sources don't give a consistent account of what exactly he believed, but they show clearly enough that he reveled in a world of majestic comprehensibility, plus a fair amount of strangeness.

He preached, for instance, the transmigration of souls—that people's spirits could be reincarnated in the bodies of animals. To avoid harming their ancestors, therefore, Pythagoreans wouldn't eat meat or beat a disobedient dog. Like the Zoroastrians in Persia, they believed that the world is locked in a contest between light and darkness, good and evil. Pythagorean communities were the monasteries of the ancient world, holding property in common and living by a rigid code. Several centuries after Pythagoras, Iamblichus of Chalcis wrote, "The aim of all the Pythagorean precision about what should and should not be done is association with the divine. This is their starting-point, and their way of life has been wholly organized with a view to following God."[3] To them, the evil in the world was the imprecise and the uncertain, which is why math was so important. Again, Iamblichus: "The Pythagoreans devoted themselves to mathematics and admired the accuracy of its reasonings, because it alone among human activities knows of proofs."[4]

Most mathematical proofs in those days took form in pictures of abstract shapes; the algebraic notation we use now wasn't invented yet. The Pythagoreans considered these pictures sacred, combining geometry and mystery cult in a single scientific-religious mélange. The correspondence between mathematical ratios and musical scales especially fascinated Pythagoras. He believed that the movements of the stars and planets make a beautiful sound, playing always, which we don't notice only because we've been hearing it our entire lives.

The idea of mixing mathematics with mythology seems odd to us today. We memorize formulas, use them to do problem sets, and forget most of it when the test is over. But that's not the way mathematics was, and continues to be, created. It's a foray into the unknown that borders on mysticism. Polls suggest that among scientists mathematicians are most likely to believe in a God.[5] Maybe spending one's life immersed in abstractions makes a divine mind seem more plausible. But I wouldn't really be one to know.

Math didn't come easily to me growing up. My father did his best to help. For a time in middle school, I would wake up each morning and find waiting for me a paper with a set of problems in his delicate, hieroglyphic handwriting. But math problems were the last thing I wanted to do in my first waking minutes, and downstairs I would hand them to him with dashed-off answers, if any.

Dad was a real estate agent—of heroic ability, as his clients have always told me. Work kept him out late, and he would eventually come in the front door with a pile of papers in his arms, topped by a clunky old HP-12C calculator. His mind seemed like a calculator too. Given a date, he could instantly say how old somebody was at the time; given a price, he would produce the tax or interest as if by reflex. He always counted steps as he walked up and down them, automatically and insuppressibly. If it weren't for him telling me that each flight in our house had eight steps, on dark nights I would have been content to feel each with my sock to tell if it was the last.

A hobby of Dad's was to make family trees of English royalty with his computer. They became dot-matrix murals that covered the long wall of his study. He had traveled to castles and cathedrals, and he would tell wonderful stories about them over dinner if something got him started. We had no blood of Stuarts or Hanovers or Windsors ourselves, of course, but they became a sort of extended family.

As I was getting ready for bed, I might hear him singing part of a Verdi aria, accompanying himself on the piano, and after he went silent, if I crept out of bed, I would see him lying on the couch with headphones on. Maybe this time it was Wagner, or Puccini. On other nights he would ramble around the backyard in the dark, planning the next part of his garden.

In high school geometry, math finally started to become something I could wrap my mind around; we started learning about proofs. We learned how to construct arguments from basic principles. All of a sudden math class was not simply a matter of calculating, but of discovering, and my attitude about it changed entirely. I took calculus my senior year and felt the exhilaration of late-night group study sessions, when the solution to a problem would finally come loose for us after hours of tugging at it from every direction. We learned to derive important theorems, masterpieces that had been composed in great minds of centuries past, and then used those theorems to derive more. In physics class, we used the math to predict the motion of tangible objects. I worked my way twice through a floppy paperback of Einstein's *Relativity*. Like the correspondence Pythagoreans found between mathematics and musical scales, Einstein's equations declared that the universe is not what it seems.

Around the time Pythagoras died, at the beginning of the fifth century B.C.E., another Greek thinker of strange notions and lasting influence was born, also in southern Italy. Like Pythagoras, Parmenides of Elea treaded in the brackish region between religion and philosophy, myth and logos, and politics. The laws he established in Elea survived him by five hundred years. He wrote his treatise in the form of a poem, though its verses strain to accommodate their meticulousness. They seem ready to burst into prose at any moment. As did the epic poets, he attributed his inspiration to the whispers of a goddess who opened his eyes and moved his pen. But like the philosophers he strove to make no claim without reasons.

The goddess guided him to divide his poem into two parts: the Way of Truth and the Way of Appearance. The second is a compendium of what he takes to be false opinions that people have about the world; it resembles Pythagoreanism. The first is an all-out attack on common sense, in the name of banishing logical contradiction. Nothing, Parmenides claims, cannot exist. Everything conceivable exists, unchangeably, eternally, in perfect unity, and in the shape of a sphere. What we see in the world that appears to change, to cease to exist, and to differ from other things is all illusion. That anything could not exist is a contradiction; if you conceive of a thing not existing, it then exists in the very conception. In this weird way, the goddess gets him to trust his mind before his eyes. Thoughts are the reality of the world, and logic is its native language.

Among his fellow Greek sages, such totalizing notions were commonplace. Thales claimed that everything is really water, Anaximenes said everything is air, and Heraclitus answered that everything is like an ever-burning fire. Parmenides was different; a century and a half later, a commentator named Eudemus wrote, "Parmenides would not agree with anything unless it seemed necessary, whereas his predecessors used to come up with unsubstantiated assertions."[6]

Human minds make imperfect looms for pure reason. Even when such careful thinking doesn't turn into an affront to the obvious, as it did for him, it gets tangled up often enough. Philosophy, for me, started to be of interest after forcing myself to go cold turkey on a years-long obsession with *Star Trek* and the show's vision of a future made better by human reason. Yet the words of Spock to a precocious younger Vulcan in *Star Trek VI* seem apropos here: "Logic is the beginning of wisdom, Valeris, not the end." Behind them, in Spock's quarters, hung a Marc Chagall painting of Adam and Eve's expulsion from Paradise.

∴

A hundred years after Parmenides, in the early fourth century B.C.E., the young Plato arrived in Syracuse, Sicily. Athens had only recently executed Socrates, his obstreperous mentor, and Plato had already earned a reputation as a sage in his own right. In Syracuse, he began what would be a decades-long entanglement with the royal court in an attempt to test his ideas in practice, to put philosophy in charge of a whole society. There, he came into contact with followers of Pythagoras and Parmenides, who lived not far away on the boot of Italy, and kneaded their philosophies into his own. If there's any doubt about the place of abstract reason, of logos, in Plato's mind, one need only recall the sign over the door to the Academy he founded, just outside the walls of Athens: LET NO ONE IGNORANT OF GEOMETRY ENTER.

Plato, like his predecessors, taught that genuine Truth and Reason—capital *T* and capital *R*—aren't to be found in the visible world. Instead, he believed there are higher "forms," or "ideas": eternal, unchanging, and perfect molds from which the stuff that surrounds us is cast. The *Timaeus,* a dialogue written forty years after his teacher's death, is Plato's most ambitious effort to explain the nature of the universe. And there is a proof in it for the semblance of a God, culled from habits of mind he learned in Italy and in the Athenian agora.

Look around. Everything in the world is always changing and becoming. Then, look inside your mind, to mathematics, logic, shapes, abstractions. These never change. They're among the ideal forms, fixed inalterably in the universe's structure. Among the temporal and the passing, notice something else: everything must have a cause. If it exists, and once did not exist, it was created somehow. The dialogue's main speaker, after whom the *Timaeus* is named, surmises that there must be a divine creator who makes the world according to a blueprint of preexisting forms. He calls this creator *dēmiourgos,* meaning "craftsman" or "common worker," but its nature and identity remain mostly a mystery: "The father and maker of all this universe is past finding out; and even if we found him, to tell of him to all men would be impossible."[7] If anything can be learned about the creator, it will be through esoteric proofs, accessible only to philosophers.

I learned about Plato's forms from my first philosophy teacher, Ken Knisley, a taxi driver who occasionally taught elective classes at my high school. He had untamable curly hair and a matching beard, ringed with the beads of sweat brought on by his full-body gestures. He also had a show on community access TV, on which he wore a navy blue jumpsuit that said

PHILOSOPHER on the breast—except when he wore a toga to act out Plato's famous cave allegory.

We all live, says Plato, as if we're prisoners in a cave. There is a fire at our backs, casting the shadows of objects on the wall before us. Truth is something we're unaccustomed to seeing; we see just shadows. Visible, transitory things are reflections of an invisible reality.

What, then, would happen if a prisoner of the cave escaped and climbed up into the sunlight? There, he finds an entirely new kind of light, blinding him at first. With time, though, the prisoner looks up from the shadows and objects and reflections to the sun itself: "He will contemplate him"—this sun god—"as he is."

> He will then proceed to argue that this is he who gives the season and the years, and is the guardian of all that is in the visible world, and in a certain way the cause of all things which he and his fellows have been accustomed to behold.[8]

That sun stands for the Good, the highest of the forms, whose light shines on everything that is True, with a capital T.

It was in Ken's classes that I first felt the tug of exalted ideas. We read philosophers supposedly too difficult for us, and he pushed us to give an account of ourselves in terms of them. Some days, he would forget the assigned text entirely and, in amazement, tell us stories about his toddler son. He taught the pleasure and the payoff of thinking, and the responsibility each of us has to seek out undying truth. The upshot: I had a job to do, to figure out the universe for myself.

The philosophy that Ken offered was one of meaning in the face of meaninglessness. Instead of biblical salvation, we learned about Greek drinking parties and German angst. Mention of God would sneak into our discussions only because of how the existentialists mourned God's death. These readings certainly suited my emotional state. For one homework assignment, I composed a distortion-drenched, power-chord song on my guitar to accompany a passage from Nietzsche's *Thus Spoke Zarathustra*. When I put my recording in the cassette player, Ken leaped to the front of the room and started reciting the text with appropriate vigor: "One must have chaos within oneself to give birth to a dancing star!"

Some years later, I learned that Ken had died of cancer without much warning. Later still, I came across a makeshift online eulogy, tacked to the comments of a blog he had started in his last days. A friend of his captured a bit of Plato's eternal forms when she wrote there, "Some conversations, some ideas, really deserve to continue, even when the person who started them . . . ends."[9] The shadows of human life pass away, but the ideas that we wrestle with never do. Ken would have liked that. But he also refused the consolation of pure ideas. He titled the blog's first and only post "No Abstraction."

Plato may have looked to ideas beyond, too, but he did so in this-worldly ways. He wrote down his philosophy in dialogues, conversations among people seeking after truths together. For him philosophizing was inseparable from the love between fellow seekers, between student and teacher, and among friends. Through discussion, one's soul investigates itself. It thinks about thinking. By reaching for eternal ideas, beyond the cave of the material world, human souls can touch divinity.[10] A conversation among philosophers is a council of gods. That was another thing I learned first from Ken: the pleasure of philosophy when done with others. He taught us what was in books, but he also made us his friends. The off-topic talk about his son was on-topic after all.

Near the end of his life, Plato lost faith in the utopian projects that had brought him to Sicily; the Syracusan kings turned out to be irredeemable tyrants. His final, unfinished book, the *Laws,* describes a city that would be "second best" to perfection, though more realistic in practice. Socrates, who appears in most of Plato's dialogues, is absent in the *Laws.* It's noticeable, and unsettling, as if Plato felt that the teacher of his youth—capitally punished on the charge of impiety—might disapprove.

While his earlier books tended to handle the traditional gods ambiguously, even playfully, here they have a very serious job to do. Plato tells us, in chapter 10 of the *Laws,* that the root of all crime in society is disbelief in the existence, attention, or integrity of the gods. It's that simple. "No one who in obedience to the laws believed that there were gods," he writes, "ever intentionally did any unholy act, or uttered any unlawful word."[11] Lawbreakers, therefore, should endure not only regular punishment for their crimes; they must also listen to lectures containing proofs of the existence and significance of the gods. One of the first recorded instances of proof for divine beings, it seems, is as a correctional device.

Speaking on behalf of civic order, Plato's Athenian Stranger sounds tired and impatient. He complains, "Who can be calm when he is called upon to prove the existence of the gods? Who can avoid hating and abhorring the men who are and have been the cause of this argument?" He complains about the impertinence of these common criminals "who will not believe the tales which they have heard as babes and sucklings from their mothers and nurses," and who therefore must be subjected to philosophy. Still, Plato allows, "the attempt must be made."[12]

His first two arguments for the existence of the gods are terse and hurried; the first is from the order of the natural world, and the second is from the fact that people of all cultures seem to be in general agreement.

> In the first place, the earth and the sun, and the stars and the universe, and the fair order of the seasons, and the division of them into years and months, furnish proofs of their existence; and also there is the fact that all Hellenes and barbarians believe in them.[13]

Later on, the Athenian Stranger unveils a more detailed argument, which relies on the nature of motion.

There are ten kinds of motion, he explains, but only one, the motion of a living soul, doesn't depend on being moved by something else. A soul—the soul of an immaterial god—must therefore have been the first motion of all. (Actually, there must be at least two such souls: one causing good order and another causing erratic evil.) "And judging from what has been said," Plato concludes, "there would be impiety in asserting that any but the most perfect soul or souls carries round the heavens."[14] These souls, as human souls must, obey the eternal laws of the universe—which include the laws of the city. When you believe in such gods, you can't help but believe in the city's laws too.

For the earlier Plato, arguments about the gods were a matter of pleasurable, rational speculation, a conversation among philosophers. Here, proofs are servants to the social order. But the underlying idea is the same: pure reason is what rules the world, not the whims of an Olympian soap opera. As Frederick Copleston puts it in his canonical history of philosophy, "'Atheist' means for Plato, first and foremost, the man who denies the operation of Reason in the world."[15] It is a definition that might rub many actual atheists nowadays the wrong way. What's more, in the eyes of his own society, it was Plato who could seem like an atheist for exchanging the meddlesome gods of the poets for law-abiding, reasonable ones. But others, in the centuries to come, would conclude he must have had inspiration from above.

∴

When I was in middle school, my parents decided that we should begin taking family trips to Europe. Planned summer activities were unfortunately a doomed proposition where I was concerned; I hated every summer camp I was ever sent to, and being stuck with my parents, together with whichever grand-parents could come along, was sure to bring out the brat in me, and it did.

Each trip had some special significance. Paris, for one, gave my mother a chance to revisit the years she had spent in France studying medieval French epics. Germany, I found when we got there, was my father's turn. He had taken German as a student and spent a summer hunting down in situ altar-pieces by the medieval sculptor Tilman Riemenschneider. (He was able to show me why, at a fortuitous exhibition in Munich: faces with joy disguised in melancholy.) His choice to go there, and to learn that language, was espe-cially rebellious for someone coming from a post-Holocaust Jewish family, as he did, that avoided buying German-made things.

The idea of a trip to Italy came from my father's mother, but a last-minute medical mishap prevented her from coming. In Florence, Venice, and Rome, we did what you would expect; we went to a lot of museums and churches. The churches were especially a problem because there was one around every corner, and it was hard (for everyone but me) to resist going inside. It turned out, though, that my parents were really good at visiting churches. They stayed away from the tour groups and found some piece of art that even I would have to admit was interesting, especially when one of them explained it to me. They were still always too slow. But even through my boredom I got the message: *Something about this is important.*

The day in Italy I have the hardest time forgetting was when we went to Vatican City, mainly because of its unpleasantness. The crowds are over-whelming—thousands of people from who-knows-where who mostly only care to see the Sistine Chapel, yet have to soldier through nearly the entire Vatican Museums on the way. Until, that is, they find something that catches them, something they've seen in books a million times and are pleased and surprised—once they push through the huddle of others around it—to encounter the real thing. One of those is relevant here. It's Raphael's fresco *The School of Athens,* on the wall behind you and to the left, as I recall, when you enter the Apostolic Palace's Room of the Segnatura.

Among the many heroes of ancient thought that the fresco gathers under marble arches, Plato and Aristotle stand at the center. They are side by side, with the younger Aristotle slightly to the fore of white-bearded Plato. They speak with their gestures. Plato holds the *Timaeus* to his body and points his right index finger to the sky. Aristotle, who was once Plato's student, looks back at the master and, balancing his *Ethics* outward against his thigh, holds the palm of his hand toward the earth.

This is the standard caricature of the two prototypical philosophers: Plato sought truth and order in the utopian clouds, while Aristotle cataloged marine life on the shores of the Aegean. For both, however, the cosmos is basically rational, mathematical, teachable, and learnable. They preferred clear argumentation to epic poetry and believed in a truth higher than the gods of temples and legends. The job of their philosophy was to seek after that truth, that universal reason. They had no scripture, bishops, or savior, yet still their God would land them in the heart of the popes' palace centuries after they had died.

The foundation of Aristotle's philosophy is the system of logic that, for almost two thousand years, provided Europe with its definition of reason. His best-known principle is the syllogism, the basic unit of deduction and proof, whereby a conclusion can be safely and inescapably drawn from accepted premises. Take the simple example that philosophy students inevitably encounter:

1) Socrates is a man.
2) All men are mortal.
3) Therefore, Socrates is mortal.

This kind of reasoning promised to escape the flaws of human bias, frailty, and confusion, lending authority to all that he wrote. If he can be trusted with logic, why not trust what he says about the universe?

Building on the logical works are Aristotle's theories of physics and what came to be called metaphysics—literally, "what comes after physics." Aristotelian cosmology eventually ascends to a divine being he claimed to know neither by faith nor tradition but exclusively by thinking.

Like Plato's *Laws,* Aristotle begins with a meditation on movement in the world. One thing moves another. Moving things form a chain reaction of causes and effects and effects becoming causes, a churning and eternal cycle. There was no beginning; motion cannot have come from nonmotion, he reasons, so the universe must always have existed, always in motion. But every motion has to be caused by something. This is important. Wisdom, says Aristotle, is knowledge of causes.

The sequence of things causing other things cannot be infinitely long, however, even if it goes on eternally; you can turn a chain necklace round and round your neck but only because it has a finite number of links. Aristotle held that an infinite number of anything is impossible, for any number of things will still be less than infinity. Besides, if you start counting infinitely many causes away, you'll never reach the effect. So if there's a finite number of causes, one of them has to be first, and it holds all the others in place. To stay on your neck, a necklace needs to have a clasp.

The journey upward, through the sequence of causes he finds in the world, brings Aristotle past the stars and planets. He takes them to be the eternal gods hinted at in the myths of tradition, going about their orbits in perfect order, forever. When he reaches what moves them, the journey comes to its destination: that which is also eternal but eternally unmoved by anything else. He wonders, in a tangent, whether there could be many such beings (47 or 49, or maybe 55) but concludes not, repeating a line from the *Iliad:* "Too many kings are bad—let there be one!"[16]

This unmoved mover isn't simply the finger pushing over the first in a line of dominoes at the beginning of time. This mover—call it God—is the whole purpose of the whole game, through all eternity. It's the final cause of everything, though never by physically, materially acting on the world. As every domino falls, this is the overriding reason, the gravity. While "all other things move by being moved," Aristotle explains, the first and final cause isn't moved by anything else, even while it moves everything. It "produces motion as being loved."[17] His God is pure thought, pure purpose, and the sum of all that the universe aspires to.

This is a God mired in the daunting system of the theories, definitions, and assumptions of Aristotle's entire corpus, veiled from the uninitiated like the secrets of a mystery religion. And for what? There can be no friendship between people and God, and there is no need to bother with prayer or worship. Though Aristotle describes God as a soul something like human souls, it doesn't condescend to commune with us. Though it acts as the benevolent governor of the natural order, it offers no hope of special miracles.

What, then, does God do? The most perfect thing one could do, says Aristotle: God thinks. But God can't think about just anything. This perfect God can only think about what is perfect. "Therefore," he concludes, "it must be of itself that the divine thought thinks, since it is the most excellent of things, and its thinking is a thinking on thinking."[18] With this formulation comes the ultimate apotheosis of the philosophers' logos culture, a mind without a body, a self-thinking thought. At least so far as we mortals can know, this God *is* proof and nothing else.

∴

The Gospel of John, written toward the end of the first century, starts out this way: "In the beginning was the *logos,* and the *logos* was with God, and the *logos* was God." It is a passage, with *logos* translated as "Word," that I first discovered in high school, in the pages of an old King James Bible my mother had been given by her father in his late-life pious phase—compact and quaintly illustrated, between beige leather covers that could zipper closed. These peculiar phrases caught me with their poetry and what I could make of their meaning. Recalling the first words of Genesis, the act of creation, the language of John's Gospel implies that the whole fabric of the universe is reason, language, and logic—what the Greek philosophers were talking about. I kept reading more and more from the Bible and its exotic promises. A few verses later: "Behold the Lamb of God, which taketh away the sin of the world!"[19]

A problem with trying to record this "history of my religious opinions"— in John Henry Newman's phrase, betraying the narcissism of the task—is that they disappear. I began keeping a journal only a few days after my sixteenth birthday, which is the beginning of a record that can confirm or deny what fragments I actually remember. It started as an assignment in my first writing class. At night, before bed, I would sit with that spiral-bound blue notebook and do battle against the pages, scribbling one claim and denying it a sentence later, or twisting what was at first dead serious into a bad joke. I had something to say that only writing could draw out—something important, it felt like—but I didn't know what yet. Day after day I tried.

God was a question I kept clear of at first. When forced to consider religion by something I had read or seen, the sentences became even more contorted than usual. Once, I went to a concert at a local Baptist church with a friend and wrote, *I felt like we had just entered hostile territory.* But the place reminded me, if only by contrast, of a thick book I had just read and barely understood, *The Brothers Karamazov.* I remembered some things the monk Zosima said about his love for his God. *Maybe they should read this shit,* I cussed. *Believe in it or not, it is as true as anything could ever be.* What in the book is true exactly, or how, I don't say.

One of the very earliest entries I find in my journals opens bluntly: *Today, my parents told me they are separating.* They had brought me to my father's office in the basement of our house to say so. I sat in the squeaky leather chair and listened as my father, mainly, talked from the far corner of the room and my mother, beside me, mainly stayed silent. That night my world bifurcated.

This was on top of the already shaky foundations of an uncomfortable body, an erratic mind, and the malaise of suburban life. I wrote about having this feeling of "skin hurting"—*when I feel like there's absolutely nothing I can do to make my life bearable again.* It came and went, without warning or good reason, except adolescence. It's a story familiar to many of us in this generation, we "millennials": two houses, lonely neighborhoods, and the feeling of being at the mercy of forces beyond our understanding. From initial conditions like these, spelled out in the details of each particular case, each of us has our own story. Really—divorce or not, millennial or not—nobody evades this basic problem: out of the multitude of stage sets, other people, and stray ideas, a person must be made and a mind must be made up.

I could recognize myself in that word from John's Gospel, *sin;* it was my private shame about one thing or another, and the universal but surprisingly difficult process of discovering that I was a mess. Through all this, I wrote and wrote in my journal. *I've been playing with ideas of sin,* I recorded one day. I never liked to say anything too specific, for fear of who might someday read it, but you can imagine. Religious words started becoming a code to myself. *In confession, in absolution, and in starting anew I am recognizing with every moment my sins and my failures and my own cruelty to myself in expectation and of the world*—and so on. These pages are tough going. *Why do I burn so unsatisfied?* I beg. *I cannot imagine what satisfaction I require, what could possibly soothe my desires, what could bring me some peace.*

I wasn't sure I believed in God, exactly, but I could say "God" this and "God" that, writing to the word, with it, and through it. God, as logos, was a word before becoming a being or a belief. It was infinite love, the opposite of that irrepressible sin. Somehow the theological idiom started to work. It gave me a license to forgive myself that I didn't have otherwise, and to keep trying to be better. Scattered pieces of thoughts coalesced into sense, and into sentences, making the entries gradually more readable to my eye today. It was as if John's promise were coming true; there really was hope against sin to be found in a certain divine Word and, through it, a means of expression.

In early Christianity, Greek philosophy found both a challenger and a new lease on life. This new religion had one God (kind of like Aristotle's unmoved mover) who created the world (kind of like Plato's dēmiourgos) and promises eternal life (as, much of the time, did Plato). It became a popular speculation that the pagan philosophers, aided by the divine logos, must somehow have perceived the truth that Christ would reveal. But philosophy alone was not sufficient.

"Jews demand signs and Greeks desire wisdom," the apostle Paul wrote to his followers in the Greek city of Corinth, "but we proclaim Christ crucified."[20] *So there,* he's saying, *love unto death.* The image is shocking. It's hard to do ordinary philosophy with a bloodied and tortured and executed God, one who forgave his executioners, who commands us to love our enemies. This is seemingly unthinkable. Yet, for Paul, "We have the mind of Christ."[21] Mind, logos—he's preaching philosophy, crucified. Its first axiom is that act of self-sacrifice, made out of love.

∴

The new Christian synthesis found decisive expression in Augustine of Hippo, a fourth- and fifth-century North African bishop. He would become the most influential theologian of Latin Christendom. Augustine ended up placing grace-given faith on a pedestal above reason, but he didn't do so for lack of thinking. In his *Confessions,* we meet a man who searches for truth through intellectual mazes, reading this, hearing that, and discussing this. Before becoming a Christian, Augustine had been a follower of

Manicheanism, whose adherents professed to believe about God o
could be known through reason. But after meeting the famous M;
leader Faustus, Augustine decided this claim was a fraud. "Notl
wrote, "would remain stable in human society if we determined t
only what can be held with absolute certainty."[22] Life cannot be lived by
proof alone.

The *Confessions* itself attests to this. It takes ideas seriously but refuses
to wrest them from personal history. It begins with his childhood and ends
with a commentary on Genesis. Memories mix with a treatise about memory.
He comes to his God by seeing what is so fragile and disordered in himself.
Sound familiar? I can't help but imitate it.

In one essay, "Concerning Faith of Things Not Seen," Augustine compares
believing in an unseen God to trusting a friend. We trust our friends because
we want to and have to, before we really know they're as good as their word.
If we didn't, they would have no chance to prove themselves. "And thus," he
writes, "when you commit yourself in order to prove, you believe before you
prove."[23] He wanted to tame the longing for proof, to temper it.

This doesn't mean, though, that there's nothing to go on at all. In *The Free
Choice of the Will,* he offers something more like an actual, and actually quite
detailed, argument for God's existence.[24] It's written as a dialogue. Like
Plato's cave, it takes the light of the sun as a metaphor for the one truth—and
good and beauty—that illuminates the world. This truth must be a reality
higher than any human mind, everlasting and unchanging. He reflects on
numbers, on how arithmetic is the same for everybody. And on wisdom,
which chooses what is more perfect over what is less. Plato would be nodding
at every step. Augustine goes on to talk about the pleasure of discovering the
truth that is highest and most perfect, and how truth is our guide to happiness. This universal truth, he says, is God.

He seems to like the proof, and even rejoices at the end of it—but only for
a moment. Ultimately, he doesn't want a religion made of proofs. There's no
Christ in there, for one thing; one must hold to Christ by faith, Augustine
instructs. Human reason has limits, and it depends above all on divine revelation and grace. Christians before and after him therefore had to worry that
proofs might be a sin against humility, against the proper posture of human
beings before their crucified God.

The major character in the *Confessions,* besides Augustine himself, is his
mother, Monica. She was a Christian and hoped that her wayward son would
become one too. He finally did convert while far away in Italy, where his

thoughts caught up with her influence; Monica was made a saint for the role she played in his conversion. But she didn't lead him by proofs—instead, by her faith, her love, and those powers and pressures that only a mother can exert. It turns out that my own mother's birthday, August 27, is Monica's feast day.

I was still little when Mom discovered Ramana Maharshi—not to be confused with the Beatles' Maharishi—a man who had spent his life on a mountain in southern India, as little concerned with metaphysical proofs as with material possessions. Maharshi sat in silence, composed hymns to his mountain, Arunachala, and answered the questions people asked him. Though he had died fifty years earlier, my mother was growing more and more devoted to him and his teachings. I witnessed her turn to meditation, to walks in the woods, and to learning Sanskrit, determined to find the peace that she believed must lie beneath the pain of divorce. A hundred different ways, she would tell me that no search is more worthwhile than the search for the highest.

Meanwhile, what my father turned to was more of this world. He remarried, designed gardens for his clients, took up poker, and adopted a cat. He started going on trips back to Italy, and switched from making family trees of the English royals to even more magnificent, full-color ones of the Medicis. Dad's rescue was in the people and places around him, while the help my mother sought took her further inward. I wanted some of both.

As they fell apart, my center didn't hold; I had to find one of my own. I kept on reading Mom's Bible and, when she wasn't home, borrowing her books about meditation. I remembered the few prayers that she insisted I memorize as a child—the Lord's Prayer and the Twenty-Third Psalm. I visited local churches on Sundays and during the week ducked into their prayer chapels, trying not to be seen, since I didn't know what to do in front of an altar or in a pew. The very foreignness of those places, though, was a kind of comfort. My parents had always told me that what I believe would be up to me, and now it really was. Urgently.

Plato thought that all learning is really recollection, remembering what one's soul already knew from the eternal forms before birth. Religion felt to me like a rediscovery. Even as I tried to hide what I was up to, my mother kept encouraging me. *She has given me the essentials. She has given me the search,* I wrote, after I had come to accept my new obsession. But *my mind, that is truly my father's.* I brought to the search his skepticism, his feeling, and the desire, at least, for his meticulousness. By the middle of my senior year in high school, I could hardly think about anything else.

Augustine stressed that his capacity for faith came from God. But the desire for it, the pining, and the asking—that was from his mother, Monica. These drove him into doubts so deep that the only way out would be a new kind of conviction. "I have become a question to myself," he writes in the *Confessions*.[25] God became a question for me.

During Augustine's life, the Roman Empire was collapsing, and its fall would consign the genre of proof to obscurity in the West for centuries. The end of ancient philosophy is usually marked by the murder of the philosopher Hypatia, daughter of the librarian of Alexandria, at the hands of a Christian mob in the year 415. Greek thought nearly disappeared from Europe, and away with the philosophical classics went the God of reason. Other religious genres took over instead among Christians: the suffering of martyrs, mystical prayer, cathedral building, asceticism, crusades. But wherever the Greeks were still being read, the genre of proof would live on in other guises.

TWO

The Island

MUSLIMS AND JEWS MAKE PROOF SAFE FOR REVELATION

Back in the 1950s and 1960s, there was a fad for tropical islands. This was the generation of Americans that had fought on such islands in the Pacific and had since begun blowing up some of them with nuclear tests. People couldn't get enough of island music (lap-steel guitars), island swimwear (named after the Bikini Atoll test site), or island fantasy vacations (in the country's newest state). Gilligan had an island of his own on TV. The anthropologist Margaret Mead's stories about life on distant islands described a liberated sexuality that would influence both the coming counterculture and the consumer culture that would succeed it. There's still a picture at my father's old house in San Diego of my grandmother next to Mead. Grandma would arrange for Mead to give a lecture at the university when she was in town, and then they would go shopping together.

Our truest selves live on islands—so goes the mythology—because they're free from all the junk of society, with its distractions and phonies and stale dogmas. Islands are Eden before the Fall, where we can still walk around naked, unashamed. (Eden, protected from the world outside, was itself a kind of island.) This is life as it was meant to be. Philosophy started on the islands scattered around Greece, and it was on one of those too that John the Revelator saw his visions of how the world would end.

As a teenager I used to think about islands a lot. Lonely islands. I would draw pictures of them and imagine them while I was falling asleep. This threatened to divide me into two people at once: the one I ostensibly was— with this family, these friends, these expectations—and the one I would be if finally left on my own, just me and my island, alone with the melodrama of existence. It became an Occam's razor for cutting down on habits and possessions; I would try to minimize what I would miss if I were instantly transported there; things like contact lenses and coffee became sins against it.

I mention all this to give some indication of the feeling that rises up in me when I read a singular book about an island, written in twelfth-century Granada by a Muslim philosopher named Abu Bakr ibn Tufayl. It's called *Hayy Ibn Yaqzan*. The title is also the protagonist's name, which means "Alive, son of Awake." His story was popular and cosmopolitan, even while describing just about the most solitary kind of life imaginable. It also happened to be a pithy summary of what philosophers at the height of medieval Islamic civilization longed for with their proofs, and what they thought proofs could accomplish.

In the centuries after Rome fell, the ancient Greek classics found a new home in the world under Muslim rule. More than ever before, the genre of proof familiar today began to take shape in earnest. There was a God that some people felt the longing to prove, and there were ancient proofs in need of a God. The reappearance of the genre later on in Christian Europe owed a lot to what happened there and then, in the cities of the Muslim world.

It's fitting, I think, that one of the world's first philosophical novels can't decide between science fiction and plagiarizing scripture; Ibn Tufayl gives two possible explanations for how his hero came to be, from infancy, the only human being on his entire island. Initially we learn that, by a convergence of natural forces explained in poetically licensed pseudoscience, Hayy comes about through spontaneous generation, from a mix of supernal sunlight and island mud. But Ibn Tufayl realizes that not everyone will think this plausible. So as not to obstruct the narrative at its outset, he offers a second alternative: Hayy is born elsewhere under suspicious circumstances and set adrift in the sea by his mother, like Moses in the Bible and the Qur'an, entrusted to God's care. Natural or mythic: take your pick.

In either case, the mystique necessary to suspend our disbelief comes by way of the story's location. We're told that Hayy's island lies in the equatorial seas near the coast of India. This was, for Ibn Tufayl, like setting a novel in low Earth orbit would be now. India was at the edge of the familiar; the Islamic dominion stretched from where he was in Andalusia—southern Spain on today's map—along the Mediterranean, to the Levant and Persia, but it stopped at the Indus River. India was at the eastern edge of his world. East is also where the sun rises, and the light-as-truth symbolism in that fact meant a lot to Ibn Tufayl—as much as anyone a fugitive from Plato's cave. Ibn Tufayl was, so to speak, an orientalist: a Westerner who looked to the East for a more spiritual, exotic alternative to the familiar humdrum. People there in Andalusia knew math and science, perhaps, but they were deaf to deeper meanings, to the hidden unity in everything. His mission was to explain the secrets of "oriental philosophy," and to reconcile them with ideas that were more familiar, and more conventionally orthodox.

An orientalist impulse like this filled my family's religion when I was growing up. We would take trips out to California to visit an Indian guru, and I got my first pomegranates and mangoes from his hands. We went there for an escape, or a return, to something less restrictive and more pure than the ordinary and familiar. I took to the quest. One night, at the guru's ashram, my parents heard me saying through a dream, *Keep the lights on forever,* which would've made Ibn Tufayl proud. He had a very serious affection for light.

India deserves a further digression from Hayy's story. At the time that Ibn Tufayl was writing, India was in a golden age of proofs. Westerners today tend to gravitate toward India's more unfamiliar outgrowths—pantheist and polytheist forms of Hinduism, or Buddhism. But medieval India didn't just have proofs; it had a personal, transcendent God, one not so different from what you would find in the West. There were debates about suffering, bodiless minds, and eternity.[1]

The heyday of theistic proofs in India came during the tenth and eleventh centuries—about the same time as in the Islamic world—with roots going back at least to the fourth. In debates against atheistic Buddhists and materialist Hindus, the Nyaya school of Hinduism honed a doctrine of God and the proofs to defend it. The titles of Nyaya scholars' books hint at what it all meant to them: Udayana's *Flower-Offering of Logic,* Jayanta Bhatta's *Bouquet of Reasoning.* Proofs were an act of devotion as well as disputation. There was a moral argument that there must be a lord over the law of karma; an argument that language could only have arisen from divine tutelage; and one that the Vedas—the ancient Hindu scriptures—could only have had a divine author.

The best-developed Nyaya proof was one from "composition"; just as the pieces of a clay pot need a potter to join them—this was a favorite Nyaya analogy—the pieces of the world must have had someone to put them together. The Nyaya school had no doctrine of creation-from-nothing, as in the West, but its scholars argued that an intelligent agent must have fastened composite things as we find them, or at least fastened what in turn fastened them. They went on to reason that this first fastener must also be bodiless, omniscient, omnipotent, and perfectly good. More or less, it's the familiar God of monotheism.

Rediscovering the familiar is as much a part of the allure of the East— or of the Moon, or of an island, or of the ancients—as encountering the exotic. I saw this early on by way of Indian gurus who succeeded in acclimating to California culture. Americans were drawn to these gurus by what seemed familiar as well as by what was new. It's what Ibn Tufayl saw, as an Andalusian reading strange Persian books. When you're between worlds, you look for what little they share. If something is true there and true here, its proof is that much stronger.

.·.

The diverging stories of Hayy's origin converge at his infancy, and his journey begins in earnest. A doe finds him, adopts him, and suckles him into childhood. He grows up at her side, imitating her and the other animals on their island. His sole concern is to live like them at this stage, taking care of material needs and nothing else. The doe teaches him to eat wild fruit and drink from streams. She keeps him warm in the cold. He learns no human language, but he can mimic birdcalls and grasp their meaning. Soon, though, he begins to need more than the animals can teach.

By his seventh year, Hayy starts realizing that there's something different about himself. He learns to use sharpened sticks to ward off hostile creatures. Troubled by his private parts, he covers them and eventually makes himself a costume of eagle feathers. Finally, childhood proper comes to an end when the doe grows ill. She stops moving, and Hayy tries to save her by doing surgery on her insides. But, rooting around in there, he finds that her life force—her sunlike heat—is already gone. She has moved on from her body. The best he can do is autopsy.

He doesn't know it yet himself, but Hayy's entrée into medicine also marks the start of his career as a philosopher. Ibn Tufayl's readers would have recognized this. What medical knowledge was available at the time came mostly from the Greek textbooks that Muslims had collected in their conquests around the Mediterranean. It was a small step from the Greeks' medical teachings to their theories about the nature of the universe, and each informed the other. The cosmos and the body were intertwined. Ibn Tufayl reflects this belief in his book. He divides Hayy's life into seven-year segments, a formula that came from Galen, the Roman-era Greek physician. As Hayy's body matures, he steadily gets wiser about ultimate things.

There were other reasons for the affinity between philosophy and medicine in those days. Philosophy was sometimes considered a suspect activity, a foreign science, spoken of in Arabic using a Greek loanword: *falsafa*. (Ibn Tufayl judiciously uses *hikma* instead, a native Arabic word for "wisdom.") Philosophy attracted Muslims as well as the Jews and Christians who lived among them—making their conversations both rich and potentially subversive. But philosophers often had friends in high places; many of the most famous ones were physicians in royal courts. Ibn Tufayl himself served as doctor to the sultan in Granada, which helped legitimize his speculations. In turn, pronouncing on cosmic truths must have lent some needed gravitas to the medieval physicians' rather primitive business. Thus it was fitting for Hayy's career as a philosopher to begin with a surgery.

After the doe's death, Hayy studies and dissects other animals. He moves into a cave, discovers fire, and learns to cook meat. At twenty-one years old— 7×3—he begins to venture into metaphysics, speculating on abstractions like variety, unity, the elements, size, forms, and measurement. He discovers the existence of the soul and, by extension, the baseness of his body. Observing the stars, at age twenty-eight— 7×4—he charts their movements, and they lead him to infer a hidden unity. But the defining moment for Hayy comes at age thirty-five— 7×5—when he becomes convinced of the existence of a God. Nothing is the same afterward.

The proof doesn't come all at once. Hayy's mind has to reason its way through a replay of the history of proofs so far. First, with echoes of Plato's *Timaeus,* he concludes that anything that comes into existence must have a cause, beginning with a being who created them according to the blueprints of eternal, perfect forms. He also marvels at the order of the natural world. Like Aristotle, looking up at the stars, he reasons that everything in motion must have been moved by something else; since the sequence can't go on to infinity, there has to be a first mover. Each of these observations seems to point at the same thing, though even if he could speak he doesn't know its name. The book's readers did. This was God, more or less like the God of Islam, but made out of island reason, without a Qur'an or prophets or the law.

Hayy's speculations start to get even more adventurous, beyond just repeating the ancients. Through him, Ibn Tufayl shows us what Islamic civi-

CONTINGENCY

NECESSITY

lization had already added to the Greek proofs. Nobody impressed him more than Ibn Sina, the great eleventh-century Persian, also a physician. Ibn Sina provided the core of the oriental philosophy that Hayy, alone on his oriental island, would discover. Actually, *Hayy Ibn Yaqzan* is the also name of a book by Ibn Sina, and Ibn Tufayl cribbed it as a tribute.

Ibn Sina, too, began with Aristotle. He was especially interested in the idea of something existing *necessarily, by virtue of itself.* Aristotle used this concept to argue for an eternal universe, but for Ibn Sina it alluded to more. It sounded like God.[2]

Nothing has to cause a thing like this to exist. It just exists, and it has to. The universe wouldn't make sense if it didn't, like a painting with no surface. Other things either exist *contingently,* having been caused by something else, or are merely *possible* and don't exist at all—though in principle they could. Contingent things can cause contingent things, and they'll go from being possible to actual. Take, for instance, the book you're reading. As I write, the words begin as only possibilities, blinking one by one into actual existence. I, the one writing, am a contingent being if there ever was one. I follow this story, from one contingency to another, in the hope of reaching a ground beneath them all. Whatever lurks there, as something must: that's necessity.

Ibn Sina then collects these concepts into a proof, similar to Aristotle's argument from motion. An infinite regress of contingent things causing other things is absurd. There must, at the end of the line, be a necessary being, one that depends on nothing else to account for its existence.

What's really distinctive—and really "oriental," in Ibn Tufayl's view—is Ibn Sina's interpretation of what it all means. He analyzes this concept of necessity and finds a God of pure intellect who is unitary, good, and beautiful. Intellect, in particular, is key. By contemplating a proof of such a God, one can actually reach its object. One can see, feel, and know God. This is contact. This is for real. As he reached the climax of his proof, Ibn Tufayl's Hayy started to feel its power.

But first Hayy ran into a hitch, which plagued him for years on end. For all his persistence of thought on that little island, he knew of just one question that wouldn't lead him to an answer.

∴

The man who would become Ibn Tufayl's successor as Andalusia's leading philosopher, Ibn Rushd, used to tell a story.[3] Still young and inexperienced, Ibn Rushd arrived at his first audience with Sultan Abu Ya'qub—the exalted Commander of the Faithful, and so on—to find him talking alone with Ibn Tufayl. The first thing the sultan said to Ibn Rushd as he entered terrified him. "What do the philosophers believe about the heavens?" he demanded. "Are they eternal or created?"

This was a loaded question, a test. Ibn Rushd probably knew something about the answer—he would later write a definitive commentary on Aristotle—but the problem was whether to admit it. Aristotle's unmoved mover appealed to Muslims, along with Christians and Jews, except for one big problem: it presides over an eternal universe. That would contradict the first verse of Genesis, for one, as well as what passages about creation seem to be saying throughout the Qur'an. The God of scripture was supposed to have created the universe with a beginning in time, out of nothing. Sultan Abu Ya'qub's question, for this time and place, was philosophy at its most dangerous. It didn't help that the sultan's Almohad dynasty had a brutal policy of intolerance for whatever didn't fit their literalistic kind of Islam.

The authority of ancient philosophy and that of Muhammad's revelations were at odds: one seemed to say the universe is eternal, the other that it had a definite beginning. Ibn Sina had brought the God of philosophy a bit closer to one recognizable by his fellow Muslims, but it wasn't close enough. His God still exists coeternally with its universe, like Aristotle's, and against the most common interpretation of the Qur'an.

Ibn Rushd knew this well enough to keep his mouth shut. Could he be punished for studying Aristotle's heretical teachings? "I was seized with consternation and did not know what to say," Ibn Rushd wrote. At first he pretended not to know. For all the awkwardness of the moment, though, Ibn Tufayl seemed curiously unconcerned.

Proofs for the existence of God in the medieval Islamic world always hinged on whether to insist on creation from nothing or follow Aristotle back through eternity; you had to choose one or the other. The argument for creation had a head start thanks to the sixth-century Christian philosopher John Philoponus, who lived in Alexandria in the decades before it came under Muslim rule.[4] He used Aristotelian methods to derive a seemingly un-Aristotelian conclusion.

Aristotle's mathematics held that there can't be an infinite number of any things in existence, or anything infinitely large. It would lead to unconscionable absurdities—for instance, $\infty - 1 = \infty$. An infinitely long sequence of causes couldn't happen either, for similar reasons. (This occurs to Hayy on his island.) But if Aristotle was right about infinity, as John Philoponus saw it, he must have been wrong about the eternity of the universe. Just as there can't be infinitely many causes, there can't be an infinite quantity of time or events or motions. Matter, too, is changeable and fickle—how can it be coeternal with the divine mind? The universe must be finite. Time must be finite. There must have been, therefore, a beginning, a creation, and a creator.

Aristotle himself feared that if he was wrong about the eternal universe, "there is no alternative to the world's generation being from night and everything being together and from that which is not."[5] Creation from nothing—from "night"—wasn't a prospect he relished. But John Philoponus, a Christian, emphatically did. So did a lot of those who read him in the medieval Middle East. Among the first of Islam's philosophers, al-Kindi, introduced his ideas to Muslims, while Sa'adia ben Yosef brought them to Arabic-speaking Jews. As opposed to Aristotle's physics, they came closer to the logic of Plato: the universe itself must have a cause. From such parts, these men assembled proofs—not for the eternal God of the ancients, but for the creator in scripture.

This was a task most famously carried on by Abu Hamid Muhammad ibn Muhammad at-Tusi al-Ghazali, who died early in the twelfth century. Rather than an eccentric courtier, he was a theology professor and legal scholar with an important teaching post, well poised for his influence to spread and to last.

In his famous polemic, *The Incoherence of the Philosophers,* al-Ghazali lists twenty of philosophy's most grievous mistakes. The first and the worst, from which the others flow, is the eternity of the universe. He mounts his attack against it on several fronts, refuting the philosophers' interpretation of celestial motions and, in the footsteps of Philoponus and al-Kindi, showing the absurdity of an infinite past. Using philosophy against philosophy, he lists self-contradiction after self-contradiction. Al-Ghazali's chief targets were Ibn Sina and his predecessor, al-Farabi, whose followers—"Muslims in name only"—he accuses of moral depravity as well as philosophical error.[6] While al-Ghazali ultimately adopts the basic structure of Ibn Sina's proof for God's existence, he's careful to insist that this God is the creator of the universe, from nothing.

He wasn't interested in bending Islam around philosophy. People called al-Ghazali himself the "proof of Islam," so fully did he embody orthodox religion. The God he was after was a God who would make a difference, who made a world that couldn't be confused with a godless one, or with one run by some distant narcissist like Aristotle described. A God that didn't create the universe from nothing was not worth his time.

The medieval proof from creation found an unlikely defender much more recently in the evangelical philosopher William Lane Craig. Even as a boy, growing up in a not especially pious family, Craig remembers—proverbially enough—looking up at the stars at night and intuiting that all of it must point back, somehow, to a first cause. That cause got a name when, thanks to a girl in his high school German class, he became a born-again Christian. He studied philosophy at Wheaton, an evangelical college. But only a bit later, while trudging through Frederick Copleston's nine-volume *History of Philosophy,* did he learn that his childhood intuition had been thought of before by medieval Arabs and Jews. He decided he had to go back to school and study it.

"I wanted to resolve once and for all in my own mind whether this was a sound argument," he says. "It captivated me."

When he began doctoral work in philosophy during the mid-1970s, Craig read everything he could about the argument from creation. In translation, he studied versions of it by al-Kindi, Sa'adia, and al-Ghazali. He measured what they said against the latest science—the big bang, the expanding universe, the mathematics of infinity—and he concluded that they were right. In thousand-year-old Arabic texts, this evangelical from the American Midwest found a simple, powerful syllogism he could work with. He summarized what they had said and added modern evidence to support it, step by step:

1. Whatever begins to exist has a cause.
   a. Intuition suggests that from nothing, nothing comes.
   b. Nothing we know of came from nothing.
2. The universe began to exist.
   a. An infinity of past events is impossible.
   b. It is impossible to form an infinite by successive addition.
   c. Scientific cosmology describes a universe with a beginning.
3. Therefore, the universe has a cause, and that cause is God.
   a. The cause must transcend space and time.
   b. The cause must be changeless and immaterial.
   c. The cause must be unimaginably powerful.
   d. Causes are either scientific or personal; this one cannot be scientific, so it must be personal.

Craig's dissertation appeared in print as *The Kalam Cosmological Argument* in 1979—*kalam* roughly means "theology" in Arabic—and it would become the most argued about philosophy of religion text in recent memory.[7] "If our discussion has been more than a mere academic exercise," the book concludes, "this conclusion ought to stagger us, ought to fill us with a sense of awe and wonder at the knowledge that our whole universe was caused to exist by *something* beyond it or greater than it."[8] For Craig, this was never merely academic. He would turn the argument into his opening volley in public debates. Proclaiming it became his ministry. When you're confronted with the logic, if a proof like this means anything, he thought, it changes you.

And on that note the great dilemma of creation and eternity brings us back to Hayy, alone on the island. Assembling these proofs changes everything for him. But it does so only when he finally realizes that the dilemma isn't worth his worry.

Hayy's mind thinks its way to a proof of the first cause, and to something like Ibn Sina's being that is necessary-by-virtue-of-itself with an eternal universe. Each, like al-Ghazali and Ibn Rushd, pokes objections at the other. From where Hayy stands on his island, and in his short island of time, he can't decide which story is really true—eternity or creation. He has no revelation or ancient authorities to incline him one way or another. But what he finally discovers is that the implications are the same. A God worthy of worship awaits him at the end of either proof: a cause without a body and a perfect, unchangeable ground of being. It dawns on Hayy that, no matter what, he can be sure there is a God, and that's assurance enough for him.

It was also enough, evidently, for Ibn Tufayl and the sultan when Ibn Rushd found them talking together and when the sultan raised his question about the universe. This sultan was a reactionary ruler who sought to purge his society of heretics and unbelievers. But as philosophers alone in a quiet room—their little island, away from the mainland public—they could confess to one another that the truth might be more ambiguous than they would publicly admit. Ibn Tufayl finally managed to calm the younger Ibn Rushd, who told them what he knew about the ancients' opinions. The sultan sent him home with money and a robe and a horse to carry them.

∴

With thirty-five years behind him, Hayy's life takes a sudden turn. It's all because of the God he found in proofs. He had become possessed.

> By now thought of this Subject was so deeply rooted in his heart that he could think of nothing else. He was distracted from his prior investigation of created being. For now his eye fell on nothing without immediately detecting in it signs of His workmanship—then instantly his thoughts would shift from craft to Craftsman, deepening his love of Him, totally detaching his heart from the sensory world, and binding it to the world of mind.[9]

This God makes him lose interest in the things around him and even in taking care of his body beyond what it needs to keep the ecstasies coming. He gets better and better at making the periods of bliss last longer and longer. He learns that it helps to spin in circles—like a Sufi dervish, or pilgrims circumambulating the Ka'ba in Mecca, or the stars overhead.

This is just the kind of experience that Ibn Sina's oriental philosophy promised, drawing in part from those we now call the Neoplatonists. Chief among them was Plotinus, a third-century Greek-speaking Egyptian who developed what he found in Plato into an elaborate doctrine, with an eternal and perfect One at its summit. Plotinus experienced mystical union with this One on several occasions, apparently. He described these in terms that make it seem like he had Hayy in mind: "The flight of the alone to the Alone."[10]

Hayy's visions don't fit well into words. Ibn Tufayl actually warns us not to take any of his images too literally. But Hayy travels through the celestial spheres of planets and stars and sees countless faces all praising God in unison. He sees the torment of souls who don't heed their divine source. This might sound to us like a mescaline trip, but its cause is proof and proof alone. The whole cosmic order comes to him on his island. Now, Hayy is perfectly and never alone in the divine company. "He has gained an understanding as unshakable as that of an old friendship," says Ibn Tufayl, quoting Ibn Sina.[11] After seven seven-year periods, in his fiftieth year, Hayy's ecstasies become so intense that he loses interest in living entirely: "Hayy longed that God—glory to Him—would ease him altogether of his body."[12] But his body perseveres, and the story continues.

It turns out that there is another island nearby, and one not so lonely. It's full of people. They've received news of God's prophets and made a religion out of it. Where Hayy has only hard-won, direct experience, the people on this other island teach each other about the necessary being with symbols and laws. Or, at least, they try.

There is a man on this other island named Absal. Having had a small taste of mystical adventures like Hayy's, life in society doesn't satisfy him anymore. He sets off into the ocean in search of solitude, and he lands you-know-where.

At first when they see each other, Absal runs away. Hayy chases him down and catches him, and they become friends. Absal teaches Hayy language, and Hayy reciprocates by talking about his visions. Absal explains how religion works back on his island. There are certain basic practices: faith, prayer, alms, fasting, and pilgrimage. He describes the stories of heaven and hell, of judgment and resurrection—stories that came to earth through a messenger. Basically, he teaches Hayy about Islam.

Parts of these lessons seemed familiar to Hayy, consistent with the visions he had been having and with his longings. And it's familiar to me. When I took an introductory class on Islam, during my first semester in college, things that didn't make sense before in other contexts started to cohere for me in the context of that religion. Again: the exotic can shake one into a fresh look at the familiar. We learned about Islam's Five Pillars—the same practices that Absal taught Hayy—and about the medieval empires and modern revolutions. One thing that especially stuck with me was an article by an anthropologist we had to read about conservative Muslim women in Cairo.[13] She describes conversations among them about praying the five-times daily *salat* prayer: they do it not because they want to, necessarily, but because they want to want to. This was a revelation—a simple idea, though far from obvious to me. I had expected faith to arrive more or less prepackaged and rock-solid from the start. But these women knew it isn't automatic; some of us have to prepare ourselves through discipline and practice.

When Absal tells him about popular religion, however, with all these trappings of ritual and law, Hayy doesn't exactly see the point. Why bother? Why doesn't everyone just live in perpetual ecstasy like he does? Absal has to explain human nature. He has to explain how society works. It's hard for Hayy to grasp, having no idea what people become like when they live together. He needs to see it for himself.

They sail for the other island, and on arrival Hayy starts preaching about what he had discovered from his thinking and visions. People gather around him and listen at first out of curiosity, but their attention hits a limit. Those who understand a little get stuck in arguments and confusion, while the rest understand nothing. Most are interested in religion only so far as it can win them possessions and power over each other. His teachings cause chaos.

"Hayy now understood the human condition," writes Ibn Tufayl, probably parroting the cynicism of the Almohad rulers. "He saw that most men are no better than unreasoning animals."[14]

Popular religion, for all its faults, is the best these poor creatures can be expected to handle. There's no sense trying to show them something better and purer. Frustrated, Hayy and Absal decide to return to the island Hayy came from. Hayy tells the people that he's seen the fundamentalist light, that he was wrong all along. He adjures them: Submit to tradition, as literally as you can; shun innovation; observe the laws and statutes; and don't meddle in things that don't concern you. Then Hayy and Absal sail back to where they can have their ecstasies in peace. That's where their story ends.

Condescension like this was common among those who dealt with philosophy in Ibn Tufayl's time. Al-Ghazali, for instance, liked to repeat Muhammad's saying, "Hold fast to the religion of old women"[15]—old women being simple, pious, and practical. Al-Ghazali saw fit for himself to cull through Aristotle and Ibn Sina, and to construct proofs for the God of the Qur'an, but he didn't intend it for popular consumption. Ibn Tufayl says he discloses his light-bearing truths through Hayy's story only reluctantly.

Still, he does. He won't buy into Hayy's cynicism completely. "I had risen to pinnacles higher than the eye can see," Ibn Tufayl says at the end of the book, "and I wanted to try, at least, to approach them in words so as to excite desire and inspire a passion to start out along this road."[16] Most people probably aren't ready for these precious secrets, yet here he is writing them down. And, actually, the elitism becomes just part of their allure.

∴

As Islamic philosophy flourished, Arabic-speaking Jews were paying attention and making parts of it their own: Sa'adia, Solomon ibn Gabriol, and Musa ibn Maimun—Moses Maimonides. Maimonides played the elitism game too, just as Hayy felt forced to do. But this was no islander; he suffered too much and bore too much responsibility to mistake himself for that.

THINKER	DATE OF DEATH	CREATION OR ETERNITY?	PREFERRED PROOF
Al-Kindi	871	Creation	From temporality
Sa'adia	942	Creation	From temporality
Al-Farabi	950	Eternity	From degree and perfection
Ibn Sina	1037	Eternity	From necessity
Al-Ghazali	1111	Creation	From experience and from cause
Ibn Tufayl	1185	Undecided	From cause
Ibn Rushd	1198	Eternity	From motion and from design
Maimonides	1204	Creation	From motion, composition, cause, and necessity

Like Ibn Tufayl and Ibn Rushd, Maimonides grew up in Andalusia. During his twentieth year the Almohad dynasty took over, the same one to which Sultan Abu Ya'qub belonged. While Muslim philosophers could float above trouble in the sultan's company, Maimonides saw the business end of Almohad repression. He endured exile, humiliation, and forced conversion to Islam. After almost twenty years of it, his family moved, eventually settling in what is now Cairo, Egypt. Maimonides stayed there until his death in 1204. Having come from half a world away didn't prevent him from becoming head of the Jewish community there, and—philosopher that he was—he served as a physician to the local Muslim rulers. Maimonides remained indelibly a Jew, and an especially pious one. But as a thinker, writing mostly in Arabic, he belonged to the Mediterranean milieu. His concerns were as much those of the Islamic philosophers and their Greek antecedents as those of the Bible and the rabbis.

Maimonides thus thought between worlds: between philosophy and scripture, between community and cosmopolis. As both a leader of Jews and a doctor among Muslims, the stakes were especially high. "Truths should be at one time apparent," he wrote, "and at another time concealed."[17] The twentieth-century philosopher Leo Strauss took Maimonides as an exemplar of writing between the lines, one who tried to defend the practice of philosophy even while protecting the religion of the multitudes and the powerful from its hazards. At the start of Maimonides' magnum opus, *The Guide for the Perplexed*, he warns that if you haven't studied enough religion yet, or you're not mature enough to know what's at stake, he would prefer you to put the book down before you start.

Maimonides is vicious against those who would abandon philosophy to save divine creation. "Consider the fate of these speculators and the result of their labors; observe how they rushed, as it were, from the ashes into the fire." People obsessed with proving creation ex nihilo, he continues, "have weakened the arguments for the existence, the unity, and the incorporeality of God."[18] Maimonides affirmed creation himself. But, like Ibn Tufayl, he wanted to ensure that the proofs for God's existence wouldn't hinge on that fragile question of whether the universe is eternal or created. If we have only an argument like William Lane Craig's for God from creation in time, and its assumptions about the nature of the universe turn out wrong (as they might), we would be left proofless, doubting whether God really exists.

The first chapter of the *Guide*'s second book gives four proofs. The first and most rigorous is a version of Aristotle's argument from motion in the world and among the celestial spheres, up to the top: "This prime mover of the sphere is God, praised be His name!"[19]

Next comes an argument from composition, which resembles what the Nyaya school was doing in India. Things in the universe, it says, are evidently composed of other things—honey vinegar is his example—and such combinations require a combiner; the sequence of combinations leads, again, to a first combiner, itself uncombined. Third is an argument from necessity, along the lines laid by Ibn Sina, and fourth follows the logic of causation to a first willful agent, like Plato. At each step Maimonides takes care to demonstrate what Aristotle couldn't do very convincingly—that there is only one God. Good philosophy leads back to the God of the Torah, he meant to show; fear not. But bad philosophy is a different matter.

The Jewish Talmud tells stories about the damage foreign notions can do. There's an antihero named Elisha ben Abuya, often called just *acher*, "other." A brilliant student who seemed sure to be a great rabbi, Elisha falls prey to Greek culture, and it seduces him away from Judaism. The rabbis scorn and condemn him, but they also betray a little sympathy. He is an elusive character, as ambivalent as the feelings Jews have often had for what lies beyond their own community-in-exile. But for Maimonides, Elisha's problem was being a sloppy philosopher—sloppy in particular about creation and eternity—and he doesn't intend to follow suit.

This archetype of Elisha is one I've known and felt and repeated. I grew up with trace amounts of Judaism, but it was the religion my teenage curiosity most carefully ignored. My father made some attempts, during that time, to remind me of our ancestors' traditions. He gave me the yellowed copy of the *Sayings of the Fathers* he had gotten as a boy in Hebrew school. Soon after he moved away, with our wounds still fresh, we took a road trip, and he surprised me with a Passover Seder in plastic containers for us to share in the car: matzoh, charoset, bitter herbs, and everything—more than any other Passover I can remember, it was authentically exilic and resolutely hopeful. The first Hanukkah after he left, I lit the candles with my mother and was surprised to find that I remembered the blessings well enough to sing them. I still thought of myself as Jewish, but I didn't go much further than that.

There is, in this omission, a certain history. Since the time of Elisha and before, Jews have lived among the nations, adrift, between worlds, never sure when tolerance would turn to persecution. The love of studying and questioning that has bound Jewish culture together like the pages of its books has also led some to drift outside the canon. The Judaism I learned from my father had in it a sense of resignation. If the choice was between being Jewish and being himself, he seemed to take the latter, even if it meant becoming part of the quiet attrition that every generation of Jews has known. The Arabic-speaking philosophers liked to repeat a maxim that came to them jointly from ancient Greece and early Islam: truth is truth, regardless of its source.[20]

Looking for truth, I careened everywhere I could. A weekend retreat at a Buddhist monastery. Hindu scriptures. Metaphysical bookstores. Evangelical churches. No matter how scattershot the options were, each experience seemed to lead to the next, with the sensation of overriding reason. But my grandparents on my father's side learned something about what I was up to, and it worried them. Myopic me, I couldn't understand why they felt that way. I felt shocked in turn. My experiments weren't about them, or my father, or Judaism. Why weren't they happy that I was fashioning my proof?

The Judaism I had learned from them before didn't go far beyond matzoh ball soup, anyway. Their house was a place for more ordinary forms of love. I would come downstairs in the morning and find Grandma, still in her night-gown, making eggs. I was her only grandchild. If everyone piled into the car, I would sit with her in the back, and her soft, bony hand would hold mine the whole way while we whispered to each other underneath whatever con-versation the others were having. When I left for home, she would hold me still, looking long and hard in my eyes; when it became too much, she would borrow a line and an expression on her face from some old movie actress and then let go, trying to laugh. Our family thought of her in cosmic terms, as a being whose presence held the universe—or ours, at least—together against the natural urge to dissolution.

Grandma pleaded for me to spend some time at the campus Hillel, but her agitation only made me afraid of how the other Jews there would see me. I didn't go.

As she lay on her dying bed two years later, unable to speak, I could only hope she heard me say, *I haven't rejected you. All that you gave me, I will keep . . .*

∴

Translated into Latin in the seventeenth century, Ibn Tufayl's little book about Hayy would become part of the European Enlightenment, influencing Spinoza, Locke, Boyle, and, of course, Daniel Defoe's *Robinson Crusoe*. It portrays a fetching if deceptive version of the human ideal and the ideal religion: rational, self-sufficient, mystical, and emphatically male, living and thinking with no need for anyone else. Hayy finds a philosophical friend in Absal, finally, but only after he has found himself. There are no better conditions than an island, it would seem, for proof.

Hayy is the template of so much in the genre of proof that would follow. He's a blank slate and thinks pure, male, prepolitical, asocial thoughts. No mother whispers prayers into his ear as a child to steer his grown-up reason. We may not all get to be spontaneously generated like Hayy, but through proofs perhaps we too can have a new birth—bloodless and pure, into an invisible brotherhood of minds who've touched the divine.[21]

So, which is the real person, finally? The islander? Or the creature at the mercy of a life among others? Jacques Derrida—another philosopher from the borderlands between North Africa and Europe—discussed *Robinson Crusoe* in a seminar near the end of his life, when he was already diagnosed with the pancreatic cancer that would kill him. He spoke of how separate we all are from each other, in our own worlds—"forever uncrossable." We see shadows of other people, but nothing more. We live in societies together, but do we really hold anything in common? Is the planet I live on really the same as yours? One can't know. "There is no world, there are only islands," Derrida said.[22]

As if against Derrida, centuries earlier, John Donne wrote and prayed that "no man is an island." And, with time, the idea of an island came to me less and less the way it had before. The gospel's command to love started compelling me to believe Donne. Christians pray, in relevantly geographic terms, "Forgive us our trespasses, as we forgive those who trespass against us." Mercy comes to our islands when we give it to others. There have to be others, since it's in them that we find God's image on earth. My island alone wouldn't do.

Or maybe it was this: the God I was discovering would be my portable island—an unworldly presence, yet closer than my jugular vein, in the words of the Qur'an. Maybe I longed less for islands because I was really beginning to live on one. This path I was taking, and the decision it was leading toward, was turning more and more solitary.

THREE

Grammars of Assent

A COMEBACK IN CHRISTENDOM

Anselm couldn't sit still. Rising before the sun, even on the coldest winter mornings, he and the other monks would gather in the church to chant psalms. They all wore the same habit, and their voices all sang the same tones, whose echoes cascaded through the stale air and against the stone walls. But Anselm was distracted. The prayers on his lips couldn't compete with his thoughts, and his thoughts were stuck. "I hoped for gladness," he wrote, "and, lo, my sighs come thick and fast!"[1]

The Benedictine abbey at Bec, in what is now northern France, was less than a century old in 1077, but it had already become famous thanks to its celebrity abbot, Lanfranc of Pavia. Anselm—whom history calls Anselm of Canterbury—came from the Italian Alps. Back home, he and his father differed in every way but their stubbornness, and living together turned unbearable. After his mother's death when he was in his early twenties, he set off northward. He traveled through all of France, past the universities at Chartres and Paris, arriving at Bec in 1060. Becoming a monk wasn't his plan at first, but word of Lanfranc's school there captured Anselm's imagination. He entered Bec as a novice, and under Lanfranc he mastered the medieval curriculum's catalog of doctrines, categories, and distinctions, held together by church authority and the daily ritual of liturgy. Anselm became a teacher in his own right. But his own assent to faith didn't fill him as he thought it should. It didn't saturate his mind and will the way a living God deserves.

He wrote a book called *An Example of Meditation on the Grounds of Faith,* which begins with an Augustine-style proof from the degrees of perfection. Some things in the world are more perfect than others; a horse's nature is better than a tree's, in one example Anselm gave, but human nature is better than a horse's. These degrees make sense only if at the top of the scale there is a most perfect God. Adducing other familiar proofs, he further reasoned that this God is uncaused and the source of every other thing's existence. But these didn't satisfy him—too worldly and piecemeal, unequal to what he believed must be the simplicity and elegance of the supreme being. "I began to wonder," he recalled, "if perhaps it might be possible to find one single argument that for its proof required no other save itself."[2] The problem nagged at him and wouldn't let go. He lost the desire to eat, to drink, and to sleep. Worst of all, as he would piously tell his biographer Eadmer, it distracted his attention from prayers.

Yet it was during Matins, while the monks' voices mingled with darkness, that Anselm's rupture of insight finally came. Recounted Eadmer, "The grace of God shone on his heart, the whole matter became clear to his mind, and a great joy and jubilation filled his inmost being."[3] This grace may have been in the form of a proof, but it entered into his world like a trance.

His idea, and his way of explaining it, would blow through the schools where monks studied and debated over their hand-copied texts. There had been arguments for the existence of God circulating before, but this was something new. It was simple and puzzling and ecstatic. If Anselm was right, no longer would proof be an affront to humility or a substitute for faith; it would be their fulfillment.

Anselm proceeded to record his discovery in a short treatise. He called it *Fides Quaerens Intellectum—Faith in Search of Understanding*. It was a phrase found in Christian literature since antiquity. But for Anselm, the words aren't quite right. More than searching for it, he *craved* understanding. He pined for it.

After this second work was completed in 1078, however, he changed the names of both his books. The first he called *Monologion,* meaning "monologue" or "soliloquy." The second became the *Proslogion,* meaning "discourse" or "discussion." It was not just Anselm speaking now; God had entered the conversation.

∴

The house I grew up in had a monastic character. In a neighborhood full of ramblers, it was the lone modernist cube. My mother loves that kind of architecture, so it's what she got: yellow-brick walls inside and out, enormous panes of south-facing glass, and a leaky flat roof, full of skylights. The interior, though, was more my father's doing: antiques, as many medieval ones as he could afford. Most of the furniture was made of dark wood, standing against the light walls of the house. There were a few uncomfortable black thrones. In one corner, on a tall, columned base, stood an old statue of Christ victorious, with the paint long gone, arms missing, and wounds in the feet. Basically, I spent my childhood in a museum. When I go back home now and step through that door, I whisper to myself the name I've given it: the House of Great Silence.

Frank Lloyd Wright, my mother's architectural hero, used to design clothes for the people—the women, at least—who lived in his houses. In a house so carefully and consciously made, you're not just living there. You're part of a work of art that serves the higher purpose of the whole.

The house was big enough that we could all be there and not really notice one another's presence. This happened a lot—one person per floor, each going about what we were doing, more or less quietly. In the back was a woods, with a little stream that led to a bigger one, which led to the Potomac River. We were right under a flight path, but when you grow up with the sound of airplanes, you learn to tune it out.

The house became especially quiet, and especially monastic, when my father moved out, taking many of his antiques with him. Thus stripped, it was my mother's ship, the vessel of her salvation. Like Anselm, she would wake up early in the morning to meditate. The peace and order and abundant light of the house was what she wanted. And it was there and then, in the House of Great Silence, that the urges in me began calling for a decision, for my own assent.

That's a heavy word, *assent*. It's a bit like "belief" but thicker, more demanding. It's social, and it's volitional. Assent is what belief looks like in the flesh—the intertwining of person and proposition, when the two become inseparable. Decisions shape beliefs and beliefs make decisions.

The idea of going to an actual monastery came to me during the last months of high school. My mother had recently been on a retreat at Holy Cross Abbey in Berryville, Virginia, at the suggestion of the wife of my father's business partner. Though anything but a Catholic herself, Mom enjoyed the silence of the place and hinted that maybe I should go sometime too. The idea didn't make much sense to me until some weeks later—I think it was in the shower—when it suddenly, momentously, did. For the past year or so I had been reading my way around religion without clear reasons how or why, and here was an opportunity to test that curiosity on experience. *I think it is an interesting place to put myself,* I wrote in my journal, *an interesting context to throw myself into and see what happens.* The timing worked out well. In the last months of senior year, my school gave us the chance to do an independent study project, and I decided to do mine at Holy Cross.

The monastic life isn't for everyone, least of all an unbaptized teenager. You can't just slip in. I called up the abbot, Father Robert, told him about my idea, and he allowed me to come for a meeting. In all, I had to make the hour-and-a-half drive west three times for interviews with different monks. Each questioned me about my reasons and my motives. One steely old monk in particular thought that it was a terrible idea, and he made sure I knew it—I didn't have the maturity, and I didn't know what I was getting into. But finally they agreed to even more than I had hoped for: a two-week stay, and not even in the guest house but in a cloistered cell, living, working, and praying as they do. By that time, I had fallen permanently in love with the place, set on hilly green pastures, studded with jagged outcroppings. The Shenandoah River runs along one side of the property, and the Blue Ridge Mountains stand just beyond.

Back home, waiting for the project to begin, my reading and thinking intensified. I wrote, still sorting out the meanings of the words, *I want to know who I am with respect to the monastery, to the discipline, and perhaps to God.* I read *The Seven Storey Mountain,* the early memoir of Thomas Merton. He was a Catholic convert, monk, artist, and activist—and an extraordinary writer. Later in life, when he discovered sixties radical politics and Eastern mysticism, and fell in love with a woman, that book made him cringe. It does a little for me now. How could anyone think that the monastery would wipe away one's doubts and passions, once and for all? How could I? But at the time, his certainty and self-denial had me in a thrall. Merton became my patron saint.

I enlisted everything around me in my preparation, which became ever more haphazard and frantic. I summoned the resources of calculus, seemingly the closest among my classes in school to the transcendent: *God is the conception of the infinite in things,* I mused a few days before leaving for the abbey, imagining some exalted integral of integrals. I alternated between reading my mother's books on Eastern meditation and whatever I could find from the Western mystics. It was a relief to discover how much they had in common. The Eastern practices of self-emptying and self-discovery my mother had been exploring had counterparts in the West too, forgotten in most ordinary synagogues and churches but remembered in the monasteries, where my father's antiques would have fit in nicely. It helped that in Catholicism divorce doesn't exist.

∴

Holy Cross belongs to the Order of Cistercians of the Strict Observance—the Trappists. It follows much the same code of life as Anselm did at Bec, set out in the sixth century by Benedict of Nursia. The monks live in an eternal return of manual labor and study, punctuated every few hours by prayer together, beginning at 3:30 in the morning, and ending, in midsummer, a little before sunset.

When I first arrived, the sound of monks chanting psalms in unadorned unison terrified me. Their words—calling on God with praise and for help and for deliverance from enemies—only brought into relief what these monks believed and I did not. The men clothed in white habit and black scapular, nearly all gray-haired and wrinkled, loomed over me in the dark choir like shadows, like ghosts, until one showed me a passing, understanding smile. I felt that I needed to know what they knew, which meant learning to believe what they believed.

At Holy Cross, the cottage industry is a fruitcake factory. On a given day I would decorate cakes with red and green cherries, or sift through the yellow raisins for seeds, or spray brandy on top. (The monks cracked up when they gave me the brandy job, since I was still under drinking age.) Afterward we would mop. With the young Merton in mind, I chased opportunities to exercise my humility and obedience, to give myself over to the work, to the community, and through it to the will of their God. I sat in the church on my own for hours waiting for an invisible presence to arrive through the body on the crucifix, curled in literal anguish, hanging in front of a rough-hewn stone sculpture of the Virgin Mother presenting her child. But mainly what I noticed was the ticking clock over the door. I spent too much time reading, consuming book after spiritual book, hoping one or the next would finally tell me what I was doing there. Each lit me up somehow but usually at cross-purposes with the others.

Monasteries are not places for lofty philosophy; in their extraordinary way, they're built for ordinary life. Monastic thought and literature dwell in the practical matters of prayer, liturgy, community, and sanity, in tune with the silence and monotony. Anselm was unusual among monastic authors for his metaphysical speculation, which was usually the work of scholastics in the cities. Still, his ideas came ensconced in the routine of psalms and contemplation. They were tailored for that life. And that life, in itself, is a living proof; nothing makes sense in the monastery if God doesn't exist.

One of the monks assumed watch over me while I was there, Brother Benedict.[4] Before taking his vows, Benedict had lived a busy life in the world, having worked on a Mississippi riverboat, as an archivist at the New York Public Library, and as editor for the collected works of George Balanchine. He knew great writers and artists, and he had been married. Each day, he would leave a stack of books for me outside the door of my room with a kind note, but he never seemed to be trying to persuade me of anything in particular. I knew I could come to him with my questions. He had been through plenty of his own, though his slight, collected bearing belied it. As I talked and talked half-aimlessly, his eyes followed me through the oversized bifocals that hung above his white beard. I tried to tell him about my fears and doubts and worries there, and how confused I'd been feeling. That's when something he said changed everything.

"Well, of *course,* Nathan," Benedict told me. "We all doubt. We question."

It was that simple: the idea that their faith is a process, not a possession. A way of living. The monastery, says St. Benedict's *Rule,* is to be "a school for the Lord's service"—for "beginners," it says, not saints. "As we progress in this way of life and in faith," it promises, "we shall run on the path of God's commandments, our hearts overflowing with the inexpressible delight of love."[5] A *path.* A faith that you don't take for granted. You mold yourself for it, patiently, with hope and love. The barrier between the monks and me began to dissolve. Their prayers, anyway, had already been finding their way into my sleep after Compline.

The monks sang not just out of certainty, but out of desire. They were living out a relationship, with Jesus among them as a brother, God their father, and Mary the mother of all. It was a family I could belong to, to strengthen

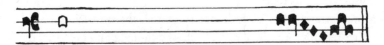

℣. GUARD US, LORD, AS THE APPLE OF YOUR EYE.
℟. HIDE US IN THE SHADOW OF YOUR WINGS.

me for my family at home. I continued torturing myself with books and unanswered prayers, but I wasn't alone in it now. Chanting in the choir or working in the bakery, we were building our proofs together. *There are moments when I really believe I could love this God,* I wrote.

Another week passed, and it was time to get in my car and go home. I was ready. All the thinking and reading had taken a toll. I wanted to drive back fast and see my friends, so I put Bob Dylan's *Desire* in the CD player, and that's what I did. The image that sticks with me, though, is of looking in the rearview mirror at the long road through the abbey's fields, back to the buildings in the distance that were already blending in with the mountains. No matter what other songs might play over them, those prayers would keep ringing in my head.

∴

Anselm originally sketched his beloved proof in only a few short pages. He begins with a psalm, the verse that opens Psalm 14: "The fool has said in his heart, 'There is no God.'" (It's also in Psalm 54, and Augustine used it in his proof as well.) So what is it that makes this fool, as the Bible says, a fool? Everyone can agree, Anselm explains, that "God" means "a being than which nothing greater can be conceived."[6] People disagree only about whether the God they're talking about actually exists.

This difference, says Anselm, makes all the difference: the unbelieving fool's concept of God has a problem. A God who exists out there in real-ity, and not just in the mind, is greater than one who is just a concept. An existing God has to be better than a nonexisting one, Anselm thinks. To claim that God doesn't exist, therefore, contradicts the very concept of God we're talking about—again, the "being than which nothing greater can be conceived." Nothing is better than this God, as a rule, and that's why the fool

is a fool. His God is a contradiction. The moment you really grasp the idea of God in your mind, you have proof that God is real.

This simple idea did for Anselm exactly what he hoped it would. In a single stroke, it declared that the God of his faith and hope, the sum of all perfection, has to exist. Knowing *what* God is, then, becomes the same as knowing *that* God is. God's nature and existence are the same. There could be no more fitting proof for the one, true God whose self-disclosure to Moses was in the words "I AM THAT I AM."[7]

Usually, when I describe this to people for the first time, they give me a sour look, like I've got to be kidding. There were those in Anselm's time, too, who weren't buying it. Soon after copies of the *Proslogion* began circulating, a fellow monk named Gaunilo composed an objection.

Twice his age, and with a soberer cast of mind, Gaunilo believed in God no less than Anselm did; what he didn't like was Anselm's reasoning. Their exchange was a considerate one, between two monks with a common cause and a common faith. Gaunilo chose a playful title for his essay: "On Behalf of the Fool"—the same fool of Psalm 14.

The essence of the critique is simple: just because something seems like it should exist doesn't mean that it actually does, out there in the world. He gives an example to illustrate. Say we're told of an island—another island!— out in the ocean, so far away that it can't be reached. That's a shame, because there's no island more perfect than this one. It has bounty and wealth undisturbed by people. Gaunilo then claims that, according to Anselm's logic, this island really exists. It must, right? If it didn't, we could think of an island just as excellent that did exist, and it would be better. But nobody is going to claim that such an island, or what-have-you, is really out there. How, then, could the same kind of reasoning be a trustworthy proof for God's existence? Thus Gaunilo builds a reductio ad absurdum—the whole thing collapses in absurdity.

Nothing Gaunilo wrote could make Anselm back down or lose confidence in his first flash of insight at Matins. He was so confident, in fact, that he circulated the critique together with his own reply. The reply clarifies a subtler part of the proof in the *Proslogion,* which Gaunilo, and others since him, overlooked.[8] See if this helps.

God, Anselm explains, is not in the same class as an enchanted island. The single thing "than which nothing greater can be conceived" must be always and everywhere, with no possibility of not existing. Everything depends on it. As the height of perfection, it's the measure against which we judge the good in all else. As things in the world come and go, it's the steady ground beneath them. It's not simply, as Gaunilo wrote, something "greater than all other beings," much less other islands; an island may be paradise, but it is still only an island, and greater things than that can be conceived. God, on the other hand, is uniquely unsurpassable. No other thing could qualify. "You alone, then," he prays, "of all things most truly exist and therefore of all things possess existence to the highest degree."[9] Gaunilo was out of his depth.

Anselm didn't know it, but he had precursors in this kind of thinking. Recall, for instance, that Ibn Sina wrote of that which exists necessarily, by virtue of itself. Abu Nasr al-Farabi, a tenth-century Turk, came especially close to Anselm's phrasing when he described "a perfect being nothing more perfect than which can exist." "It is not possible to conceive," al-Farabi added elsewhere, "a being more complete than his being; a reality greater than his reality; or a unity greater than his unity."[10]

Anselm had no access to the writings of his Muslim counterparts. Their only common denominator was the Greek heritage, but even the Greeks were still largely missing from Anselm's world. There may have been a copy of the *Timaeus* at Bec, though little else even of Plato. It was from Augustine, mainly, that Anselm got the Platonic themes that show up in his proof. Against the advice of Lanfranc and the convention of the time, however, he refused to pepper his treatises with quotations from earlier authors. Like so many others who work in the genre of proof, he felt the anxiety of influence. How can one claim to speak for pure reason while relying on the authority of those who came before?

What's striking about Anselm's proof, even more than the motions of its logic, is how he describes it. Doing justice to what he had discovered by the grace of God meant inventing a literary device. The *Proslogion* mixes treatise and devotion, reason and emotion. It takes the form of a prayer—or a letter, as if to a friend. Thinking and feeling meet, the basic ingredients of assent.

In Anselm's world, letter writing bridged distances and soothed absences. An informal postal system of couriers carried letters, inscribed on rolls of parchment, between the monasteries.[11] When a new batch arrived, someone would read what was in it out loud to the whole community. Letters, whether bearing a greeting or a matter of contention, were public documents in private form. The more intimate one sounded, the better the show.

Until he eventually succeeded Lanfranc as archbishop of Canterbury in Britain, monastic discipline kept Anselm at Bec. Letters were his contact with the outside world. Most of the early works we have from him are letters and prayers, written for the far-flung monks and noblewomen who asked for his advice or blessing.[12] Even while expounding on theological ideas, these are drenched with feeling and imagery, anticipating the worldly, romantic passions of the troubadour poets who were then coming on the scene. They were widely copied and circulated.

Anselm thought, as Plato did, that friendship could be an ecstatic, salvific undertaking. His passion in letters to friends is so palpable, and so unusual for its time, that modern interpreters have wondered whether his relations with other monks were actually celibate.[13] Take, for instance, this passage from a letter to another monk named Gundulf.

> When I sit down to write to you, oh soul most dear to my soul, when I sit down to write to you, I am uncertain how best to begin what I have to say. Everything I feel about you is sweet and pleasant to my heart; whatever I desire for you is the best that my mind can conceive.[14]

There it is: a variant of the central formula of his proof—"the best that my mind can conceive"—appearing, years earlier, as a token of affection. In turn, the kind of language he uses in friendship turns up in prayers and treatises. Anselm felt his God, like his friends, more as absence than presence. Addressed to the silence of the mind, his proof answers much the same longing as the letters; it insists that all along, though unseen, God is with him. In the first chapter of the *Proslogion* he writes, "Lord my God, teach my heart where and how to seek You, where and how to find You. Lord, if You are not present here, where, since You are absent, shall I look for you?" And with the proof, he says in the book's last chapter, "I have discovered a joy that is complete and more than complete"—from absence to presence, from longing to consummation.

Anselm's proof "is mysterious," wrote the French Jewish-and-almost-Catholic mystic Simone Weil, "because it doesn't address itself to the intelligence, but to love."[15] Like love, you've got to sit with it, and also struggle.

Even in his worst despair, Anselm gives no indication that he ever actually doubted the existence of his God. It was God's silence, not nonexistence, that troubled him. "I do not seek to understand so that I may believe," he writes, "but I believe so that I may understand."[16] The proof was that understanding. He saw a glimpse of God, more clearly than he ever had before. It was a taste of the eschaton, the final condition that souls striving for blessedness will one day reach. Proof meant certainty, assurance, and ammunition for persuading others, sure. But before those, Anselm was simply grasping at his God, and that grasping led him to joy.

∴

The difference between what I had come to know in the monastery and the Catholicism I found going to churches afterward was a shock. At the monastery there had been quiet, study, and simple work. In the churches, though, I found the remnants of an organization built to shepherd certain immigrant communities into the American middle class. There were Knights of Columbus in faux-military uniforms, sermons that dealt more with football than with the gospel, and pews filled with people who could barely leave their busyness at the door. If nothing made sense without God at the monastery, outside, God seemed superfluous. Or worse.

In my first semester of college that fall, in one of our many long, wrenching conversations late at night in a dorm lounge, a friend tried to tell me that my interest in Catholicism was an insult to him, as a Jew. He was also gay, and he thought maybe I was trying to repress the fact that I was too. I wondered whether he could be right—though the agonizing records I kept on various efforts to manage and temper my desires suggested otherwise. Meanwhile, the *Boston Globe*'s revelations of sexual abuse by priests had started an ever-worsening chain reaction around the country. None of this had been a problem at the monastery. I was dealing with all the anxieties and hang-ups basically common to eighteen-year-olds, all of a sudden amplified by the ancient anxieties and hang-ups of an ascetic, legalistic religion.

Sexuality is always somewhere in the background with proofs but always in a way that belies exactly how. Proofs never mention it. They don't need to; that's the point. The proofs supposedly begin where extrarational forces and urges end. The proof claims, *I'm more than that, I'm better than that. I'm more sensible than the sensual.* It's a claim to a certain dignity over undignified flesh, the promise of some clarity, at last, beyond fleshy confusion.

In those days, the whole color of life could turn from one shade to another in a matter of hours; I went to sleep each night hoping—and, increasingly, praying—that I wouldn't wake up depressed. College freshmen usually have some sorting out to do about who and what they are, but the urge for reinvention was especially strong in me. Alongside my course in Islam that first semester, and my visits to every religious service I could find, I was taking formal logic in the philosophy department, multivariable calculus in math, and introductory fiction writing. It amounted to a lot of ways of thinking at once. At night, as I tried to sleep, stories blended with doctrines, then morphed into theorems.

Though I remember that period like forever, I wasn't on campus very long before some clarity began to arrive. An ad in the school paper led me, on the last Sunday night in September, to a small meeting in an upper room, above an arch. With me were a few others interested in making their way into the Catholic Church through the Rite of Christian Initiation for Adults, or RCIA. (I had been legally an adult for only a month.) The grandfather clock in the corner of the room was stuck at the eleventh hour, and that seemed a mighty sign. *I think I might do it, I might actually do it,* I scribbled that night after getting back to my room.

Father Bodah, the Catholic chaplain, led the discussion. As he often did at these meetings, he was probably wearing his black clerical shirt and collar with a dull blue fleece half buttoned up over it. His goatee was dark, though speckled with gray, on a slim, pensive face beneath a pair of glasses. While he spoke, with a voice as possessed of its doctrine as of old novels and dry ecclesial jokes, I wished he would never stop. There was none of the condescending enthusiasm one might expect from a campus chaplain; the very grammar of his sentences declared their seriousness, as did his melancholy. In that room, with each story and each Latin motto that his terrific memory produced, the whole universe settled into itself, and so too did the assent I was moving toward.

Brother Benedict would help me phrase my questions, but Father Bodah could answer them. He would quote Cardinal Newman: "Ten thousand difficulties do not make one doubt." We marched through the difficulties, one at a time, to solutions that were elegant, intricate, and satisfying. With him I first encountered the Catholic systematic imagination that is the legacy of Thomas Aquinas.

∴

Aquinas's *Summa Theologica,* the enormous treatise he labored over for the last decade of his life, is composed entirely of short articles, arranged like bricks. Each makes only a single point, building on the points of articles preceding it, always following the same structure:

1. A question is stated.

2. Several possible answers follow, which Aquinas doesn't accept; they might be arguments made by his contemporaries or misunderstandings of scripture.

3. He gives his answer and arguments to support it.

4. One by one comes a reply to each of the objections stated in (2)— then on to the next article.

Together, these bricks make an imposing wall. One at a time, every question Aquinas could think of finds an answer, and each answer has a spot in the system—exhaustive, exhausting, mesmerizing.

Two hundred years had passed since Anselm. The thirteenth century was a momentous time for trying to figure out the universe; ancient wisdom was back. Through crusades in the Holy Land and Muslim neighbors in Spain, Christian Europe discovered the Greek learning preserved by Islamic and Byzantine libraries, especially the works of Aristotle. Latin translations from Arabic, and then from the original Greek, began in the previous century. With the ancient texts, too, came translations of the Arabic commentaries by Muslims and Jews. The commentators' Latinized names—Averroes (Ibn Rushd), Avicenna (Ibn Sina), and Maimonides among them—were bywords for authority and controversy alongside that of "the Philosopher," Aristotle. He was, as Dante would soon put it, "the master of those who know."[17] A revolution was under way, and Thomas Aquinas, a young student from Sicily who was newly professed in the Dominican order, couldn't have been better poised to take part.

Aquinas's world didn't welcome the revolution with open arms. In 1215 Aristotle's speculative works had been banned for fear of a threat to orthodox theology. Theories from Muslim Aristotelians about the eternity of the universe and the oneness of all minds circulated among scholars and students, showing Europe's bishops how real the threat could be. But the spread of Aristotle's books was impossible to stop; by midcentury they were everywhere. In order to control the Aristotelian tide, new professorships were created for scholars from the Dominican and Franciscan orders, which Rome felt could be trusted to sift through the material with allegiance to right belief. Aquinas's work was always under suspicion of heresy during his lifetime. Studying Aristotle meant playing with fire.

Together with his teacher, Albert the Great, Aquinas argued hard against those who would dismiss the new ideas entirely. They adjured their church and their society not to fear the advance of knowledge, that God had made this universe a reasonable one. But they weren't afraid to correct Aristotle when he appeared to be in error.

Aquinas was said to live perpetually in intense thought. At a royal banquet in 1269, he was so lost in contemplation that he didn't notice when the king was speaking to him. He could dictate to his secretaries even while sleeping. Meanwhile, he ascended to the heights of magical mysticism. Tears streamed down his face as he said morning mass. While thinking through difficult problems, he prayed to talking crucifixes and levitated off the floor. He poured all these energies, mental and mystical, into amassing the fullest synthesis of Christian doctrine and philosophy ever created. But following a stroke near the end of his life he saw a vision so powerful that he stopped working and went around telling people, "All that I have written seems like straw."[18] Few found this convincing, of course; rarely has an author been taken quite so seriously as Aquinas.

Not long after his death, a condemnation was issued in Paris that targeted parts of Aquinas's Aristotelianism. But the resistance didn't last long. In 1323, less than half a century later, Rome canonized Thomas Aquinas a saint, and during the crisis of the Reformation, his books were held up as an authority next to the Bible at the Catholics' Council of Trent. His embrace of Aristotle made way for a revival of ancient art and science in the Renaissance. And the Catholic Church, even as I encountered it with Father Bodah, still struggles with whether to imitate Aquinas in his daring or accept his words as second to scripture.

That first night of RCIA classes, and in the weeks and months that followed, each answer took its place, comfortably and immovably, among the rest. The Trinity. The sacraments. The miserable death of Jesus, and his radiant reappearance afterward. Sin and grace, life and death. I welcomed them all. RCIA became the part of my week when, in Father Bodah's presence, everything would come together and make sense. He recommended more books for me to read. In my journal I increasingly adopted the vocabulary of a believer and, in my head, the propositions of belief. It was like an experience Thomas Merton describes, before his own conversion, upon discovering Aquinas. "Here was a notion of God," Merton would remember, "that was at the same time deep, precise, simple, and accurate and, what is more, charged with implications which I could not even begin to appreciate."[19] Yes—that.

My heart, if I can presume to speak for it, didn't want to wait for baptism. Small things I can wait for, but for the big ones, I've always been impatient.

Having baptism as a destination, though, didn't take away the wavering. On a good day, everything felt guided, reasoned, and purposeful, leading me upward to glory or, at least, some equanimity. Something miraculous would happen involving a rosary. I would read the Bible and hear the Word of God. Waking up the next morning, it could all be gone.

I flatly decided that there is no God, says one journal entry. Then later on it continues, *Okay. Then a moment of truth burst through the open window from the falling snow outside and then, okay, there is a God.* Answering doubts with order, I organized a regimen of solitary morning and nighttime prayers, based on what I had learned at the monastery. When I could, I went to weekday mass at noon on campus. *Maybe the key is in something Father Bodah said,* I wrote. *In our tradition, God finds us, he extends His being to us. And all I have to do is take hold.*

∴

The order of things is no accident with a thinker like Aquinas, least of all in the *Summa Theologica.* Its architecture is part of its message. The *Summa*'s outline traces the circle of Aquinas's universe: God exists, and makes the world and its people, who through Christ and the sacraments of the church return to God. Throughout, he weeds through the promise and pitfalls of Aristotle, in conversation with Catholic tradition and the Bible. Every part is in its proper spot.

The *Summa* begins, after a prefatory section, with the existence of God. This question he divides, in turn, into three: whether God's existence is self-evident (no), whether God's existence can be proved (yes), and then whether God exists (yes).

Proof of God's existence came to Aquinas in no fit of divine revelation, as Anselm's did. Instead, he distilled his Five Ways—five separate, consilient arguments—from Aristotle and his successors. In the West, they're sometimes treated as if Aquinas invented them. In fact, he did little more than curate and reformulate what he thought to be the Islamic world's soundest proofs, largely in agreement with Maimonides. But probably no compendium of proofs has been more influential, thanks to the subsequent megalith of the *Summa* that the Ways help set in motion.

Motion, actually, is the method of the First Way, just as it was Maimonides' first argument in the *Guide.* This comes straight from Aristotle. "In the world some things are in motion," Aquinas begins.[20] Everything in motion was made to move by something else, which itself must already be moving, having been moved by another. But the chain of movers can't go on to infinity. If there were no first unmoved mover, there could be no motion at all. "And this," Aquinas concludes, "everyone understands to be God."

The next three arguments follow a pattern much like the first, relying on aspects of Aristotelian science and the impossibility of an infinite regress.

Number two deals with *efficient cause,* which for him means the cause of something's existence. There are things that exist, right? Since there can't be an endless progression of causes going on to infinity, there must be a first one. If there weren't a first, there would be no others. Following Plato, by way of Maimonides and the Arabic tradition, he concludes that there must be a first cause of the world. To this, "everyone gives the name of God."

The Third Way is about *possibility* and *necessity.* It's an Aristotelian distinction but one developed much more fully in the Muslim world, especially by Ibn Sina and Maimonides. To start, Aquinas observes that there are things in the world whose existence could be merely possible, and such things come to be only through what already exists. If everything were merely possible, though, Aquinas reasons, there could have been a moment when nothing existed at all. If this ever happened, as it thereby might, nothing could be caused to exist thereafter. This prospect of an eternal nothing is intolerable for him, and he takes it to be absurd. Like motion and cause, the existence of all the things in the world that could be merely possible makes sense only if there's also some being beyond the fray. There must be at least something that exists as pure necessity and pure existence, by its own necessity, upon which all the rest of creation hangs. Again, "this all men speak of as God."

Now, note well: Aquinas still makes no commitment to the universe having been created in time, against eternity. These finite chains of motion, cause, and contingency could happen over a finite past, or an infinite one. He means to describe the structure of how things in the universe relate to one another, not narrate a sequence of events. His reasoning leaves the question of creation or eternity up to God, and in God's revelation he sees that God chose creation, in the finite past.

Aquinas's Fourth Way deals with *degrees.* It's that old idea of perfection-in-the-abstract just as Anselm argued for early on: that some things are more good, true, and beautiful than other things implies that there exists something that is the most perfectly good, true, and beautiful of all. They're like the rungs of a ladder that can only stand if there's something at the top—"this we call God"—to rest against.

The last of the Five Ways deals with *purpose.* Its antecedents are plenty, and we'll get to more of them later. Aquinas agrees with Aristotle that all things act toward a goal, toward certain ends. The goal of a rock is to sit, and the goal of a person is to be happy. Now, it is clear that lots of things, such as rocks, don't think up these goals for themselves. Even people, who can think, don't decide that they want to be happy; they just do. To Aquinas it's obvious that this order cannot come from the things in nature but must be the work of an orchestrator, a final cause. And of course, for the fifth time, "this being we call God"—as I was beginning to more and more.

Now, where do these *Quinque Viae* leave us?

In the structure of the *Summa,* as well as in their meaning, the Five Ways are only a beginning. Unlike Anselm, Aquinas found no bliss in his proofs. He held that ultimate happiness comes from contemplating God,[21] and that's not really something he thought proofs enable one to do. Each Way gives only very general knowledge, gesturing toward certain facts about some kind of God but saying little about God as such. We *call* the proofs' object God, we *give it that name,* but they're just the faintest outline of who God must be. Aquinas thought that a really complete proof, and thus real happiness, isn't possible in this life. In the *Summa* he repeats a famous passage from First Corinthians: "For now we see in a mirror, dimly, but then we will see face to face."[22] Just when you think you've got everything figured out, you come up against your limits.

Straw.

When it was time to go home for winter break after my first semester at school, I discovered just how much had changed in me. I had already told my parents about what, in the act of telling them, became my decision to go through with baptism. One at a time, they listened more than they gave advice. My mom and I traded book recommendations. She actually seemed happy about it, that I was inclining toward a spiritual practice of my own; for her, in these matters, different paths can reach the same goal. When I told my dad, he said he would be there at my baptism. That night, the two of us walked around the city for hours talking—books, classes, possibilities. I wrote in my journal of *a release,* of *a massive weight lifted so perfectly off my shoulders.* I wrote, *I am not entirely crazy, I need no longer to live a lie.* It wasn't supposed to, but what they thought mattered a lot.

Back home for winter break, I told my friends, one by one, what I was about to do. Some were more surprised than others. I sensed that my explanations didn't really satisfy them. By day I tried to write down the proofs I had been thinking through, and at night I would try to explain myself to friends again. They didn't even seem to care, in the sort of day-in-day-out sense that I apparently had to, whether God exists. Was that their blessing or their curse? One can come down awfully hard in condemnation against those not putting all their waking energy into finding out the meaning of life and the universe, and that which animates them both. But it wasn't clear to me whether my friends were the ones trapped in Plato's cave or whether I was. I wrote a story called "St. Thomas" in which the main character is a student who discovers a proof for the existence of God—a satire on myself.

That winter, I thought I could understand why Jesus had been so powerless in his hometown; there, everyone knows you too well as you were, not as what you realize you're becoming. Arguments—to say nothing of miracles— don't work.

∴

Together, Anselm and Aquinas made the genre of proof respectable again in Europe. But that doesn't mean they agreed about how to do it. Anselm's earlier book, the *Monologion,* had rudiments of the Five Ways, but such hodgepodge was exactly what he didn't like about it. Aquinas dismissed Anselm's proof with a single paragraph of the *Summa,* just before introducing the Ways. He thought the whole idea of proving God from a mere concept is fraught: people might have different concepts of God, for one, and existence in the mind can't entail actual existence. It seemed like more of the same cloistered thinking that reigned around him, and against which he proclaimed Aristotle.

Anselm built his proof entirely in his mind, with no reference to the outside world. This kind of reasoning is called *a priori*—literally, "from what comes before." It's hardly surprising from a man who so loved the quiet of his monastery. Aquinas's proofs, however, were *a posteriori*—"from what comes later"—beginning with how the world works. Anselm looked within, but

Aquinas wanted to show that signs of Christianity's God await us in nature. They devised two very different grammars of assent.

During Aquinas's time, the new mendicant orders—the Dominicans and the Franciscans—were gaining influence in Europe's universities, and as they did, the two became rivals. One of the things they disagreed about was the proper method of proving God's existence.[23] Aquinas's worldly, didactic approach resonated with his Dominican community, devoted to preaching against heresy and convincing the unconverted. Compared to Aquinas's Five Ways, Anselm's proof was hopelessly lost in the a priori clouds.

Franciscan thinkers, generally, were warmer toward Anselm. Their order's founder, Francis of Assisi, was known for works of love, not study. His example seems to have made them more open to Anselm's fusion of reason with mystic longing than to the colder Aristotelian alternative. Finally, it would be a late medieval Franciscan, the "Subtle Doctor" John Duns Scotus, who tried to reconcile the two approaches. "For accuracy and depth and scope," gushed the young Thomas Merton, "this is the most perfect and complete and thorough proof for the existence of God that has ever been worked out by any man."[24]

Duns Scotus had Anselmian instincts. He wanted not a cluster of independent arguments but a single, all-in-one proof for the one God. He takes pieces of the Five Ways, and he shows that they converge in something like Anselm's necessary being. He grounds Anselm's idea, in turn, with the Ways' a posteriori roots in nature. Aquinas and Anselm seem to be not opposed to one another, as they themselves seem to have thought, but mutually supportive.

This Scotist synthesis was an epic in the genre of proof, but Duns Scotus died young and was never made a saint like his predecessors. His scholastic contrivance soon became a paragon of what more modern thinkers would be eager to set aside. Its intricacy and breadth, however, says something true about what it takes to believe fully and deeply: it requires combining both Anselm and Aquinas, uniting the inward with the outward. Assent, like this, is a convergence—a meeting of circumstances, choices, and the best of one's knowledge. It is complicated. But then, when it happens, it's also simple. It just is. One's assent becomes yet another fact upon which everything else depends.

Although that night has defined my whole life since, I have only a few scattered memories of the Easter vigil when finally I was baptized in the campus chapel. Sacramentally, spiritually, and officially, I became a Christian and a Roman Catholic, a person responsible to a God. The water trickled over my head from Father Bodah's hand. Some friends came to watch, and my parents too, sitting in separate pews. Afterward, I had dinner with my father; religion separated us now like the table between us, and we fumbled to reach across it. The following day, my first Easter, I went to church again with my mother, trying to show her what it meant to me. After she left, I felt full of private happiness, full of resurrection.

That night I remembered something Brother Benedict had once said about his own conversion being "suspect." *Well mine is,* I wrote. *They all are. We all are. God works in us anyway.*

I wrote a letter the following week to my friend Corinne from high school—who had been patient, if perplexed, as I dragged her to churches and then ran off to a monastery. *Probably for the rest of my life I will question that water and that night,* I said, *but I am comfortable at least to have something certain to question.* The letter continued, *In the eyes of faith, that moment changed what I am, though all else remains painfully the same.* I wanted to assure Corinne that I was still myself, only more so.

Like love stories that end with the first kiss, conversion stories usually stop with the conversion. But I have more chapters ahead. Proof is what comes afterward, after birth and rebirth, through practice and entropy. It is the reconstruction, the tale we tell ourselves and those privy to our terminology, in the years and centuries that follow. Now I was starting again to build up arguments and conclusions of my own from a new foundation—but not, despite myself, from scratch.

FOUR

On Certainty

EARLY MODERNITY UPENDS A FAMILIAR PROOF

The story almost repeats itself: another dim room, another silent flash of insight in the mind of a man. Yet while Anselm was alone among his brother monks and under the roof of his church, this solitude, five centuries later, was more complete.

René Descartes, a slight, sickly Frenchman in his early twenties, was in Germany serving as a volunteer in the Bavarian prince Maximilian's army. A war was on, and would be for thirty years. Its lines were drawn along the same ones that, over the past century, had divided Europe: Catholic on one side—Maximilian's side—and Protestant on the other. Descartes was traveling back to camp from the coronation of Holy Roman Emperor Ferdinand II when a spell of bad weather held him at the town of Neuberg for the winter, in late 1619. He found a room to rent that had a warm stove in it. With no company but his own, tucked away from the war outside, he devoted himself to thoughts and dreams that would have an outsized effect on the subsequent history of ideas.

What he found there was not the faith of Anselm but doubt. He began questioning what he thought about God, the world, and everything in between, until only certainty remained. Then, from that precipice, with no help but the help of proof, he would build it all up again.

There's a tantalizing magic in the prospect of being alone. We've seen this already on islands and among monks, and I felt it during the months after my baptism. I had a lot to think about, a lot of doubts to dispel. Solitude seemed like just the means for making headway. I had just spent an unusually eventful school year boxed up on a too-pleasant campus, where I daydreamed about monasteries and, only somewhat oppositely, going "on the road" like Jack Kerouac. That summer, I chose the latter.

I got in my white '93 Corolla and hardly left it for a month, the stated purpose being to Discover America. But really I did it for the quiet in between. I drove south from Virginia to New Orleans, then west, up the coast of California, and back east by a more northerly route. I stopped at one monastery above the clouds at Big Sur and another among the Rockies. I made a friend at a Mormon food pantry in Salt Lake City. The trip took me past landmarks and landscapes and several of my new college friends in their native habitats, though most of the time it was just my car and me.

When traveling in those years, I would sometimes bring along a used paperback copy of *On Certainty,* by the philosopher (and solitary) Ludwig Wittgenstein. It's a collection of notes he jotted down in the last years of his life, after a visit to the United States in 1949. It begins with a claim that another philosopher had recently made, about how noticing one's own hand constitutes proof that there really is an external world. ("This fellow isn't insane," Wittgenstein imagines a voice replying to anyone surprised by the topic. "We are only doing philosophy.")[1] From there the book meanders around the difficulties of thinking and speaking about being certain, enmeshed as it all is in "language games" and shadows of doubt. As I traveled, I followed, writing down notes of my own from Wittgenstein's in a booklet I had made from scrap paper, scotch tape, and two staples.

"Doesn't it come out here that knowledge is related to a decision?" he asks. Yes, it does. For me it did. I had made a decision, and followed through, and now my reasoning would have to rest on that. What I would know, I would know with respect to it. Certainties don't stand alone. They're always among other certainties, decisions, appearances, and questions. But still, like Descartes, I couldn't shake the idea that the real truth of the matter will make itself known when you're by yourself. So, by myself, I kept driving.

On that trip, in the town of Golden, on the mountain side of Denver, I found another devotee of solitude: my uncle, my mother's brother. He was living with two dogs—humanly alone—in a dingy motor inn. Stuck there on probation for a DUI bust, he had managed to quit drinking. He spent his days watching Turner Classic Movies and programming on his computer. As soon as I arrived, he began talking about both. There were start-to-finish retellings of old movie story lines. Much more, though, he showed me what was on the computer.

With an obsolete PC running DOS and a programming language named TurboPascal, he had spent the past decade building a universe. At its heart was a text editor—a place for reading, writing, and organizing in hypertext. Every feature had a purpose and a deeper meaning. Words could do actions. A special dictionary was learning how to interpret them. True to the promise of the Greeks' logos, he was trying to cross the divide between words and mind. The trouble was getting caught up in Wittgenstein's language games— the worlds of words that trick us into reality.

"Certainty resides in the nature of the language game," Wittgenstein surmised.[2]

My uncle and I had been out of touch for a long time. Years before, he had been a scientist at the National Institutes of Health, and much else: a carpenter, an encyclopedia salesman, a saxophonist, an activist, a father. Now he had few possessions that couldn't fit into the small room he was renting or in the back of his Bronco. He had been through a lot. You could see it in his wrinkles, in his towering, thin frame, in his long and graying hair, and in the teeth now missing from his gums. He spoke in a raspy voice, without breaths or pauses, like someone who'd been out of practice with conversation. But in Golden I could see that he was also fearless and generous like no one else I knew. His past was heavy, but his burden was light.

We walked the dogs on an empty golf course under the mountains, talking about consciousness. He showed me simulations of cellular automata, simple algorithms that could model complicated evolutionary processes. He talked about wanting to put them to music. Piece by piece, he was describing a world out of bits and instructions, making it seem like the real world might have been made that way too.

The journal entries from those days are scattershot. Short, stray remarks. Lists. There was too much happening to do any better. My uncle, an avowed atheist, might not like how much he and his creations drew my mind to God.

This is the most real, crazy, visceral, serene art I've ever seen in the act of creation.

All extended to include the meaning of the whole universe.

note. We have always been seeking God by infinity, the Western way, the same that dominates, the male.

This is the revelation of a sort-of gnostic place where the scientific and the spiritual have no conflict, no disunity.

Well, that is, God, the God in itself; itself.

I remained there longer than planned. But then I had to push on.

A few days later it was Chicago, where I stayed with my aunt, my father's sister, a yoga teacher and professor whose website calls her the "Thinking Doctor." I can't remember what we talked about during that visit, exactly, but it's usually just about everything. For all that my uncle can talk, this aunt knows how to listen, to ask questions that make what feels important to you seem important to her. We went on like that for hours, until again I had to leave. I had to drive back to Virginia.

I liked the solitude of that month, though not much was clearer afterward than when I left. I had seen more of the country. But of all the people I had encountered, it was those in my own scattered family who made the biggest impression on me. In them, I saw that I had come by all my anxious thinking honestly, by way of bloodline. I wasn't so alone with it anymore. At risk of a platitude: it's as if the real point of the trip was not so much taking off, like I'd assumed, but coming home.

.˙.

So, home—Descartes again. The town where he was born in 1596, in central France, has since been renamed for him. He passed his teenage years at the Jesuit college of La Flèche, where Aquinas's synthesis of Aristotle and Catholic teaching organized the curriculum. From La Flèche he followed his father and older brother in earning a law degree and then, experience-hungry, enlisted at the first sign of war. Of his parents he would write, in a passage of metaphysics no less suggestive as autobiography, "It is certainly not they who preserve me; nor is it they who in any way brought me into being, insofar as I am a thinking thing."[3] The kind of thinker he intended to be could depend only on himself. He also ditched the doctrines of the Scholastics that he had learned at La Flèche. In a world being torn apart by war and Reformation, they were no good anymore. Something different was needed, and he thought he had glimpsed it that winter in Neuberg. The challenge was to write it down.

Out of the army for a decade or so, he found a new hiding place: Amsterdam. It was perfect. Amsterdam had become a busy trading port, too bustling to notice a quiet foreigner. He went there to live "as solitary and as withdrawn a life as I could in the remotest deserts"[4]—solitary except, that is, for his servant-lover Hélène and their daughter, Francine. The two decades after he and his clandestine family first moved there gave him the most productive years of his life. They were cut short only after he accepted a position

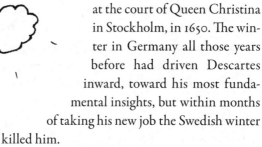

at the court of Queen Christina in Stockholm, in 1650. The winter in Germany all those years before had driven Descartes inward, toward his most fundamental insights, but within months of taking his new job the Swedish winter killed him.

The words that nevertheless made Descartes immortal are found in his *Discourse on Method,* published in 1637: *"Je pense donc je suis"*—"I think, therefore I am."[5] Another self-thinking thought, prefigured in the stove-heated room of Neuberg. There, Descartes had tried to renounce all but the single most undeniable fact. Doubt can banish everything else, but he realized it has to stop at the thinker doing the doubting. (Wittgenstein, again: "Our *doubts* depend on the fact that some propositions are exempt from doubt.")[6] From there, from this sensation of pure and solitary consciousness, before he is even ready to believe in his body or a world outside, Descartes finds God.[7]

First, an intuition: there is some perfect being, one that is omniscient, omnipotent, eternal, and infinite. He trusts this idea immediately; it seems "clear and distinct." But where could it have come from? How, in such total emptiness, could it appear like this?

It's a matter of fact for him that something more perfect can't come from something less so. (That's Plato's forms again.) Since this perfect being is obviously more perfect than he, it can't possibly be a phantom of his own mind. Actually, it couldn't come from anywhere but that most perfect being itself. Therefore, it must exist.

Before long, to buttress his case, he's retracing the route of Anselm's argument: it would be a contradiction for this God not to exist, since existence is part and parcel of a most perfect being's perfection.

> I found that existence was contained in it in the same way in which the equality of its three angles to two right angles is contained in the idea of a triangle, or that the equidistance of all its parts from its center is contained in the idea of a sphere.[8]

That Descartes's mind drifts to geometry here is no innocent association. As well as a philosopher, he was one of history's greatest mathematicians;

the Cartesian x and y coordinate grid that we all learn today comes from an appendix to the *Discourse*. He saw his mathematics as issuing from this same exercise of doubt and reasoning—but God was even more certain than math. "The existence of God," he wrote in a letter, "is the first and most eternal of all the truths there can be, and the only one from which all the others flow."[9] God, in fact, was the gateway from knowledge of himself to that of everything else.

True to his word, Descartes assembled an entire system of thought on God's existence. The physics of motion, the reality of contingent things, and the connection between mind and body—all depend on God's constant intervention. Without God to vouchsafe it, nothing else that we think we know is reliable. Descartes turns these features of everyday experience—which we doubt only on pain of utter paralysis—into little proofs for God's existence. Even to trust common sense is to believe in God. A perfect God must be good, and a good God would never deceive us, so all clear and distinct ideas we have must be true. It's a notorious feat of roundabout reasoning that later critics have dubbed the "Cartesian Circle": God ensures the truth of clear and distinct ideas, while the truth of God's existence rests on being a clear and distinct idea itself. "One might almost say that these foundation-walls are carried by the whole house," wrote Wittgenstein, capturing Descartes's paradox, unintentionally, in a phrase.[10] Descartes, for his part, was unperturbed.

The Cartesian argument for God owes a lot to that of Anselm, both in its approach and in the experience of solitary insight that brewed it. But the whole orientation is different. This is not "faith in search of understanding" but doubt in search of certainty. There's no prerequisite devotion or authority, or the apparatus of a monastery. After Descartes, the starting point would be not God but one's own self; God's existence was a reality for each person to discover. It's therefore no accident that, in his wake, the genre of proof passed mainly over to the custody of Protestants, erring as they did on the side of individualism—though Descartes remained a Catholic.

As a Catholic, he had to be careful. Upon hearing of how the Inquisition was handling Galileo in Italy, he revised his own work to avoid trouble. Still, the Dutch schools banned his works during his lifetime, and they appeared on Rome's new Index of prohibited books a decade after his death. As usual, though, the Index didn't really have the intended effect. Within fifty years, Descartes was being read in schools all over Europe, Catholic and Protestant alike. His method of doubt and abstract reason became, for a while, *the* method, and his version of the a priori proof became the standard assurance that God exists.

.·.

In his letters Descartes was fond of repeating a Latin motto from Ovid, meaning "he lives well who hides well." It's summed up even more briefly on the signet ring used by another exile in Holland; alongside the picture of a thorny rose, it warned, *"caute"*—"caution." The man who wore it followed this advice hardly better than Descartes. You let your guard down when you're all alone—on your island, or in your monastery cell, or in a city too busy to notice you. Both these men knew they needed the reminder. But they also knew that one can only be careful for so long.

Remarks Wittgenstein, "These rules of caution only make sense if they come to an end somewhere."[11]

Baruch Spinoza was born in 1632, in an enclave of Amsterdam Jews who had only recently escaped centuries of persecution and forced conversion in Portugal. During Descartes's years in that city, Spinoza was the brightest student his community had. But, like Elisha ben Abuya, he began reaching for knowledge beyond Torah and Talmud. In this case, it was the siren song of Descartes's books that drew him—books of pure reason, not of rules and rituals.

Spinoza kept quiet about all this at first. Only after his father and stepmother died when he was in his early twenties did he start talking, and talking got him in trouble. His people had spent centuries sacrificing to preserve their beliefs. The rabbis tried him. When he refused to recant or reform, they banished him from his family, his business, and his tribe, for "evil opinions and acts," with acid that still stings:

> By decree of the angels and by the command of the holy men, we excommunicate, expel, curse and damn Baruch de Espinoza, with the consent of God, Blessed be He, and with the consent of the entire congregation. . . . Cursed be he by day and cursed be he by night; cursed be he when he lies down and cursed be he when he rises up.[12]

Spinoza embraced his new condition. He began to go by the Latin "Benedictus" rather than the Hebrew "Baruch"—both meaning "blessed." He spent the rest of his life in solitude, broken only by visits with friends and admirers. To support himself he took up lens grinding, making sought-after precision instruments for scientists like the astronomer Christiaan Huygens. All the while he worked at his philosophy. Neither a Jew, nor a Catholic, nor a Protestant, he was freer from the constraints of others' opinions than even Descartes had been. Some would call him an atheist, a heretic, and worse, making the *Ethics,* Spinoza's masterwork, unpublishable during his lifetime. Yet the German poet Novalis spoke of him as the "God-intoxicated man." All his philosophy began with God, or a God of a certain sort.

Spinoza's debt to Descartes is evident on the first page of an early draft of the *Ethics,* from around 1661: "We can know clearly and distinctly that existence belongs to the nature of God."[13] It's a priori reasoning, with "clear and distinct" ideas, and from there all other knowledge comes. He structured the final version of the *Ethics* like a piece of pure geometry. Definitions, axioms, and propositions, each built on the others, in stacks of reasons upon reasons. "For the eyes of the mind, whereby it sees and observes things," Spinoza wrote, "are none other than proofs."[14]

By the eleventh proposition of the *Ethics,* only a few pages in, he's ready to demonstrate that God exists. It begins with a familiar argument by necessity, with echoes of Ibn Sina and Aquinas's Third Way: something must exist that isn't caused by anything, existing by virtue of itself. Then it converges on more Anselmian language, by way of Descartes. He tries to imagine God not existing: "It is absurd to affirm this of a Being absolutely infinite and supremely perfect."[15]

On their own, Spinoza's moves sound much like what has gone before— another perfect, necessary God who exists. But the way he arranges definitions and axioms around words like *infinite, substance,* and *existence* would have already troubled the astute. The crux of it comes a few propositions later:

PROPOSITION 14: "EXCEPT GOD, NO SUBSTANCE CAN BE OR BE CONCEIVED"

- Corollary 1: "in Nature there is only one substance, and ... it is absolutely infinite"
- Corollary 2: "an extended thing and a thinking thing are either attributes of God, or (by Axiom 1) affections of God's attributes"[16]

All substance is God. We are part of God, we thinking things. Nothing but substance is real, and substance is God. "All things, I say, are in God, and all things that happen, happen only through the laws of God's infinite nature."[17] There are no miracles, only natural laws. He wrote, in passing, of "God, *or* Nature," as the "eternal and infinite being."[18] God is the universe and not apart from it—a universe alive with creative, active force. Many at the time and afterward would say that his idea of God made him an atheist. But Spinoza denied it. The way he thought of "Nature" was as something great enough to be worthy of calling God. Interjects Wittgenstein: "It is always by favor of Nature that one knows something."[19]

Scientists centuries later would speak of "the mind of God" in much this way; Albert Einstein said outright that he believed in Spinoza's God. But it's not a God of the normal religious passions, or rites, or scriptures at all. It's another God of thought, a universe whose essence is intellect.

∴

My childhood next-door neighbor, one of my best and oldest friends, is named Mat—or so he named himself. When he was a teenager, away went the second *t* after he recognized its superfluity. When he came home from his first semester at college, and I was still a high school senior, Mat had an idea: we should celebrate the winter solstice. We would do it by staying awake all night in his parents' basement, with the help of bottled Frappuccinos and a dose of Ritalin. No electric lights allowed. I had followed him through everything else growing up, from *Star Trek* to guitar playing, and I was happy to take him up on this. It fit well with my religious experiments at the time. Two other friends came too, women actually, though they became tired of us and didn't make it through the night awake.

I think the solstice was well served by our tribute anyway. Over the course of hours that passed like a quick eternity, Mat and I sat on the floor, talking through a theory of everything that he had been working out. Spinoza probably would have smiled on it. Mat wanted an idea of God within the bounds of science—one that, like his name, had nothing superfluous. Any entity's will, said Mat, is the sum total of the natural forces acting upon and within it. Mind permeates everything, and with mind comes the possibility of consciousness. God, then, is the conscious will of the sum total of everything. I was deep into my year of physics and calculus in school, and we brought those to the mix as well: if individual wills are the points, we decided, God is like the equation.

We took that in. It was awesome.

We worked through the consequences of this for one thing and another. What constitutes an entity? Any collection of atoms, but some are more conscious than others. The human nervous system, for instance, is one especially well suited for self-awareness. What is this God like? Ask science. Ask

Spinoza. That night, at least, we reveled in it all. Dawn came, and we greeted the sun together on the deck.

The next year we were both back from college for winter break. It had been my first semester away, and so much had happened. But this time I was the one with something to say, and I suggested repeating our solstice ritual.

There in the dark, stuck with each other and the hours ahead of us, I said what had been going on in me those past months, that I was becoming a Catholic. Mat, the best of friends, challenged me and questioned me harder than anyone. Rather than a shared project, this solstice we had an unwinnable argument, point after point. It was more tiring than exhilarating. He said that Christianity would trap me in its backwardness, while I tried to say that it was saving me. He had chosen the God of Spinoza, and I was moving back, or forward, toward Anselm.

With respect to Anselm, Spinoza made a move in the *Ethics* that was really quite audacious. He began with the kind of a priori argument that, for Anselm, then for Descartes, proved the transcendent, personal, biblical God. But he claimed for it a different meaning—the opposite, almost. Anselm's reasoning, guided to its fullest expression, and with the unwitting help of Descartes, led Spinoza not to the existence of a supernatural creator but to a God inseparable from creation, from the universe, and from us. It was a different kind of God, and a different notion of existence. He hijacked that venerable proof and steered it away from the heaven promised at Bec, away from the metaphysics of La Flèche, and into a world that is itself a mind.

He could be mistaken for Aristotle in asserting that "God loves himself with an infinite intellectual love."[20] Another self-thinking thought; a self-loving love. Happiness is the goal of the whole system in the *Ethics,* and Spinoza finds it in his God, through unassailable geometric proofs. "Love toward the eternal and infinite thing feeds the mind with a joy entirely exempt from sadness," he wrote.[21] To the dismay of his many detractors, Spinoza became renowned as the "virtuous atheist"—chaste, frugal, honest, and gracious. But he knew that contemplating proofs isn't something for everyone. The *Ethics* ends with a warning to those who would try this higher path: "All things excellent are as difficult as they are rare." Certainty of this kind takes work. While on the road I came across a line in Susan Sontag's *Against Interpretation* that puts the matter crudely:

Jerking off the universe is perhaps what all philosophy, all abstract thought is about: an intense, and not very sociable pleasure, which has to be repeated again and again.

.·.

Where did the monasteries, decisions, prayers, and arguments lead me? A nondescript room on campus. A dozen or so Catholic college students are seated in a rectangular circle, attempting to enact what is wishfully called "fellowship." Father Bodah says a prayer over the carryout Indian food on paper plates in our laps. Then we're left to our own devices. For far too long I'm in a conversation mostly about the weather—at least that, I think to myself, is something above and beyond us. A metaphor, maybe, a code for speaking about the highest? Or numbing awkwardness.

Almost all the students are so-called cradle Catholics. God comes easily to them, an inheritance implanted before their earliest memories and tilled by parents and churches. The truth of our religion is so obvious to them that there's no need even to mention it. Or at least that's how these new sisters and brothers in Christ seemed to me.

Life at college—a college better known for naked parties and poststructuralism than for old-time religion—meant that I had to hone my beliefs while being constantly called on to question. The effort to shore up my newfound faith wound up making me among the more active Catholics on campus. This is the logic of any ritual, or of *The Secret* self-help series, or of *Field of Dreams:* act like it's true, and the truth will take care of itself. One day, after receiving some tortured letter I had written him, Brother Benedict sent me a sheet of paper in the mail, photocopied from the *Oxford English Dictionary*. Underlined, in light red ink, were parts of the definition for *pretend*.

Etymology: from the Latin *tendere,* "to stretch, extend."

Definition 2: "To bring or put forward, set forth, hold out, offer for action, consideration, or acceptance."

And 3: "To put oneself forward in some character; to profess or claim." It's not a lie—banish the thought—but a test. And a test that goes well, remember, is a proof.

"Acting," says Wittgenstein, "lies at the bottom of the language game."[22]

I attended daily mass as often as I could and found a few new friends to share mumbled rosaries and silent meditation. We would talk for hours about our attempts at what the theologian William Stringfellow would call "living humanly in the Fall," in a post-Edenic world full of broken people: prayer, politics, work, love, sex, and being present to the forgotten. One friend was planning a revolution, and another was inviting girls at Saturday night parties to mass. I shared the eucharist with them, and with all sorts of people at churches I visited around the city.

There was the man I would see at the Methodist soup kitchen sometimes who would tell everyone they look like movie stars; the woman born in Mozambique, left by her husband forty years ago in Trinidad, who wanted me to help her tend a garden; and the same, silent man who would be the only other person in the cathedral downtown on Saturday afternoons. I had a friend who saw angels, and another who could sing like one.

I joined the campus pastoral council and took part in interfaith dialogues. By myself, I kept at my monastic prayers, every morning and every night, hoping to make the words so familiar that my mind would hold on to them throughout the day. For stretches, it did. God's presence could seem to arrive, to descend, to prevail, with the Queen of Heaven standing over me and the peace of Christ inside. But then all that would disappear—as I knew it would, as the mystics have always warned. "Doubt comes after belief," says Wittgenstein.[23] This could be terrifying, and isolating, in ways I had never imagined before I tried believing.

"We have all known the long loneliness," I read in the autobiography of Dorothy Day, founder of the Catholic Worker movement. The problem sounded familiar, and her answer made sense: "The only solution is love and that love comes with community."[24] Like Christ and the poor, though, community is mostly left out by proofs. They're another kind of solution for loneliness. I tried both at once; I would try anything. I thought sometimes of running back to the monastery in Virginia, but it was little more than a thought. Then I found the next best thing there in college: a packed-full co-op house, where a handful of us were praying in as many different ways. When we wanted to pray together, the silence of a nearby Quaker meeting was an adequate compromise.

Then there's the departed community—the tradition—which is so much a part of what drew me into the Catholic Church and an even bigger part of why I stayed. If one century's answer to a particular question doesn't satisfy you, try that of another. If the theologians don't help, ask the mystics, or the hymns, or the monks. The saints point your eyes toward God by their company and example. There is so much. There are liberals and conservatives, literalists and exegetes, rationalists and fideists, sinners, heretics, ruins, and rumors. It made sense that this is how God's community should be: mixed up. I fit in well.

The mood swings of the time before my baptism settled. All the prayer and practice and the passing of time did their work on me. But if God is real, I knew, it isn't to be my pet, or worse. A God worth believing in would have to pull me out of myself, beyond what delusions my head could conjure for its own comfort. Baptism hadn't cured me of my doubts, nor had anything else, so what remained was a gradual, purgatorial, and more interesting kind of faith.

This meant not shutting out the questioning. I couldn't just dismiss the secular instincts in my classes and among most of my friends. While some other Christians at college chose to see themselves as an embattled minority, under siege and on the defensive, I wanted to disassemble the walls. Speaking once at a Sunday mass, I recited an old maxim of popes: "Truth cannot contradict truth." Hearing those words carry through the chapel put a chill through me. I went on, "When what my faith rests on has been shaken here, better to rest it on something stronger and keep going, better to challenge myself further to rest it not on myself but on that which is above all else."

There were times when this ideal actually worked for me, and paid dividends. But then a challenge would come, from a classmate or friend with a notch more confidence in his or her ideas than I had in mine, and I would flip into anger, tight-lipped and hot-bodied. These were such young convictions. People would make me defend official Catholic pronouncements that I was uncomfortable with myself. The gospel would go unannounced and undefended. I wished that I could stifle the sacrilege and that everyone would give themselves to the plain God of love I had found. The challenges became exhausting. But, ideally, yes: openness to truth is the best policy.

The first major I declared, as a sophomore, was computer science. The department was essentially an engineering program, but I was there to do metaphysics. It was all because of what my uncle had showed me in Golden. On a computer, abstraction is more than abstraction; proof becomes not just an idea, but a mechanism. It seemed like a good gauntlet for faith, if a roundabout one. Computers are certainty machines. You can't fool one with sophisms the way you can fool yourself. If the logic doesn't work, neither does your program. I learned more about how people were using computers to model complexity, as my uncle was—neural networks, ecosystems, economies, societies. The mind of a God like Spinoza's would be computable too.

Each summer during college I made sure to have some weeks to spend in the basement of my mother's house creating something—an unfinished novel, a website, an album of songs. One of those summers produced a 131-page treatise called *A Theology of Scale*. It's tedious and unforthcoming, even with the help of the interlocking definitions in the glossary at the back. There are harrowing sentences, like *The gestalt principle maintains the categories of prejudice as they are required by the demands of social aggregate or human consciousness.* It revolves around a computer program, an algorithm first devised by a Cold War–era game theorist. Mixed in with the text are fragments of code and pictures of the program's output. From there, the range of reference is idiosyncratic—from the Bhagavad Gita to the arrival of Vulcans in *Star Trek: First Contact* to Michael Heizer's enormous geometric structures in the Nevada desert, *City*. I seem to have been intent on leaving nothing out.

This *Theology of Scale* was an effort to explain why the God of the universe—in my peculiar lexicon, the "aggregate infinite"—seemed to me so hard to believe in and why it mattered so much to try. Religion, I decided, is what the infinite looks like through our eyes, in space and time at the human scale. Mat's solstice Spinozism runs throughout the book but reconciled with my Catholicism. (Mat was also studying computers in school, much more successfully.) I pressed on, almost until school started again in September, and finished a draft. But then I spent an airplane flight trying to explain the whole thing to my friend Alexa, who had also become a convert to philosophy in Ken Knisley's classes. She wasn't seeing it. If the test of philosophy is a conversation between friends, my treatise failed. I hoped that at least the time spent thinking that summer would lead, in some unknown way, where I needed to go. As Jesus reminded those who crucified him, we know not what we do; I sure didn't.

What I had been aiming at was an infinite God I could reach with my finite mind. It's what Anselm, Descartes, and Spinoza were after too; knowing them better then might have saved me some effort.

∴

Reason alone, one way or another, eventually turns into reasoning together. It sees the light of day, it meets its own history, it strikes up a conversation and is never the same afterward. Being certain can be easier among others. But others pose a risk to certainty too.

Reflected in the mind of someone else, an idea becomes something else, if only slightly. And slight changes mean a lot for a proof. From Anselm to Descartes, Descartes to Spinoza, and so on—philosophers have played a game of Telephone with Anselm's original argument. It changes with each iteration, in each generation. There's an uncertainty principle at work: to perceive the idea is to transform it. As each of these thinkers discovered certainty for himself, he did so differently.

Spinoza died in February 1677, peacefully, of a lung ailment exacerbated by the glass dust he inhaled while grinding lenses. Three months before, though, he had hosted an encounter with one of his few contemporaries whose influence on philosophy would rival his own.[25] The visitor was Gottfried Wilhelm Leibniz, a frenetic, younger genius who was taking the long way back to Germany after an extended stay at the Parisian court. Leibniz had already discovered calculus, including the notation we still use today for integrals and derivatives, and was assembling the philosophical system that, together with Descartes and Spinoza, would make him the third of the great rationalists. Only one piece of material evidence remains from the meeting, a scrap of paper with Leibniz's notes written in Latin. What it describes, and what the two discussed together, is a proof for the existence of God.

Like Descartes, Leibniz hoped that a new kind of shared certainty could reconcile a divided world. (If philosophy failed, warfare might not; what brought Leibniz to Paris was a ruse to persuade Louis XIV to join a new crusade against Muslim Egypt, uniting Catholics and Protestants in a common cause against the infidels.) His ideas were adventuresome and original—well paired with his notoriously extravagant wigs—but he intended them as a defense of familiar religion, despite giving no expression of outward religiosity himself. Proofs were about the extent of his piety.

"Why is there something rather than nothing?" Leibniz would famously ask. The question is basic enough to risk absurdity or childishness; his answer is the philosophers' God. He coined what is still called the "principle of sufficient reason," which means, simply, that everything must have an explanation. Just about everything can be explained by other contingent things—except the fact that there is anything at all. The only sufficient reason for there being anything at all, he thought, must be an infinite and necessary being whose cause is in itself.

The system that Leibniz went on to develop relies, next, on this being's intrinsic perfection. He reasoned, for instance, that God must have made this the best of all possible worlds. (It's an easy claim to caricature; I once met an American man in Costa Rica who cited this phrase to justify spending all day with prostitutes.) Any evil in the world can't be God's doing but only the result of freely acting, created beings.

Thirty years old, and approaching The Hague for an audience with the great heretic, he was inclining toward Spinozism, which he would confess in later writings as a momentary error. Fragments of the *Ethics* had been circulating, and what Leibniz had seen seduced him, even as he tried to resist it. When Leibniz arrived, he came bearing a proof.

"I showed this reasoning to D. Spinoza when I was in The Hague, who thought it solid," Leibniz claims on that sole relic of the encounter. "For when at first he opposed it, I put it in writing and read this paper before him."[26] What they discussed was an a priori argument from God's perfection, resounding back through Descartes and Anselm to Plato. The absolute perfection of any one quality, said Leibniz, cannot contradict that of any other perfection. All perfections are compatible with one another, and they naturally converge. The most good, for instance, must also be the all-knowing. He argued that a most perfect being like this is logically possible. And since existence is itself a perfection, that being actually, necessarily, exists.

Leibniz's twist on Anselm's proof, building on what Descartes and Spinoza had already fashioned, was to put it in terms of modal logic, of possibility and necessity: if God is possible, God must necessarily exist. The perfection that's wrapped up in the concept implies existence, so if the concept of God isn't totally self-contradictory, what it refers to is real.

This simple formula fascinated Kurt Gödel, probably the twentieth century's greatest logician. The incompleteness theorems he proved in his early twenties shattered the hope that all of mathematics could be fixed on a purely logical foundation, a hope that had its roots in Spinoza's everything-God: no logical system can be so complete as to prove its own consistency. Yet logic remained Gödel's master. Late in life, having grown ever more reclusive, he confided to a few friends that decades earlier he had composed a proof of God's existence.[27] It was essentially Leibniz's proof, expressed entirely in symbolic logic.

Like Leibniz, Gödel was not an outwardly religious man outside of his proofs. He and Einstein, the Spinozist, used to go on long walks together in Princeton; says a passage in the papers found after his death, "My belief is theistic, not pantheistic, following Leibniz rather than Spinoza." Like Leibniz, too, Gödel was anxious to fend off Spinozism.

ONTOLOGISCHER BEWEIS
KURT GÖDEL, 1941

$$\Phi(\varphi) \equiv N\,(\exists x)\varphi(x)$$
$$A(x) \equiv (\exists x\,[(x)[\varphi(x) \equiv_N A(x)].\Phi(\varphi)]$$
$$G(x).\varphi\epsilon+ \rightarrow \varphi(x)$$
$$(\exists x)\,G(x) \rightarrow N(\exists x)\,G(x)$$
$$G = \hat{x}\,[\,(\varphi)\,\varphi\epsilon+ \rightarrow \varphi(x)]$$
$$\psi\epsilon+ \rightarrow \psi(G)$$

The cost of Spinoza's certainty was higher than either Descartes or Leibniz would accept: a God no longer resembling the one his parents worshiped. This God, altered beyond recognition by philosophy, is an ever-present danger for the genre of proof. Leibniz once insinuated, "Descartes thinks in a whisper what Spinoza says at the top of his voice";[28] the latter's heresies, that is, are also in the former, only less cautiously expressed. But it's a judgment that could come back onto Leibniz himself. He, in his devotion to a God of proof alone, was closer to Spinoza than he wanted to admit.

Twenty years before the two met in The Hague, a third star mathematician renounced pure reason altogether. Blaise Pascal had published an important treatise on conic sections and invented a precursor to the computer (which explains why my uncle's programming language is named after him). But by his thirties, Pascal and much of his family found religion in a serious way. He put aside mathematical pursuits and instead focused on composing religious polemics—most famously the *Pensées,* the notes for an unfinished treatise that he left behind at his death, at thirty-nine, in 1662.

"To laugh at philosophy is to be a true philosopher," writes Pascal.[29] He's at odds with the mathematician in himself. (So was Wittgenstein: "The propositions of mathematics might be said to be fossilized.")[30] Out of this tension, Pascal dreamed up his famous "wager," another kind of proposal for the solitary thinker, the would-be believer, around whose certainty all else revolves.

Without God, Pascal proposed, there is no judgment after death; a finite life passes, and the question doesn't matter. But if there is a God who grants eternal life to believers and damnation to the rest, that God matters infinitely more than any lifetime on Earth. The promise of the infinite instantly

∃ GOD   ¬ GOD

∃ BELIEF   ∞

¬ BELIEF   ∞

overwhelms any finite alternative. "If you win, you win all; if you lose, you lose nothing," he calculated. "Wager, therefore, that He is, without hesitating." It is a proof for a man without proof, one facing "the infinite distance between the certainty of what is ventured and the uncertainty of what will be gained."[31]

So, then? Before and after his wager, Pascal goes to his knees in prayer. That is where, when the need for faith is clear, he directs us to actually find it: prayer, piety, repentance. "It is the heart which is conscious of God, not the reason," he wrote.[32] Proofs in the head are no good unless they reach the heart to be lived and felt and given.

∴

Like Pascal, I gave up on calculating machines. By the end of a year studying computer science, after I had forced a handful of programming languages into my head and spent night after night in the lab, the metaphysics wasn't getting any clearer. It was time to work out what was happening to me elsewhere. So when I returned to school for my junior year, I switched my major for good to religious studies.

When I told people I studied computers, they would ask me to fix something; when I said religion, they started telling me about what matters most in their lives. I remember the receptionist at my dentist's office asking what I studied, and I answered. Immediately she pulled out the Bible from under her desk and let loose, explaining her daily reading and prayer regimen. She loved that someone might care to listen. This would be annoying to a lot of people, I realize, but not to me.

Don't mistake a modern, secular religious studies department for some kind of seminary, like the receptionist probably did. As I was trained to study it, religion is a human phenomenon. The point is less to evaluate the truth of its claims than to understand their meanings and functions. We'd suspend the questions of truth and proof, for the time being, and simply describe. There was even a Greek word we'd use as shorthand for this: *epoché*. I kept experimenting with proofs mostly on my own time, but even that I was learning to do in a new way.

In religious studies, the tools of sociology, psychology, philosophy, and textual criticism are supposed to make the discussion open to people of all backgrounds and convictions. Instead of fixating on whether certain religious doctrines are true or not, we would talk about how they fit in social life, how they adapt to new circumstances, and how they take form in ritual. (Even the most solitary religious pursuits, we read in Émile Durkheim's century-old *Elementary Forms of Religious Life,* are "collective forces in individualized forms"; "impersonal reason is but collective thought by another name.")[33] We would ask why some religions are so concerned with beliefs in the first place while others are less so. We would think a lot about how women and foreigners and the poor have been marginalized and stricken from traditional narratives. These were really interesting questions. I couldn't get enough of it.

I loved going to conferences along with robed Buddhist monks and collared priests among hordes of tweedy professors. It looked to me like the world that Descartes and Leibniz had dreamed of in their time of religious wars, a world of sympathy and tolerance built on holding reason in common. It was a relief from the political climate of the early 2000s, when narrow religious agendas were having a lot of influence. There, in those classrooms and conferences, I saw that truth could be a shared possession, not a sectarian one. Religious studies let me take a more catholic approach to thinking about religion—catholic with a small *c,* meaning "universal." The big *C* Catholicism I had found for myself was there, too, but so was my mother's guru and my father's secular turn. I even studied Hebrew. On vacations I started going again to religious places of different kinds, like I had before baptism, but this time as a student. I could be one thing without turning my back on everything and everyone else.

The ground rules of religious studies, though, weren't as cozy for others. Our teachers wouldn't accept some of the explanations that believers might offer—because scripture says so, or because God exists, for instance. A few of my Christian classmates couldn't stand it and dropped the major. Some teachers were outright dismissive of belief; rather than suspend the question, they would try to simply reduce it to a social force or a logical mistake. But most of the time, thinking about religion this way was a relief for me. It let the pressure off. Everything didn't depend on my own precarious logic anymore. There was a faith to be found, also, in learning about the faith of others: not vicariously, one would hope, but as accompaniment. I could forgive myself for uncertainty as long as I was studying, asking, and listening. It's a curious liberation, a backdoor kind of certainty; "A doubt without an end," says Wittgenstein, "is not even a doubt."[34]

FIVE

Coming of Age

FROM THE ALL-DESTROYER
TO AN ABSOLUTE IDEA

My conversion started smack-dab in the middle of the time when these sorts of things tend to happen, statistically speaking: the major identity formation years, as the puberty fires begin to cool and congeal. I have a theory that this period of radical doubt and radical impressionability is a mechanism built into human nature to test our belief systems, ensuring that they haven't gotten stale with later-life obfuscation and complacency. To impress a teenager, an idea has to satisfy certain criteria. It has to be simple enough to grasp quickly while also having huge explanatory scope. It should make one feel a sense of self-possession, of confidence. It should stipulate particular activities to keep one occupied, preferably with a group of like-minded peers. If these aren't satisfied, expect the worst. My journals remind me how, in the absence of an alternative, vicious kinds of nihilism can seem astonishingly appealing at that age.

When I started trying to write poems in high school, I usually went for the biggest subjects I could think of, making myself miserable in the process. My dad noticed this and told me about the pastoral, the ancient poetic genre that takes life in the country as its subject: shepherds and sheep, grassy hills and barns, puppy love. Familiar things and common moods. Learn to write on simple topics, he said, and you can turn to bigger ones later, if you have to. He was probably right. But I'd try that for a moment—I really would—only to relapse into God, truth, and the universe before I knew it.

This is dangerous stuff. Those years have an amazing capacity to fix certainties, or unfix them, for good. If one can't find a way to make peace then with the ideas competing for one's allegiance, late adolescence can lead one down the path of causing a disproportionate amount of trouble. Take, for instance, David Hume.

Hume once wrote a letter describing a stream of his adolescent consciousness, explaining that he had grown up accepting the evidence for God in nature's order. "Any Propensity you imagine I have to the other Side," he wrote, "crept in upon me against my Will," gnawing at old and comfortable intuitions, as if coming from a power beyond him. His recollection continued:

> And tis not long ago that I burn'd an old Manuscript Book, wrote before I was twenty; which contain'd, Page after Page, the gradual Progress of my Thoughts on that head. It began with an anxious Search after Arguments, to confirm the common Opinion: Doubts stole in, dissipated, return'd, were again dissipated, return'd again; and it was a perpetual Struggle of a restless Imagination against Inclination, perhaps against Reason.[1]

Like loose papers in the wind, totalizing pictures of the universe blew in and out of his mind, in adolescent solitude. That age sets the mood, or stirs the muck, that breeds conversions and commitments and so many other forms of necessary recklessness. And it isn't where one should expect to find proofs.

The data speak pretty clearly on this point. Proofs tend to come only later, after the air becomes still enough that papers stay down and work can be done, after a rational infrastructure has taken shape around whatever flared up earlier, at the decisive moments. Anselm was forty-four when he discovered his proof (though twenty-three when he set off from home), and Descartes published his *Discourse on Method* at forty-one (but was twenty-three, too, in the stove-heated room). The pattern holds even for Ibn Tufayl's fictional Hayy Ibn Yaqzan, who devotes himself to metaphysics at twenty-one but doesn't get to revel in his proof until he's thirty-five. "At fifteen, I set my mind upon learning," said Confucius, over in China, but "at forty, I became free of doubts."[2] The Jewish Talmud also pins "understanding" to the age of forty but advises reserving "counsel" for ten more years.[3] Plato thought a man would have to wait at least that long before being ready to "raise the eye of the soul to the universal light which lightens all things, and behold the absolute good."[4]

This pattern doesn't apply, for instance, with mathematical proofs. Among mathematicians, the big paradigm-shaking advances tend to come during the early crisis window, if at all. "Anything truly novel is invented only during one's youth," thought Albert Einstein. But religious proofs are different. Most of them don't arrive until middle age, in time for a different kind of

THINKER	CONVERSION	APPROX. AGE	DEVELOPMENT OF PROOF	APPROX. AGE
Alston, William	Returned to Christianity	54	Published *Perceiving God*	72
Anselm of Canterbury	Set off from home	23	Began *Proslogion*	44
Comfort, Ray	Conversion experience	23	Published *How to Know God Exists*	59
Craig, William Lane	Born-again a Christian	16	Published *The Kalam Cosmological Argument*	30
Dawkins, Richard	Rejected Christianity for atheism	16	Published *The God Delusion*	65
Descartes, René	The stove-heated room	23	Published *Discourse on Method*	41
Flew, Antony (older)	Accepted deism	81	Published *There Is a God*	84
Flew, Antony (younger)	Rejected Christianity for atheism	15	Delivered "Theology and Falsification" lecture	27
Hegel, G. W. F.	Watched the French Revolution	19	Delivered *Lectures on the Proofs*	59
Hume, David	"Doubts stole in, dissipated, return'd"	20	Began *Dialogues Concerning Natural Religion*	39
Ibn Yaqzan, Hayy	Discovered metaphysics	21	Beatific vision through his proof	35
Kant, Immanuel	Awakening by Hume	47	Published *The Only Possible Argument*	39
Lewis, C. S.	Accepted theism (Christianity at 32)	30	Began *Mere Christianity* lectures	42
Plantinga, Alvin	Transferred from Harvard to Calvin College	19	Published *God and Other Minds*	39
Spinoza, Baruch	First accused of heresy	23	Wrote the *Short Treatise*	28
Stenger, Victor	Rejected Catholicism for atheism	18	Published *Not by Design*	53
Swinburne, Richard	Confirmed in his Christianity	20	Published *The Existence of God*	45

crisis—a justification or legitimation of one's adulthood, already half-spent. I wouldn't really know, myself; I haven't been there yet. Even so, it's hard to imagine that anyone is old enough to prove a thing like God's existence. How would we know if we were? Self-assurance, after all, is immaturity's oldest trick.

Really, there are altogether too many books about proofs written in the old and settled phase, between bombast and decrepitude. We hear from wizened authors about what they know is true and false, about why their opponents and opponents' gods are wrong. Proof is a very preachy genre. Maybe it's better to hear from the sophomoric ones sometimes—those of us in between the questions and the answers. Whom are you going to trust? The person who has his life and reputation already staked on a particular result? The one who says he's sorted out the maker of the universe? Maybe the whole undertaking is sophomoric from beginning to end.

That, actually, is a point Hume's philosophy leaves us with: What can we even begin to think we can expect to say about God? Considering all the smart middle-aged minds that have gotten tripped up in the proofs before him and since, maybe he was on to something.

.·.

In his mid-twenties, in 1734, Hume left home in Scotland for fresh air, to think and write abroad. He chose La Flèche, France, the same place where Descartes had studied just over a century before; Descartes's shadow accompanied him there. With the help of the college's library, its supply of conversation partners, and the isolation of self-imposed exile, Hume set about writing his first, foundational work, *A Treatise on Human Nature*.

The *Treatise* is a daring piece of moral philosophy, principally, but there are consequences in it for just about everything else, from free will to politics. Human beings, for Hume, are hardly the noble, rational, abstract souls usually imagined by philosophers, pondering through a noble, rational, and abstract universe. Reality is trickier than that. We're ruled by our passions at least as much as by reason, and our efforts to settle on the essential nature of things are shot through with uncertainties. Speculation is mostly crazy and made up; much better is what one can actually see and experience. "A wise man," went Hume's maxim, "proportions his belief to the evidence."[5] Considering what people like Descartes and Spinoza had been claiming to discover from reason alone, this was a serious challenge.

The Cartesian legacy had already taken on a life of its own in British hands. This was the land where Francis Bacon had laid out the scientific method and Isaac Newton had discovered the laws of motion; empirical observation held sway, and how one thought about anything—including God—seemed like it should depend on this new kind of science. Hume's insistence on the evidence was also coming straight from another Brit in exile, John Locke, who had finished his *Essay Concerning Human Understanding* while living in Amsterdam during the 1680s. (He was also writing books that would in part be the basis for democratic revolutions to come.) Where truth is concerned, wrote Locke, "'Tis trial and examination must give it price, and not any antique fashion."[6] He'll believe something only when he sees it.

While he credited Descartes with his "first deliverance from the unintelligible way of talking of philosophy in use in the schools,"[7] Locke's empiricism, as his approach is called, strayed a long way from his fellow adoptive Amsterdammer. Concerning religion, for instance, Locke wouldn't accept that a true concept of God could be counted on as innate in all of us. He knew from travelers' reports that the natives of far-flung places didn't believe in a God that European Christians would recognize. A purely a priori argument won't do. You need evidence.

He begins with a Cartesian instinct: *I exist.* But from there, rather than turn to God, Locke turns to the world. Our minds perceive matter around us, right? Matter alone, he argues—with reasoning pretty much lifted from Plato's *Laws,* you'll notice—cannot bring a mind into being. Matter is inert, and mind is active; mind can act on matter but not vice versa. If the universe began with only matter, there would be no minds like our own. There would be none of the order we see in nature. The cause of both matter and minds must therefore have come from a disembodied mind: a God.

Locke's own confidence in this proof sounds at once sure and shaky; he writes in the *Essay* that "its evidence" is "(if I mistake not) equal to mathematical certainty."[8] Then, after not too many pages, he moves on to something else; he gets out of Dodge. And it's interesting that he can do so at all.

While Descartes's whole system stands or falls on God's existence, Locke treated the matter as something more like a case study, a curiosity. It appears late in the *Essay,* merely one among other stray considerations. God had drifted to the periphery. For this reason Locke's approach made him a favorite among those embracing deism, the then-fashionable belief in a distant, reason-loving God who created the universe and then left it alone. Deists recognized him as one of them, though he denied being a deist himself. And he also had followers among those trying to defend more old-fashioned ways of believing.

One of John Locke's devotees, the physician and poet Richard Blackmore, published *Creation: A Philosophical Poem* in 1712, rendering what he took to be the good news of the Lockean view in an accessible form, against the errors of Spinozists and deists. *Creation* resists any Descartes-like appeal to pure reason or innate ideas. Writes Blackmore, in the preface, "I have chosen to demonstrate the existence of a God from the marks of wisdom, design, contrivance, and the choice of ends and means, which appear in the universe." And so he musters perhaps more enthusiasm than eloquence in verses like:

> The glorious orbs, which heaven's bright host compose,
> Th' imprison'd sea, that restless ebbs and flows,
> The fluctuating fields of liquid air,
> With all the curious meteors hov'ring there,
> And the wide regions of the land, proclaim
> The power divine, that rais'd the mighty frame.[9]

Allied with Locke and Blackmore's instincts, in 1736, the Anglican clergyman Joseph Butler published his *Analogy of Religion*. While not laying out proofs for God's existence as such—his deist opponents already accepted that—Butler tried to set out to account for Christian truth on the basis of observation and probability, judging from what he could gather about what's around us in nature. David Hume was coming into himself as a thinker just as Butler's *Analogy* appeared, and Hume admired what Butler was up to—despite his own "perpetual Struggle of a restless Imagination."

Some of the boldness Hume had felt at La Flèche dissipated upon crossing the channel on his way back home. Before drumming up the moxie to send a copy of his book to Joseph Butler, he found himself "castrating" it—"that is, cutting off its nobler parts."[10] The nobler parts, of course, were those that dealt with religion. Hume took the warning of caution on Spinoza's signet ring to heart; the fullest elaboration of his ideas on the existence of God would appear in print only posthumously.

If Spinoza said "at the top of his voice" what Descartes merely implied, Hume would do the same for the empiricism of Locke: take it to its furthest—and most unsettling—implication. You could even say that in Hume the revolution Descartes had started and Locke continued was coming of age.

DEMEA

PHILO

PAMPHILUS

CLEANTHES

∴

Lying on his deathbed in 1776, Hume confessed to James Boswell that he hadn't "entertained any belief in religion" since reading Locke in his youth. He died the convivial bachelor he had always been and, like Spinoza, betrayed no indication of fear for what would or would not follow. (In the case of each notorious heretic, the moment of death was a matter of special concern—and disappointment—to his pious contemporaries.) Three years later, Hume's *Dialogues Concerning Natural Religion* finally appeared in print. He had written it over the last two decades of his life. As Hume put it in a letter to the economist Adam Smith, "Nothing can be more cautiously and more artfully written."[11] Modeled after Cicero's *On the Nature of the Gods,* the *Dialogues* is a discussion among three characters about how best to educate the young Pamphilus—the mostly silent narrator—about the basis for religious belief. How, that is, do you teach a boy to come of age about religion correctly?

One speaker, Cleanthes, would have sounded a bit like the empiricist arguments of Joseph Butler. The second, Demea, preaches Cartesian rationalism like an impatient dogmatist. Philo, the third, would be hard to identify as the mouthpiece of anyone but Hume himself; he speaks twice as much as the other two combined.

Cleanthes' arguments lead the way. In the empiricist mode, he argues for God from the appearance of design in nature, comparing the world and the creatures in it to a man-made machine. By analogy, he contends, we can infer that they were created by a divine mind vastly greater than our own. To notice the wonder and power of nature is to know, intuitively and beyond doubt, that a God created it.

Demea can't believe what he hears: "What! No demonstration of the being of a God! No abstract arguments! No proofs *a priori!*"[12] He complains that Cleanthes' design arguments are too weak for the God of religion. After all, nature could have been created by something lesser than a most perfect being, something unworthy of worship. The evidence of design alone risks leaving us with a less-than-perfect God.

What Demea proposes instead is a familiar a priori argument for a perfect and necessary first cause of the universe. But Cleanthes won't accept it. He doesn't think that any mere idea can prove anything. "Whatever we conceive as existent, we can also conceive as non-existent," says Cleanthes, swiping at the whole rationalist enterprise, from Anselm to Leibniz. "There is no Being, therefore, whose non-existence implies a contradiction."[13] Ultimately, Demea opts to stand up for a God of feeling and faith, whose existence is so obvious in one's own heart that it can't be questioned. He then storms out of the room, leaving only Cleanthes and Philo behind.

Philo, meanwhile, casts doubt at every chance he gets on both Cleanthes' empiricism and Demea's rationalism. In even trying to discuss such cosmic things, he says, "We are like foreigners in a strange country."[14] Our experience, so limited in time and place, can tell us nothing about what came before or what lies behind it. "Would the manner of a leaf's blowing, even though perfectly known," asks Philo, "afford us any instruction concerning the vegetation of a tree?"[15] Nor is any experience with human design really comparable to the design we see in nature; they're of a completely different order. Besides, if you're explaining nature's design, why stop at a divine creator? Who, one might ask, created the creator? For the sake of argument, he describes a godless picture of the universe and contends that it is equally plausible as a godly one, for all we know. He also raises the question of suffering in the world, and of evil. Could a God or an afterlife somehow justify it? Perhaps yes, perhaps no—but, again, our experience isn't sufficient to know either way.

Philo deflects every argument the others use for a God except the very weakest—that the grandeur and design in nature *seem* to bespeak *some* kind of intelligent designer. On this extremely flimsy foundation, Philo finally declares his "veneration for true religion" and the surprising thesis that "to be a philosophical sceptic is, in a man of letters, the first and most essential step towards being a sound, believing Christian."[16]

One can't but feel confused at how the *Dialogues* ends. Even from the grave, Hume doesn't declare a position outright—or not a very muscular one, at least. Philo's brazen speeches claim to refute virtually the entire roster that the genre of proof had produced up to that point. Yet, with barely a plank beneath him, he walks away claiming to be a good Christian. The narrator Pamphilus finally sides with Cleanthes against the "careless scepticism of Philo,"[17] though it's hard to dispute that Philo's position most closely resembles the author's own thinking; one only wonders how far Hume actually followed Philo's hasty about-face and Christian credo. Regardless, the damage was done. Hume and his readers knew it. As never before, there were reasons for doubting the whole canon of proofs for the existence of God.

∴

The summer after finishing college, before setting out on a long, uncertain drive from Virginia to graduate school out West, I found myself with a few weeks and nothing in particular to do. I took it as an excuse to prowl through books that had been waiting on the shelf in my old room to be read or reread—things collected at bookstands, assigned in classes, or discreetly borrowed from my father's library. It was then that, finally, I spent some real time with Anselm's proof. Stretched out on the carpeted floor of my old basement bedroom, I held the *Proslogion* open above me. I thought back on what I had wandered into when I got myself baptized. Now, as I was preparing to move far away, there was the chance of starting over again, as if in a stove-heated room, or my own lens-grinding shop. The people and the places that I had draped my faith on in college, and that had held it up, were far away and soon to be farther. Without them, could I still believe that God exists? Did I have to? This was a new stage, a new age, and, potentially, a new life.

As my eyes followed Anselm's words, I let the rapture in his proof take hold of me. It is a masterpiece of intellectual hedonism, an idea that satisfies itself. For brief eternities, I could sense the whole vastness of a God wrapped around my little mind, like a lonesome asteroid must feel touching the gentle infinity of space. Then, always, my thoughts wandered elsewhere, and I forgot some movement of the logic. The whole thing dissolved away. I started to remember the echo of other words, from Kant's devastating complaint against Anselm, which I had just come across as well: *existence is not a predicate.*

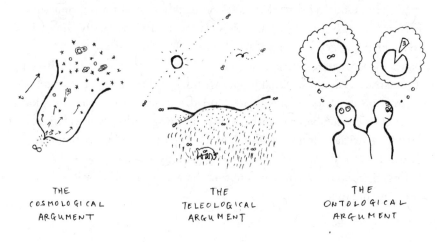

THE
COSMOLOGICAL
ARGUMENT

THE
TELEOLOGICAL
ARGUMENT

THE
ONTOLOGICAL
ARGUMENT

That sense of God, for the moment, disappeared as quickly as Anselm had summoned it.

According to the Jewish philosopher Moses Mendelssohn, his friend Immanuel Kant was *der Allzermalmende*—"the all-destroyer."[18] Heinrich Heine compared his treatment of theology to Robespierre's guillotine in the Reign of Terror. And Anselm was only one of his targets; Kant proposed to leave most of the philosophy that came before him in ruins. He didn't come to this point alone, though. He had aid and abetting. Discovering David Hume's skepticism, Kant would later say, "interrupted" his "dogmatic slumber" and woke him up.

The most common observation about Kant in the biographical notes is that his life was uneventful. He hardly ever left the Prussian city of Königsberg, where he was born in 1724 and died in 1804, with a state funeral. His critical instincts revealed themselves early; originally named Emanuel, he changed the spelling upon learning the name's original letters in Hebrew. He spent his whole life thinking, writing, and teaching, all according to a regimented daily schedule that he kept with the help of a manservant—who was eventually fired for drinking too much, perhaps understandably. Kant never married.

The decisive moment for him came in 1781, when the *Critique of Pure Reason* was published, as the first of his three *Critiques*; all that he wrote before it we now call "precritical." At first glance and long after, it's an imposing text, well guarded against the casual reader by tireless, labyrinthine German

TYPE	DESCRIPTION	ETYMOLOGY
Teleological	Arguments beginning from the appearance of purpose, design, or order in nature	*Telos*, Greek for "purpose" (Kant originally called this, following Wolff, the physico-theological)
Cosmological	Arguments taking the existence of the universe as reason to believe in the existence of a necessary being	*Kosmos*, Greek for "world"
Ontological	Arguments positing that the concept of God itself implies God's existence	*Onto-*, Greek prefix meaning "being"

sentences and scary terminology. ("This work can never be made suitable for popular use," Kant admits, or boasts, in the preface.)[19] The *Critique* partly reiterates Hume's charge against overconfident rationalism. In a rare lyrical turn, Kant writes that reason "stretches its wings in vain when it tries to soar beyond the world of sense by the mere power of speculation."[20] But his critique isn't solely a negative stroke. Reason, after all, frames experience; we know what we experience only by the way reason interprets it. Kant describes his project, rather, as a "court of appeal" for speculative reason. Between the extremes of empiricism and rationalism, he proposes a third way, complete with its own vocabulary: a "transcendental idealism," a "synthetic *a priori*." Kant's critique is meant to put thought and experience each in their place and to dictate their proper relationship. He wrote in a letter to Mendelssohn, "The true and lasting welfare of the human race depends on it."[21]

Just as for Locke, proofs for the existence of God are not at the center of the first *Critique*'s argument. They are instead just an example of its consequences; they're an ancient misunderstanding of how far pure reason can really reach. When, later, Kant would write a book titled *Religion within the Limits of Reason Alone,* they don't feature in it at all.

At the outset of his treatment of the proofs in the first *Critique*, Kant makes a huge contribution to the genre: he classifies it. While it was typical before him to distinguish between a priori and a posteriori proofs, Kant outlines three categories into which he thought every speculative proof for God's existence falls, borrowed from Christian Wolff's then-dominant synthesis of Leibnizian philosophy. They trace an ascending order, Kant explains, "which reason followed in its natural development."[22]

And so, through taxonomy, Kant made the proofs their own holy trinity, christened with venerable Greek names claiming to encompass all that had gone before. These were the names that first attracted me when I discovered them as a teenager in that green book at Corinne's house, and I've been playing with them since. Every genre needs a specialized jargon to mature and to perpetuate itself, and for proofs, these most iconic of its terms came from Kant—even as he was on the verge of dispatching their referents.

∴

What was last in arriving, according to Kant, is the first to go: the ontological proof, which had been shaped by Anselm and Descartes, inverted by Spinoza, and recovered by Leibniz. Like Gaunilo and Aquinas, and like Cleanthes in Hume's *Dialogues,* Kant won't accept that the mere idea of a thing—even the greatest and most perfect of all things—entails its own actual existence. The value of a hundred dollars, goes his example, isn't any different whether it happens to exist in your pocket or not. "Existence is evidently not a real predicate," Kant concludes, "that is, a concept of something that can be added to the concept of a thing."[23] Existence has nothing to do with *what* something is but solely *that* it is. This is the argument that snapped me out of my Anselmian reverie that summer, lying on the carpeted floor.

Kant's next move is even more devastating. Most people had assumed that they could put aside the ontological proof and still prove God by other means; he thought not. Rather, for Kant, the cosmological and teleological proofs are really ontological proofs in disguise, accompanied by the a posteriori window-dressing of apparent cause and design. Hume had shown him how little, in fact, a posteriori experience can tell us by itself. "The step leading to absolute totality is entirely impossible on the empirical road," Kant writes.[24] Experience may give you evidence for some kind of design, or some insight about causation. But to get from there all the way to an all-perfect, all-powerful God, to conclude that this designer and this cause are the same thing, we have no choice but to rely on ontological reasoning. The three types of proof are tied together, according to Kant, and together they fall under the ontological proof's dead weight.

This should not be taken to attest, however, that God's *non*existence has been proved. Not so fast. For Kant, there are good reasons to believe that God exists. In the precritical period, he actually wrote a book called *The Only Possible Argument in Support of a Demonstration of the Existence of God,* which still holds out hope for a rationalist-style proof from possibility and necessity. But by the *Critique of Pure Reason,* he turns elsewhere. "I had to suspend knowledge," he famously wrote, "in order to make room for faith."[25]

We learn most fully what he means by this in the second of the three *Critique*s, the *Critique of Practical Reason.* When the time came, his tomb would be emblazoned with words from that book about the "admiration and reverence" he felt for "the moral law within me." It's from this moral law, rather than from conventional proofs, that he ends up defending belief in God's existence.

The object of moral reasoning, Kant explains, is to seek the highest good—perfect virtue, and happiness. Actually achieving this must somehow be possible, or else our reason is unreasonable and our good behavior is in vain. But we know well enough that life rarely metes out happiness according to virtue. Far too many jerks end up winning out. So moral reason demands that there has to be a higher divine order, one in which everyone gets their due and the highest good can finally be attained. This order, in turn, implies a God, the manifestation and arbiter of the highest good we all ought to be seeking. "Only if religion is added to it," Kant writes, "can the hope arise of someday participating in happiness in proportion as we endeavored not to be unworthy of it."[26] We're obliged to hope that such a God exists; morals, he thought, wouldn't cohere otherwise.

This is a different kind of proof from the usual. It isn't another argument for what *is* but the consequence of an *ought;* belief in God is a moral responsibility, not a theoretical certainty. Together with free will and immortality, God's existence is a "postulate of practical reason," a "regulative principle." It's a belief we need to make everything else make sense. Though neither experience nor reason can confirm it, one is justified in believing in God—rather, one is required to. From that foundation, and only from it, the three classical proofs can begin to be salvaged.

The God of Kant's moral argument, thought many early readers, pales in comparison to that of earlier philosophy. God is a by-product, a mere derivative of human reason, arrived at by living ordinary life. ("This idea arises out of morality," Kant writes, "and is not its basis.")[27] His was a risky position to take. Maybe Kant had the surest way to ground religion in reason, or maybe he was a new Spinoza, an atheist in disguise. His ideas about religion were singled out for censorship. It didn't help that Kant rejected church authorities and super-rational revelation. For him, this is what it would take for religion, and civilization itself, to finally grow up.

Consider his famous 1784 essay whose title asks the question "What Is

Enlightenment?" "Enlightenment," writes Kant, "is man's emergence from his self-imposed immaturity. Immaturity is the inability to use one's understanding without guidance from another." Religion threatens to subjugate the mind when rigid dogma constrains reason and individual conscience through hierarchies and holy books. "That form of immaturity," he thinks, "is both the most pernicious and disgraceful of all." Mature faith depends on leaving behind the old religion and its old proofs.

This is the kind of thing that would have made a lot of sense to me when I was first taking Ken Knisley's philosophy class in high school. *Understanding should be gained individually, free of outside knowledge,* I riffed in a journal entry a few months after meeting Ken. *People should be taught only to be curious and to formulate their own theories in philosophy and science.*

Yes, of course we should think for ourselves. But what a lot of time wasted reinventing wheels, for one thing. For another, just imagine a life of such radical autonomy: a world of solitary grown-ups, following a God known solely by their individual reason and conscience, each outgrowing the need for anything from others. Sounds like a blast.

As the first *Critique*'s ripples spread, Moses Mendelssohn heard about what his friend Kant was doing, and it worried him. Like the interlocutors in Hume's *Dialogues,* he was worried about the young. Age and illness had left Mendelssohn unable to study the works of others and barely able to write his own. But he couldn't bear the thought of losing the rationalist proofs that both he and Kant had learned in school. What else but God can hold reason together, or explain the existence of our minds? Mendelssohn began giving his teenage son, Joseph, and some young friends a series of intimate, early-morning lectures in defense of rationalist idealism and, above all, its proofs for the existence of God. These lectures were published as *Morning Hours,* in 1785—just four years after the first *Critique.* Mendelssohn was actually a few years younger than Kant, but here he seemed like an old man, out of touch and behind the times. *Morning Hours* is an elegy for a way of believing, and a way of proving, that by then already seemed lost.

∴

During the decades following Kant's *Critiques,* German philosophy scrambled to figure out what reason might still have to say about God, if anything at all. These were growing pains. Yet it was in them that the genre of proof reached its early modern apogee; the sum total of the genre became a proof of its own. All that had been built on the intimations of the Greeks, through the caliphates and the monasteries and the schoolmen, and by minds turned in on themselves in solitary rooms, would be gathered and their parts assembled into a single, splendid edifice. That was, at least, the promise.

Reading the philosophy of Georg Wilhelm Friedrich Hegel is like stepping into a baroque alternate universe, full of meticulous, extravagant, baffling order. But it is a universe that has unquestionably shaped our own. In Berlin, Hegel was something of an official philosopher, called upon by the Prussian regime to lecture sense into students on the brink of rebellion. What he told them would stir new rebellions to come. His ideas would provide the mechanism for Karl Marx's apocalyptic socialism, even while gesturing toward the totalitarian messianism of Hitler. Not to be outdone, the champion of democratic capitalism Francis Fukuyama is a Hegelian, too, and Judith Butler found in Hegel inspiration for her radical gender theory.

Few have paid close attention to Hegel's proof for the existence of God, though it is a thread that runs through and around his whole corpus. "The explication of the proofs of God's existence," he wrote, "is the explication of religion itself."[28] It wasn't until nearly the end of his life, in 1829, that he gave a set of lectures devoted expressly to the proofs, and he signed the contract for their publication just months before dying of cholera in 1831. To Hegelian thinking, however, timing is never an accident; an end is a conclusion. Everything happens when it does for a reason.

As a young man, Hegel observed the Enlightenment's self-immolation in the French Revolution. When Napoleon arrived at the gates of where Hegel was then living in Jena, he believed he saw world historical flux incarnate. He refused to follow those, like Descartes, who made the thinker an alien in the world. Ideas shape history, and history shapes ideas. The Polish reporter Ryszard Kapuściński once wondered, "If reason ruled the world, would history even exist?" How could it? Reason is perfect, and history is not; history is change, and reason is forever. Hegel's answer, though, rejects any opposition between the two: "Reason has ruled in the world and in world history."[29] History, however untidy it may seem, is what reason looks like in time. Reason is history's meaning.

For Kant's Enlightenment, a society marks its growth and progress with ideas. The proofs it has to show for itself are its biography, or its résumé; they're the measure of how far it has come. But Hegel flips this logic upside down. *Ideas* themselves age and mature, and society develops on their behalf. Proofs are what the world is churning toward. They're the point. Whether we know it or not, we're all working to bring more of them to light.

Kant and Hegel agree that progress, both for a person and for a society, means becoming more reasonable. But they disagree about what reason itself is. Reason, for Hegel, means recognizing oneself as a participant in a huge, world historical process rather than becoming the self-sufficient individual Kant had in mind. Maturity isn't a matter of rejection and reconstruction—as Kant did with the proofs—but reconciliation and assimilation.

The Hegelian world is one of relationship, one in which all that is exists through others. Nothing, not even God, carries on by itself. There are no islands, for even they are pounded by the sea. God is the creator only because there is creation, just as there is no thinker without a thought. It's an alternative version of maturity to Kantian autonomy, one based on living among others.

Hegel's vast, all-encompassing system runs on the engine of dialectic: one thing contradicts another thing, until they merge into another that assimilates the truth in both. Repeat: thesis, antithesis, synthesis. Thought and world resolve into the idea that encompasses them. Subjective and objective resolve into the absolute. You and I resolve into we, and we are more together than we would be apart. Philosophy is the story of reconciliation upon reconciliation, as one idea answers another, and a third takes hold of them both—a progression of interwoven, isomorphic triads, each its own imitation of the Trinity. "To prove simply means to become conscious of a connection," Hegel wrote.[30] Proof connects us, and it connects us to God. Not only do we start to know God truly and fully through proofs, says Hegel, but by our proofs God comes to know God too.

∴

Hegel's teaching is as drastic as it sounds, and as confusing. I remember the whole class groaning as our professor tried to explain these twisty Hegelian phrases in graduate school—again, growing pains. But by the end, for a few of us at least, the hurt was worth it.

Part of what makes the classical proofs matter to Hegel is their history. "For the very reason that they were authoritative for more than a thousand years," he explains, "they deserve to be considered more closely."[31] The cosmological, teleological, and ontological proofs—he reverses the order that Kant

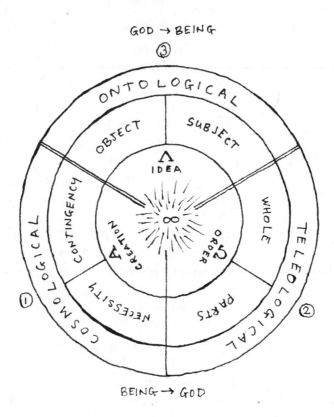

gave the first two—each reflects a particular, historical religious outlook. The cosmological represents the primitive religion of nature, standing in awe at the universe's very existence. Accounting for teleology is a further development of human reason, one that infers a unifying order in that universe. The ontological insight completes the cycle. Christianity is the highest religion, for Hegel, and the ontological argument is its equivalent in philosophy; God is not simply an idea in our heads, or a thing "out there," but an "Absolute Idea," the incarnate logos, the sole concept identical with its existence. The gospel story—the God become flesh—turns out to be just a gloss on the ontological proof. Philosophy and religion fulfill one another in this consummate self-revelation of God.

If you approach the ontological proof analytically, as simply a static abstraction, maybe Kant was right: you can't just think something into existence. But the dialectic captures, for Hegel, more than abstraction; it's movement. The idea of God's infinite perfection takes on a life of its own. It moves the thinker toward an encounter. The infinity of it negates the finitude of the thinker, and the objectivity of it negates the thinker's subjectivity. He—presumably the thinker is a he—gets pulled, dragged, and lifted, not simply into more thinking, but toward an understanding, a presence. "By means of this negation," Hegel says, "man's spirit raises itself to God, brings itself into harmony with God. The conclusion: I know that God is."[32]

The three proofs, each composed of dialectics in themselves, fold together into an even grander dialectical scheme. For this, Hegel summons the ancient distinction between a priori and a posteriori proofs, the distinction that separated Platonism from Aristotle, Anselm from Aquinas, and the rationalists from the empiricists. For him, each represents an opposing tendency: the a priori takes us from God to being, the a posteriori from being to God. The ontological proof fits into the first, while the cosmological and teleological proofs, beginning with the world and leading to God, make up the second. But these two types need each other, and they satisfy what the other is missing: the concept of God in one and, in the second, the nature of creation. Their dialectical synthesis delivers the reality of God's existence—though even to speak of "existence," he wrote, "is too low for the Absolute Idea, and unworthy of God."[33] No, God's existence is not a mere predicate. It's so much more.

This barrage of speculative moves can be hard to accept before you've bought into the rest of Hegel's imposing cosmic system, and, even then, the proof is so obscure that many since have considered it better left ignored. (Søren Kierkegaard complained that anyone who bothers to assemble such a sprawling mansion will find himself living outside in the doghouse.) Part of the appeal of writing it off as so much obfuscation was, once again, the danger of heresy. To speak of God as Hegel did—as being enmeshed in the universe rather than separate and aloof—was to invoke the specter of Spinozism, which in his time was still bandied about as a term of abuse. Together with Leibniz, Mendelssohn, and countless others, he buzzed around Spinoza's tantalizing flame, disavowing it and then trying to defend something little different, claiming to defend orthodoxy with tricks borrowed from the apostate Jew. There is always danger of heresy tucked away in the genre of proof, and Hegel definitely tempted it.

When I learned about his proof in graduate school, the arc of this book began forming across the back of my mind. Hegel showed me that proofs are not just old ideas that might be valid or not, for all time. Instead, time itself has a part to play in their validity. They are a history, a testimony, an encounter, and an experience, and their story would be inextricably bound up in mine. I might not always sense God's presence, nor could my mind always assent to the fact of it. But another fact—of my conversion, my decision—had to be dealt with, one way or another. It was an unavoidable thesis in the dialectic of my life.

There's a certain wisdom in the inarticulate, demanding, urgent impulses of youth, a wisdom worth trusting—at least in part, obliquely. Growing older would require not growing out of my conversion but into it, in new ways. My experiments with faith were becoming a faith of their own.

SIX

Grandeur in This View of Life

DESIGN AND ITS DISCONTENTS

We notice purpose around us, all the time. Cognitive scientists find that their subjects, particularly children, have a bias for seeing some kind of intentional agent at work behind events; we'll assume there is one until good reason comes along to suggest otherwise. When strange lights appear in the sky, or an economy crashes, or there's a sound in the other room, we think, *Who did it? Why?* Only later, even if by just a few moments, will we begin to wonder, *How?*

I began to see, over the course of my conversion, the hand of God in my world. Whatever gave me life, I had to thank it. Whatever made Earth and the stars, I needed to praise it. Now it had a name. This was becoming ever more God's world, existing because God exists, in place because it has a God to keep it there. If something happened, it happened for a reason, for God's reason, by God's design.

But a designed universe, as much as it might feel full of loving concern, can also seem like a prison, trapping our lives in someone else's menagerie, without any freedom, spontaneity, or serendipity. A friend, an elder novelist, once said to me in passing, "Only an atheist can believe in what is unintended." What good would novels be without the unintended? Then again, what would they be without design?

Design arguments go back as far as our story; the teleological proof has usually seemed so obvious that it didn't require as much careful attention as its cosmological and ontological counterparts. Even on the verge of confounding it, Kant wrote, "This proof will always deserve to be treated with respect. It is the proof that is oldest, clearest and most in conformity with human reason."[1]

Plato summons a design argument in the *Laws,* and his contemporary Xenophon records that their teacher, Socrates, spoke of one too. "When you see all these things constructed with such show of foresight," the old sage says, speaking of the human body, "can you doubt whether they are products of chance or intelligence?" He offers his praise to the God "who orders and holds together the universe, in which are all things beautiful and good."[2] Aristotle completed his ascent to divinity with the comfort that "all things are indeed arranged around a single purpose,"[3] and Cicero made sure to include design when he presented the Greeks' rational religion for his fellow Romans: the power of nature, its hospitality to human life, and, most of all, the regularity of the stars' and planets' motions.[4] A century later, the apostle Paul began a letter to the Christians of Rome by declaring that their invisible God can be "understood and seen through the things he has made."[5] Christian writers soon started claiming the book of nature as a divine revelation alongside scripture. Jews who didn't accept the Christians' messiah at least shared this inference; in a commentary on Genesis, *Bereshit Rabbah,* the rabbis traced the proof back to their patriarch, long before the Greeks.

> Abraham our father said, "Is it conceivable that the world is without a guide?" The Holy One, blessed be He, looked out and said to him, "I am the Guide, the Sovereign of the Universe."[6]

Muhammad, another heir of Abraham, exhorted the first hearers of his Qur'an to notice God in nature.

> He sends down water from the sky, of which you drink and irrigate the pasturage on which you feed your animals. And with it also He brings forth crops, olives, palm trees, and fruits of every kind. Surely in this there is a sign for those who reflect. He harnessed for you the night and the day, and the sun and the moon; the stars are also subservient to his command. Surely in this there are signs for men of understanding.[7]

Muslim theologians preached devotional teleology like this to the masses, even if they preferred more rigorous cosmological arguments among themselves. Maimonides wrote of design in his *Guide,* and Aquinas made it the fifth of the Five Ways. It seemed self-evident enough to him to require an explanation shorter than those of the other four. Design was simply the way of the world.

The advent of scientific natural philosophy made possible a new natural theology, out to affirm anew the empirical indications of God's existence.

By the early eighteenth century, teleological proofs were on every bookshelf, in guises that ranged from the verses of Richard Blackmore's *Creation* to the German "physico-theology" craze, producing books with titles like *Hydrotheology, Pyrotheology,* and *Insectotheology.* Pure research was still far from a paying profession, so many naturalists kept day jobs in the clergy, and they preached their sermons with the Bible in one hand and a lab notebook in the other. Arguments for God's existence—and teleological arguments above all—gained popular appeal. Even as old proofs were being called into question, these newer ones seemed more secure than ever. What sturdier assurance could there be for divine truth than the grandeur of creation, closely examined?

∴

The young Charles Darwin revered William Paley. He even lived in a room at Christ College, Cambridge, that Paley had once occupied. Paley's works were required reading at Cambridge, and *Natural Theology,* published almost thirty years earlier, in 1802, was Darwin's favorite. He knew it practically by heart—surely most of all these famous first lines:

> In crossing a heath, suppose I pitched my foot against a stone, and were asked how the *stone* came to be there; I might possibly answer, that, for anything I knew to the contrary, it had lain there forever: nor would it perhaps be very easy to show the absurdity of this answer. But suppose I had found a *watch* upon the ground, and it should be inquired how the watch happened to be in that place; I should hardly think of the answer I had before given, that for anything I knew, the watch might have always been there.

Could a watch have come about without the purpose of telling time? Of course not. All its parts fit together just so to ensure that it ticks and tocks. "The inference is inevitable," continues Paley,

> that the watch must have had a maker; that there must have existed, at some time, and at some place or other, an artificer or artificers, who formed it for the purpose which we find it actually to answer; who comprehended its construction, and designed its use.[8]

What follows, then, is a procession from plants to the parts of animals to the variety of insects and up through the elements and the distant stars to the deity whose purposes all life is designed to serve. Since childhood, Darwin had loved studying and classifying what he found outdoors; *Natural Theology* gave him more of that and then some.

Paley's book is a piece of popular science that also happens to be one long, sustained proof for a designing God. Rather than with abstract arguments, he filled his pages with the interlocking parts of the eye, the arrangements of joints, and the adaptations of animals to their respective tasks. These feats of nature attest to a majestic theology. "Whereas formerly God was seldom in our thoughts," he wrote, "we can now scarcely look upon anything without perceiving its relation to him."[9]

Natural Theology was an out-and-out best-seller for decades, though it wasn't especially original. Books of its kind had been on hand for more than a century. Even the analogy of the watch had been used to much the same effect by others before—including Cleanthes in David Hume's *Dialogues.* Paley's repetition of it posed an outright challenge to Hume: a claim that through the natural world, much more can be said about God than the doubting Scot would allow.

At the turn of the nineteenth century, England led the world in watchmaking.[10] The English were the first to build watches that could be used reliably at sea, which solved the problem of calculating longitude and enabled them to amass an empire with their navy. Nothing in Paley's readers' experience was more intently and intricately designed. A watch, like the living creatures he surveys, is a machine adapted to the laws of nature with a purpose in mind. It was also a symbol of imperial power. How could a watch, or a watchlike world, not have a powerful designer?

Yet it was Paley's onetime acolyte, Charles Darwin, who wrote the book that put the design arguments in a tailspin: *On the Origin of Species,* published in 1859. Darwin was not the first to suggest that all life evolved from common ancestors—Alfred Russel Wallace thought of much the same idea, for instance, and Darwin's grandfather Erasmus had proposed another version of it years before—but his book was by far the most plausible, comprehensive, and eloquently expressed. It drew from a lifetime of patient study and reflection, beginning with Darwin's five-year journey around the world aboard the HMS *Beagle.* At his theory's core is a simple mechanism, iterated over unthinkably long stretches of time: as organisms reproduce, their features undergo slight variations from one generation to the next; those best suited to their environments survive, while others die off; over many generations, this gives rise to new species, descended from old ones and suited to the

conditions where they live. Human beings are a part of this story too, sharing the same common ancestors as all other life on Earth.

If Darwin was right, the appearance of design that Paley reveled in could be explained without recourse to a designer. Rather than in the mind of God, nature's purposes could be searched for more immediately in the remains of fossils, in the bodies of animals, and even in human behavior. The teleological proof was no longer as obvious as it had seemed. Copies of the *Origin* sold out its first day on the shelves.

"There is grandeur in this view of life," the book concludes, that "from so simple a beginning endless forms most beautiful and most wonderful have been, and are being, evolved."[11] But, for Darwin at least, one grandeur came at the cost of another. During the forty years between reading Paley at Cambridge and publishing his theory, to the distress of his wife, Emma, he stopped attending church. When their daughter Annie died in 1851, he didn't bother imagining an afterlife for her. His posthumous autobiography confesses that "disbelief crept over me at a very slow rate, but at last was complete."[12] Without a theory of life's origins, David Hume's doubts could only lead him to skepticism, but Darwin's had a theory to grasp. Richard Dawkins has put the matter bluntly: "Darwin made it possible to be an intellectually fulfilled atheist."[13]

If it hadn't been for the worldview of design that Paley and others popularized, perhaps the *Origin* would have been simply another advance in science, not also the start of a social and religious and philosophical upheaval, as it was. Religion doesn't necessarily have to stand in evolution's way. Early Christian writers like Origen and Augustine, for instance, always urged against reading scripture too literally in matters of natural history. Paley himself might have accepted Darwinian evolution, had he lived to learn about it; he didn't insist that each species is forever fixed, and his God was one who works through natural laws, not against them.[14] But such nuance gave way to rancor. It's hard to imagine that Darwin believed himself for an instant when he wrote, in the *Origin*'s second and subsequent editions, "I see no good reason why the views given in this volume should shock the religious feelings of any one."[15]

∴

Every fall, Boston University hosts an event called the Great Debate, in which invited experts and student debaters take on a contentious matter of public interest. The auditorium is packed full of journalism students, with notepads, video cameras, and tape recorders in hand, ready to dash back to their dorm rooms afterward and produce reports for class. Booing isn't allowed, but when necessary the crowd bursts into a cry of "Shame! Shame!" At the end of closing arguments, the speakers gather in the auditorium lobby to face a barrage of questions. By design, the Great Debate is a media circus.

When I took the train up to Boston for the 2005 installment, the question at hand was whether public schools should teach "intelligent design" theory alongside evolution in science classes. The debaters included some of the most outspoken voices on each side. William Dembski, who developed much of the philosophical basis for intelligent design, stood tall and confident, with big, round glasses over a boyish face. Opposite him was Eugenie Scott, the brusque physical anthropologist who heads the National Center for Science Education, which defends the teaching of evolution in schools. Each was accompanied by another guest speaker and a very sharply dressed undergraduate from the debate team. The chairman of the journalism department presided from center stage in full academic regalia. He assured us in his opening remarks that nobody should expect to resolve the question that night; it was an old one and would continue well after this Great Debate was finished. But the stakes felt especially high. That same week marked the end of testimony in the latest high-profile court case over evolution, in Dover, Pennsylvania.

At the time, I was writing my college thesis about the Dover trial, trying to wrap my head around the arguments, politics, and performances at work in it. Walking around campus, I would look at the cultivated lawns and stray trees, muster all the wonder I could, and ask, *Designed? Evolved?* The reply sounded different from day to day. Both options tried to squeeze their way into an answer, together. But in a debate or a trial, that won't do. One side or the other has to win.

The story of the teleological proof since Darwin can be told as a sequence of such theatrics. Events like the Great Debate are commonplace on college campuses. From time to time evolution controversies flare up in a courtroom drama, its battle lines drawn around the culture wars of the moment. Evolution debates are a genre of their own, and a national pastime. While they really pose little danger to evolutionary theory's status among research biologists, who both take it for granted and consider it subject to constant revision, these conflagrations have everything to do with the challenge evolution poses to the teleological proof.

The prehistory of Dover and the Great Debate lies in old England. On a Saturday morning in the summer of 1860, Oxford's University Museum hosted a meeting of the British Association for the Advancement of Science, which climaxed in a standoff between the biologist who called himself "Darwin's bulldog," T.H. Huxley, and, clothed in purple vestments, the city's doctrinaire bishop, Samuel Wilberforce. The two were essentially proxies: Huxley for Darwin, who was sickly and had no stomach for debate; and Wilberforce for Richard Owen, the museum's founder, who had coached him to argue against evolution. Huxley came from modest means and loved abusing Victorian sensibilities. Wilberforce was a Tory in the House of Lords and stood for the establishment. Others spoke at the meeting that day, but it was for the confrontation between these two that it would be remembered. With conflicting reports and no literal transcript, the famous anecdote about what transpired that day may be more legend than fact.

Wilberforce, at one point, asked Huxley whether his ape ancestors are on his father's or mother's side. It annoyed Huxley that the bishop was turning a scientific discussion into an occasion for ridicule. He answered that, given the choice between an ape and a person like Wilberforce, the choice would be clear. Huxley later remembered his words this way: "I unhesitatingly affirm my preference for the ape."[16]

So, in the terms set by a standoff between an upstart scientist and an establishmentarian bishop, evolution got its start as an occasion for public, political theater, with science against religion, new against old, and nature against God. The metaphor that most caught on in connection with it, however unbefitting such delicate and difficult questions, was *war*. And insofar as war it was, the theater of operations soon crossed the Atlantic to the United States.

The first and greatest eruption of evolution theatrics into the American psyche was the so-called Scopes Monkey Trial of 1925. Outside powers looking to pick a fight—and spurred by local businessmen looking for a profit—descended on the town of Dayton, Tennessee. A young football coach cum substitute teacher named John Scopes stood accused of teaching that humans evolved from other species, a violation of state law. To represent the state, the three-time populist presidential candidate William Jennings Bryan arrived in Dayton. Though hardly the fundamentalist he is sometimes made to seem, Bryan detested Darwinism for the racism and irreligion that many people then were using it to justify. Against him, the American Civil Liberties Union reluctantly agreed to send Clarence Darrow, a legendary defender of organized labor—and of some heinous criminals. He wanted nothing more than the chance to topple Bryan, whom he would later call "the idol of all Morondom." Darrow was a self-described agnostic, a term first coined by the man whose shoes he was now filling, T. H. Huxley: he didn't think anyone can be sure whether God exists or not, but he tended toward the latter. Reporters from big-city newspapers followed, and it would be the first time in history a trial was broadcast live on the radio. People all over the country took sides in the contest along political, geographic, and religious lines: Prohibition against the speakeasy, tradition against progress, dogma against inquiry, rural against urban, the heartland against the coasts. Its outcome, too, the whole country would decide.

The trial made no space for subtlety or sophistication; the judge even ruled not to admit the expert testimony of scientists. But as drama, it served its purpose. The climactic moment came on the penultimate day, in a session held outdoors, when Darrow called Bryan to the stand as a "Bible expert" and questioned him directly. They sparred about Jonah and the whale, the age of Earth, and what really happened in Eden—interrupted by the noisy applause and laughter of the crowd gathered in the courtyard. The judge found technical reasons to allow the farce to go on, but Bryan had a different motivation. "The reason I am answering," he declared, "is not for the benefit of the superior court. It is to keep these gentlemen from saying I was afraid to meet them and let them question me, and I want the Christian world to know that any atheist, agnostic, unbeliever, can question me anytime as to my belief in God, and I will answer him."[17] The trial about whether to teach a particular scientific theory was really just an excuse to fight about God.

To no one's surprise, the Dayton jurors ruled against Scopes. (Darrow pretty much asked them to so the appeal could appear before a higher court.) The local favorite won, but those following the trial in newspapers elsewhere made their own judgments. The Monkey Trial became a symbol and a byword in the American mythos. "Two months ago the town was obscure and happy," the reporter H.L. Mencken wrote. "Today it is a universal joke." As if to round out the melodrama of it all, Bryan died in his sleep only days after the trial ended, before even leaving Dayton. There was victory in defeat, and defeat in victory.

After Scopes, and for decades to come, creationists shrank into quietism. Science became a matter of patriotic duty against the Axis, and then against Communism. When *Sputnik* put the Soviets ahead in the space race, Washington reacted by modernizing school curricula; in biology, this meant teaching evolution. Mainline Protestant denominations began to take an accommodating stance to Darwin. Many Catholics concluded that, just as Thomas Aquinas wasn't afraid of Aristotle, they didn't need to fear Darwin. The most radical among them, like the French Jesuit paleontologist Pierre Teilhard de Chardin, even tried to make evolution's grandeur the basis of a new kind of theology. The battle lines had blurred, and the gray area was winning out—for a while, at least.

∴

Henry Morris had hoped to study journalism at Austin, but an angel of modern fundamentalist history intervened. The Great Depression ruined his father, a realtor, and the options suddenly became much more limited— no more Austin, no more journalism. The best Morris could do was live at home and learn engineering at Houston's Rice Institute, where he wouldn't be charged tuition. This angel needed to raise up an engineer.

After graduating from Rice in 1939, Morris found a job in El Paso, leaving a fiancée behind in Houston for good. With the quiet evenings he had to himself over the months that followed, he undertook a fresh study of the Bible. All that time alone with the eternal Word made a firm conviction grow in him: the meaning of the text is plain, not open for interpretation. The six days of Genesis mean *six days,* and they were just thousands of years ago, not billions. During those lonely nights, Henry Morris was born again in the water of creationism, and he intended to take the rest of us to the river too.[18]

He went on to earn a PhD in hydraulic engineering and became a professor at Virginia Tech. But his true vocation didn't become evident until after the 1961 publication of *The Genesis Flood,* coauthored with a young theologian named John Whitcomb. It argued that the fossil record and the appearance of vast scales of time in geology could be explained by Noah's flood, as described in the Bible. This catastrophic event drowned plants and animals—including, of course, dinosaurs—covering their remains in layers of rock and sediment. Canyons, mountains, and valleys formed in the hydraulic turbulence. It was a theory that had been suggested before, and was actually taken quite seriously by seventeenth- and eighteenth-century geologists. But few scientists in Morris's day cared to give it a second chance. Among fundamentalist home schoolers and Bible study groups, however, the book marked a new beginning. Here was a man with scientific credentials taking a stand in the name of science against backsliding on the Bible. Morris launched a movement.

So far as it offered a proof for God's existence, it was less a proof from design than from correspondence: *real* science confirms the testimony of the Bible, so the Bible must have been right about its God. Morris's creationism was "creation science." Read the Bible as literally as possible, he promised, and you can expect scientific findings to follow suit, casting their eminently modern light on God's existence and revelation. No longer was the contest one of science against religion, if it ever really was; he pitted one kind of science against another.

With his career as a creationist taking off, Morris's colleagues at Virginia Tech grew uneasy, and he felt pressure to resign in 1969. But their snub turned into another opportunity. A year later, in the remote suburbs of San Diego, he founded the Institute for Creation Research, or ICR, to sponsor the development and promulgation of creation science. The ICR sought out what sympathetic scientists it could and arranged for them to write creationist tracts and debate evolutionists on college campuses.

Morris kept on writing books of his own. He saw all world history as a conflict between opposites: righteous, holy creationism on one side, evolution on the other, along with its crooked stepchildren such as racism, Nazism, communism, and nihilism. Time, for Morris, is of the essence; six days of creation prefigure six thousand years of history. As we round the second millennium after Christ, our allotment is nearly over. If the world doesn't come to accept the true creation story soon, it will be too late.[19]

The Catholic cell biologist Kenneth Miller—whom Morris considered his most formidable opponent—remembers a conversation with the elder creationist the morning after a debate in Florida. "Ken, you're intelligent, you're well-meaning, and you're energetic," Morris told him. "But you are also young, and you don't realize what's at stake."[20]

The fate of creation science and its place in American society would be settled, by and large, in two now-familiar settings: the classroom and the courtroom. As legislators and school boards attempted to insert this allegedly scientific creationism into public school science classrooms, courts repeatedly struck them down. Trials snaked around the country until finally reaching the Supreme Court in the 1987 case, *Edwards v. Aguillard*. It ended with a decision that would prove devastating: creation science is not real science, and presenting it in public schools is an improper establishment of religion, a violation of the First Amendment.

Henry Morris died in 2006. (In homage, while working on my college thesis, I wrote his obituary for one of the magazines on campus.) Under the leadership of his son John, the ICR moved its headquarters to Dallas. Its old creation museum, barely rising above the freeway in a nondescript California office park, is under new management and lives on as a relic. Church groups come through for tours, as does the occasional pack of skeptics on an extra-credit trip from the nearby state college. The docent—a thin, buoyant woman with a master's degree in creation science from the ICR—ably answers their questions. Its rooms take you through the six days of creation, showing with dioramas, recorded sounds, and murals what the Bible tells only briefly. A scale model of Noah's ark shows the sufficiency of its carrying capacity. One wall, with a row of broken pipes gushing cartoon fluid, purports to illustrate how "Natural Selection Fails." At the end lies a cross and the assurance, "Jesus Is Our True Hope."

Creation science lost among scientists, lost in court, and lost in the classroom; yet it remains hugely popular. Polls suggest that around half the U.S. population doesn't accept evolution, and most of those are young-earthers like Henry Morris. In 2007 the Australian ICR veteran Ken Ham opened a lavish creation museum in Kentucky, and he has a Noah's ark theme park in the works. But the next evolution showdown veered away from Morris's style, back to the old and venerable teleological proof, the proof from design.

∴

What first drew my attention to the intelligent design movement was discovering, at a neighborhood library one summer while back home in Virginia, a copy of William Dembski's 1998 book, *The Design Inference*. Sitting in a stack among others, on the desk in my old basement bedroom, that book came to stand for something: a presence, an appearance, an authority. I had never seen creationism like this, if it was creationism at all. The eminently respectable Cambridge University Press published it. The author boasted PhD's in both mathematics and philosophy. Even before opening it and entering its arguments, terms, and scattered formulas, I felt its force. Whether or not one is convinced by what lies within—scholarly reviewers tended not to be—the very fact of Dembski's book makes a point.

What *The Design Inference* sets out to do is give a rigorous theoretical foundation to that sensation of marvelous design in nature, assented to by everyone from Socrates to Paley. Dembski turns to a boutique branch of mathematics called information theory, together with more relatable examples from forensics, election fraud, and the search for extraterrestrial life. In each of these fields, people have to determine whether an intelligent agent is at work rather than simply blind chance or dumb repetition. One can thereby detect instances of what Dembski calls "specified complexity": arrangements of information so complex that they must have been specified by an intelligent designer. If a radio signal from Alpha Centauri were transmitting the digits of pi, we wouldn't hesitate to infer an intelligence behind it; instinct and probability would agree. Why, then, are biologists reluctant to accept that the complexity of living organisms is similarly specified? Dembski means to offer a technical, theoretical apparatus for doing just that.

Even if its dedication includes a biblical citation and its author holds a master's degree in divinity from Princeton Seminary, *The Design Inference* isn't an outright proof for the existence of a God. But it also is. Dembski insists that the designer might just as well be aliens with advanced technology, though his own inclination is clear enough. Along with the other architects of intelligent design—ID, for short—Desmbski is a Christian with Christian motivations. As he once put it to an audience of coreligionists, "Intelligent design is just the Logos theology of John's Gospel restated in the idiom of information theory."[21]

Early in 1999, months after the release of *The Design Inference,* a ten-page document called "The Wedge" surfaced on the Internet that made the movement's intentions especially clear. It came from the Center for the Renewal of Science & Culture at the Discovery Institute, a Seattle-based conservative think tank, founded in 1994, where Dembski was a fellow. Its photocopied cover showed a granulated reproduction from the Sistine Chapel fresco of God's finger touching Adam's, with a triangle above it wedging upward. Inside, it lists Dembski's book as "progress" in a twenty-year plan with an ambitious goal: "nothing less than the overthrow of materialism"—the idea that the universe is only matter, with no need for a God—"and its cultural legacies."[22] The experience of creation science in the courts showed that this wasn't going to happen just with apologetic tracts, creation museums, and a few footnotes. The "wedge," masterminded by the Stanford law professor Phillip E. Johnson, would go straight for the citadel: publications in top peer-reviewed journals, allies at elite universities, and access to mass media. At the center of the whole program was the old teleological proof for God's existence. But while the wedge did its initial work, at least, the program would downplay the God part.

Another book, described in "The Wedge" as "a breakthrough," was Michael Behe's *Darwin's Black Box,* published in 1996 by the solidly mainstream Free Press. A biology professor at Lehigh University and a Discovery Institute fellow, Behe describes immensely complicated biological systems like the clotting of blood and the bacterial flagellum as "irreducibly complex": if any one of their many parts weren't present, such systems would be useless. Since evolution is supposed to happen stepwise, with tiny modifications building and building on each other, true irreducible complexity like this would present a big problem. The best explanation, thinks Behe, is the foresight of a super-powerful, super-intelligent agent. It's Dembski's design inference, swimming under a microscope.

As ID and "The Wedge" began exploding into a public scandal, the Lehigh biology department put a notice prominently on its website; with the sole exception of Behe, the faculty declared, "It is our collective position that intelligent design has no basis in science, has not been tested experimentally, and should not be regarded as scientific."[23] The Discovery Institute listed hundreds of scientists declaring "dissent from Darwinism," and the National Center for Science Education answered with Project Steve, an even longer list of evolution-supporting scientists who happen to be named Steve and its variations. Biologists assembled litanies of all the bad design evident in nature: where's the intelligent design in vestigial limbs, shark fetuses eating each other in utero, or self-destructing wisdom teeth? Kenneth Miller, the longtime adversary of Morris and his ilk, took on Behe's examples from cell biology. Philosophers of science worried that jumping to the conclusion of design would prevent us from discovering other kinds of explanations in the future. Theologians, too, recoiled against ID's tinkering God-of-the-gaps—a God apparent only where our understanding happens to break down.

Contrary to the Discovery Institute's hopes for a wedge, intelligent design became a term of abuse among scientists and many theologians.

It was only a matter of time before this latest insurgency against evolution would end up in court. In December 2004 the ACLU turned up once again in a small town to put up a fight for evolution. The school board in Dover, Pennsylvania, had passed a rule requiring that a statement be read in biology class explaining that evolution "is not a fact" and that "gaps in the Theory exist for which there is no evidence."[24] It pointed curious students to *Of Pandas and People,* a creation science textbook hastily repurposed for ID after *Edwards v. Aguillard.*

Once again, a monkey trial. Scientists testified with the ammunition they had been building against ID for years. The Discovery Institute's lawyers sensed ill portents and chose not to enter directly, but Michael Behe nevertheless opted to take the stand against Ken Miller. Like Bryan's speech against Darrow in 1925, school board members used the opportunity to testify for their faith before a power higher than the court. *Rolling Stone*'s Matt Taibbi, Gen X's answer to H. L. Mencken, chronicled what he thought of as "just another clash with religious loonies of the same primitive sort found in the original Scopes trial."[25] People all over the world served as jury, tracking the showdown on cable news and seething blogs. The end finally came with a sweeping decision by a federal judge, who saw ID as a religious intrusion without a "secular purpose," as the law requires. Dover's schools had been going broke fighting the case, and as the trial stretched on over the latter months of 2005, voters ousted all but one of the board members responsible for it. After the election, the televangelist Pat Robertson warned the people of Dover on *The 700 Club,* "If there is a disaster in your area, don't turn to God. You just voted God out of your city."[26]

Yet Dover, like Dayton, was an ending without an ending. The biologist Richard Lewontin once observed that "creationism is an American institution"; skirmishes over evolution continue in school boards around the country. Already, too, Americans had been spreading their particular obsession with the teleological proof abroad.

∴

It was only a few years after Dover that I would find myself worrying about creationism again. This time, I was lying on the bunk bed of a crowded hostel, one of many in the neighborhood of Istanbul just down the hill from the

Blue Mosque and the Hagia Sophia. I waited there, with a notebook face-down on my chest, trying to think of questions.

By then, I had finished college and spent just enough time in graduate school to escape with a master's in religion. Restlessness had gotten hold of me there, and it took me from California to a succession of cramped apartments in Brooklyn—a change of plans. I started finding work as a writer, trying to continue my education on my own by filling the pages of magazines and websites. And it was hard to think of anything I wanted to write about more than proofs.

Thus, Istanbul.

When I first received the invitation to interview Harun Yahya in Turkey, I recognized the name immediately; I had first learned about him while working on my college thesis. Harun Yahya is the pseudonym of Adnan Oktar, Islam's most vociferous purveyor of the teleological proof. He leads a small but well-financed Turkish sect that has spent the last twenty years or so crusading against the theory of evolution. Hundreds of books have appeared under Yahya's name, bearing titles like *The Evolution Deceit* and *The Nightmare of Disbelief,* with millions of copies reportedly sold and given away per year. There is also a vast network of websites and hours of documentary films. Yahya is now best known in the West, however, for the *Atlas of Creation,* a series of seventeen-inch-high, fourteen-pound books that began appearing in the mailboxes of scientists and teachers across Europe and the United States in 2006. At more than eight hundred full-color pages each, the volumes purport to show that plants, animals, and the fossil record are all evidence of God's original design, not of evolutionary circumstance. In addition, they declare the evils that Darwinism has supposedly wrought in history, everything from the Holocaust and Islamist terrorism to the excesses of high finance.

For hundreds of pages on end, each volume of the *Atlas* presents pictures of fossils alongside critters living today and text claiming that they've remained the same for tens or hundreds of millions of years. In all that time, we're meant to understand, no evolution happened. Unchanged, intricate, and still harmonious after so many eons, they could only have been created by a God.

Rather than from the classical Muslim proofs of al-Kindi, Ibn Sina, or al-Ghazali, much of the material in the Yahya books comes from the heyday of American creation science, thanks to collaborations with Henry Morris's Institute for Creation Research during the 1990s. The tactics are classic ICR.

Straw-man versions of evolutionary theory are offered and then quickly dismissed. Passages from scientists' books are taken out of context and presented as if they express doubts that evolution is true. Qur'anic verses stand alongside recent scientific discoveries that the verses allegedly prefigure: the big bang, embryonic development, the formation of mountains, and even the structure of the brain. Those verses must, therefore, have come from a higher intelligence.

When I visited Filiz Gürel, a young genetic engineer who was teaching the introductory evolution course at Istanbul University's biology department, she showed me the copy of the *Atlas of Creation* that had come in the mail months before and that she kept under a lab table, still in the original corrugated cardboard box. "What they say is not scientific," Gürel told me.

The Council of Europe promulgated a report about the *Atlas* in 2007, warning of "the dangers of creationism in education," but meanwhile a Harun Yahya press release declared victory near: "DARWINISM HAS BEEN ANNIHILATED ACROSS THE WORLD."[27] In 2011 ads ran on London's red double-decker buses with Oktar's mug and the message, "MODERN SCIENCE DEMONSTRATES THAT GOD EXISTS." He and his followers seem convinced that their argument—and its packaging—has struck a decisive blow for God. Just don't ask any actual scientists.

Insofar as the Yahya books are successful, their success is aesthetic. Melodramatic collages portray, on page after page, the beatific harmony of God's creation—laughing children, waterfalls, blue skies, happy animals—over and against the twentieth century's dreary upshots of evolutionary thinking: concentration camps, burning crosses, starving bodies. The scenes are ridiculous even as they're appealing. On the shelves of Islamic bookstores from Istanbul to Chicago, they stand out, with glittering covers and affordable prices. The books convey an otherworldly grandeur; their design, even if not actually evidence for God's design, is their main argument.

Emre Calikoglu, who manages distribution for Harun Yahya media, picked me up at my hostel in his brand-new Volkswagen sedan, still talking on his iPhone. As the sun set, an ambient rhythm pulsated on the stereo, and we drove through the city toward the enormous suspension bridge that would take us to the Asian side of the Bosphorus. When he got off the phone, we talked about the several hundred "friends" gathered around Oktar. He told me the story of how he first joined as a college student, after hearing Oktar speak. Emre had always thought of himself as a Muslim, but religion didn't seem relevant to his life or his world. Meeting Oktar changed that.

Suddenly, the message of the Qur'an spoke to him. He came to understand that so many of society's problems are spiritual ones, stemming most of all from belief in evolution, which makes people blind to God's existence and plan for them.

It was the kind of story I heard a lot from the upwardly mobile Turks who gravitate to Oktar and figures like him. This is an Islam fit for designer clothes and Internet savvy. It traces the contours of a globalizing economy and the Turkish diaspora; the representative of Oktar's I met in New York, for instance, had also been set up to run an import-export business selling goods from Asia. Oktar is known in Turkey for recruiting the sons and daughters of the wealthy, luring them in with sex, cocaine, and spiritual fulfillment, then keeping them with blackmail.[28] They believe their leader is the Mahdi, an end-times redeemer figure who will appear alongside Jesus, according to Islamic eschatology.[29] With Mahdi-like ambition, Oktar has taken to promoting a "Turkish Islamic Union" of Muslim countries, a kind of throwback to the Ottoman Empire. He has also had some run-ins with the law and a stint in a mental hospital, which he claims as persecution by Turkey's conspiratorial secularists.

Late that night, after we ate dinner beside the Bosphorus, Emre brought me to the house of one of Oktar's friends for the interview. A pair of video cameras and their operators were already in place when we arrived, to record it for the Harun Yahya websites. The room was decorated like a page of a Yahya book, with white furniture, flowers, and gaudy appointments. Oktar came in a few minutes later, wearing black slacks and a black blazer over a black Versace T-shirt. He had on matching black shoes, though the rest of us had to leave our footwear at the door.

There was no opportunity for small talk. After we greeted one another, we sat down face-to-face in matching chairs, where glasses of peach juice were waiting on side tables. A young translator hurried to keep up with Oktar's paragraphs-long answers to my questions.

Should more science be done in the Muslim world? "Of course new proofs would be very fine to have," he replied, through the translator, "but the proofs we have in our hands right now suffice." Since the case against evolution and for divine creation is closed, he saw little need to make further discoveries—with one exception: "It is a very good idea that we might have a scientific branch which specifically deals with the existence of supernatural beings." This would include genies, he explained; angels would be more difficult to reach.

Oktar's books go on and on about the marvels that science finds in the atom and the eye, but he is clearly no scientist himself. He studied mainly at Istanbul's Mimar Sinan University of Fine Arts in the late 1970s. Never needing much sleep, Oktar began accumulating a file of notes and clippings during late nights as an art student, and that file became the basis of his message. Now, he uses his artistic talent to oversee the design of the Harun Yahya books. "The main aim of science is to help art," Oktar told me. It is "a tool which we use to make our world more beautiful every day." For him, science can be wielded like a paintbrush, revealing the grandeur of divine orchestration everywhere in nature. Darwinism is a failure to see the world as a work of art, created by an artist.

The hour got close to midnight. "How are we doing on time?" I asked.

Oktar replied, "We have time til morning."

He detailed the conspiracies working against him and promised that, within ten years or so, Jesus Christ would return. (I probably didn't look as glad to hear it as he hoped.) In the meantime, he assured me, "all of these bloody ideologies and nonsensical ways of thinking about creation will be eradicated." Oktar, like Henry Morris and so many pseudoprophets before him, has staked his campaign of mass persuasion on a cosmic endgame.

"When Jesus Christ comes I hope that we will come together again and talk things over," he said, shortly before leaving the room through the side door from which he came.

∴

Elsewhere in the Muslim world today, Oktar's obsession with refuting evolution for God's sake is an anomaly. While Morris and his colleagues have succeeded in making creationism a litmus test for fundamentalists in the United States, Muslims have tended not to be quite so concerned—yet. What the Harun Yahya media machine represents is not simply an attempt to win a fight for Islam, but to pick one that hasn't really started.

When I flew from Turkey to Jordan to meet with scientists and science policy experts, none of them was much concerned about either Yahya or evolution and religion. They were Muslims, and they more or less accepted evolutionary theory, and that was that. "I don't think we are as passionate about these things as our fellow human beings in the West are, frankly speaking," said Moneef Zoubi, director general of the Islamic World Academy of Sciences in Amman. A few days later I went to the biology department at the

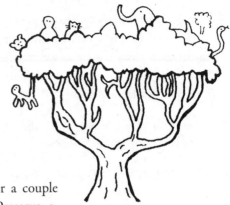

University of Jordan and asked two of the professors whether they thought the evolution of humans was compatible with their faith. One said yes, the other said no, and both thought all their colleagues agreed with them. Apparently they had never bothered to find out.

During that trip I stopped for a couple of days at Jordan's Dana Nature Preserve, a stretch of desert mountains and valleys full of rare creatures. There was a silence there so total that it was loud, as if Pythagoras's blaring harmony of the spheres were somehow seeping through. The manager of the campsite, Abu Ahmed, was an old man who said he was illiterate. I couldn't help asking him about evolution one night over supper; I wanted to compare what he would say with the experts. At first, when he finally understood what I was talking about through the language barrier, his answer was blunt: No, Islam doesn't allow it. He pointed at the scene behind us, outside the tent. There were birds soaring, cypress trees casting long shadows across the ground, and, surely not far away, a family of ibex making its way around a sheer cliff. God created nature to serve people, he said, and people have to care for it in turn. Everything is a balance, and atop it human beings were made by the hand of God—no monkeys necessary.

That was enough to get me thinking. Was it true that Harun Yahya spoke for Muslims more than I had been led to believe? But soon it became clear that what I had said had gotten Abu Ahmed thinking too.

The next day at breakfast he came to me and asked why, if evolution is true, monkeys don't turn into people all the time. It would take millions of years, I said, so we shouldn't expect to see it happening in front of us. To explain the idea of common ancestry I drew an evolutionary tree. It showed how we don't really come from the monkeys and apes alive today but that all of us descended from earlier species long ago that are now extinct. I said that many people think God could have created us *through* an evolutionary process, and Abu Ahmed lit up. He liked that. More to think about, he told me, and left me to my hard-boiled egg.

Anyway, I wasn't in the mood to press him on it. After a while in a place like the preserve, away from concrete landscapes, looming spires, and charlatan preachers, heavy questions start to shed their weight. The grandeur is simply *there*. It's just a place, with beauty and sustenance and dangers. The transcendentalists knew this well as they, a century and a half ago, taught Americans how to think in the wilderness. Their fellow traveler Walt Whitman saw fit to write:

> I say to mankind, Be not curious about God.
> For I, who am curious about each, am not curious about God.[30]

Before grandeur, isn't "each" enough? Aren't these canyons, cliffs, clouds, or their inhabitants grand enough? Must they really sum up to divine purpose or intention? There is an order in every mess, and a mess in every order. From above, Earth is small, smooth, and round, and from where we are below, vast, jagged, and flat. To either vantage our world seems to murmur, as God thundered from the burning bush, "I AM THAT I AM."[31]

SEVEN

The Deaths of God

HUMAN PROGRESS AND DIVINE ABSENCE

On October 7, 2008, twenty-two-year-old Jesse Kilgore drove out into the woods near his home, in Upstate New York, and shot himself with a rifle. In the days before the end, Jesse had been planning for the future. He reenlisted in the military and asked his father for a ticket to visit his grandparents in Florida. He was close to completing an associate's degree. As he was getting in the car to leave home for the last time, he talked about seeing a movie with his family later on. But then Jesse's father, Keith Kilgore, got a call from the state troopers. It was so sudden. He didn't understand.

The next day, a friend of Jesse's came to the house. She told Keith about a book Jesse had been reading: *The God Delusion,* by Richard Dawkins. "It destroyed him," she said.[1]

At first Keith couldn't find the book. He looked everywhere. But finally he pulled up the mattress on Jesse's bed, and there it was—where someone else might have kept *Playboys*. His favorite bookmark was on the last page. Thanks to Dawkins, Keith concluded, Jesse "had lost all hope because he was convinced that God did not exist."

Dawkins was once professor of "the Public Understanding of Science" at Oxford, having written a parade of well-regarded popular books on evolutionary biology. He's encyclopedic about science and has a knack for spinning encyclopedia into wonder. In retirement, he has turned his attention to—or, against—religion. *The God Delusion* was a best-seller when it was published in 2006 and has continued to sell well. It's caustic, merciless, and engrossing. Between the book's reflective silver covers, with a bit of science and plenty of bombast, Dawkins announces that God's existence is so improbable, and so dangerous when believed, that we would be better off banishing the thought of it altogether.

Jesse had been living with his father and stepmother since his mother succumbed to cancer in 2003. He wore closely cropped hair, glasses with transition lenses, and a big class ring on his right hand. Keith says he had a lot of friends. But just as much as he lived in the physical world, Jesse lived online, under names like Jkrapture and jesse_underdog. At various blogs and forums, through bold proclamations and viral-ready images, he argued about politics and religion. "I am a culture warrior and traditionalist," he stated on his profile at one blog, "conservative and mainly independent."[2] He posted reports about cosmic dreams he had, skepticism about global warming, and justifications for the Iraq War. Online and on the phone, he spent long hours hashing out religious questions with his maternal uncle, a seeker and drifter who had been in and out of churches down in Florida.

Up until the end, Jesse shared his father's religion. Keith, a Southern Baptist, had been a military chaplain. They went to church on Sundays, where Jesse was a leader in the youth group. When he needed help finding arguments to defend their faith, he turned to his father. I asked Keith about that faith, and he professed that Jesus of Nazareth is the incarnate son of God. "If that is not the case," he said, "then I've wasted my life on a fairy tale." Jesse wrote in blog posts that without God and an afterlife there would be no right or wrong, and no meaning in life: "It is too harsh of a reality for men to accept on their psyches, the belief there is no God."[3] To both father and son, faith was all or nothing.

Keith thinks that what in part led Jesse to the brink was the hostility to religion of his biology teacher and his fellow students at Jefferson Community College, in Watertown. "It was ridicule and it was contemptuous," says Keith. Jesse checked *The God Delusion* out from the college library, and four days later he killed himself.

Within a few weeks, Keith told his son's story to a reporter from *WorldNetDaily,* a very-right-wing Christian news website, and soon Jesse's suicide was being discussed around the Internet. The Discovery Institute produced a podcast with Keith as a spokesman for teaching intelligent design in public schools. A Discovery fund-raising letter repeated the story of Jesse to spur donations. Blogs critical of the intelligent design movement attacked Keith, floating theories about Jesse's upbringing and speculating about his sexual orientation. Keith received hate mail blaming him—and all that people felt he represents—for his own son's death. But Keith insists, "My son was his own man. His mind was his own."

There are other facts in play: Jesse's parents had split, his mother had died, and there was a girl. But through it all, arguments mattered, and God's existence mattered. These were what he talked and blogged about as whatever else bore down on him. When the reason to believe seemed gone, so was he. Jesse experienced, and Jesse's own death was, a death of God.

∴

"IS GOD DEAD?" asked the cover of *Time* magazine's April 1966 issue, in bold red letters over a black background. That issue sold more copies than any before in the magazine's history. The article inside described a new movement among a handful of young, mainly Christian theologians: death-of-God theology. Its leader was Thomas J. J. Altizer, a fiery professor at Emory University who, steeped in the most apocalyptic aspects of Hegel, William Blake, and Friedrich Nietzsche, was proclaiming a "gospel of Christian atheism." The disappearance of God, he said, is the natural conclusion of Christianity's logic, beginning with the Incarnation and ending in the secular city. Death-of-God theology was a fad that puttered out by the end of the decade, as the media hyperbole faded and all that remained were a series of eccentric, paradoxical academic texts. (The poet Anthony Towne lampooned the movement best in a 1965 *New York Times* obituary and a subsequent book, *Excerpts from the Diaries of the Late God*.) Yet the question *Time* asked on that cover continues in people like Jesse Kilgore.

The death of God is a trope usually associated with passages by Nietzsche, though it goes back long before—from the Egyptians' Osiris and the Greeks' Orpheus to the sect of Jews who claimed that their messiah had hung on a cross to the dark nights of medieval mystics' souls to the unanswered prayers of those who have perished in modern wars and genocides. Hegel wrote about God's death half a century before Nietzsche in his lectures on religion, in reference to the words of a Lutheran hymn that say, "God himself is dead."[4] In Hegel's system, this is the great lesson of Christianity: God's death is a part of God's life, and with the death of a body comes the triumph of Spirit.

Contrary to how it is sometimes remembered, the death of God Nietzsche announced is not exactly a refutation of God's existence. The "madman" of

The Gay Science who declares that "God is dead!" continues, "And we have killed him!" Nietzsche didn't claim to have killed God. Rather, it comes at the end of a long story he tells about the rise and fall of Christianity, about the faithful who killed their own God with complacent piety and self-assurance and self-satisfied reason: "What then are these churches now if not the tombs and sepulchers of God?"[5] Why? They domesticated the divine. Polite society had made God into a mere upholder of convention, buttressed by philosophy's impotent abstractions.

Though he was as much a Christian as Nietzsche was not, Søren Kierkegaard agreed. The Dane denounced Hegel's sprawling, optimistic system and "the little Cartesian dolls" that philosophy masquerades as God. For Kierkegaard, proof is an insult to faith and a waste of time. "Even if I began I would never finish," he writes, with characteristic frenzy, "and would in addition have to live constantly in suspense, lest something so terrible should suddenly happen that my bit of proof would be demolished."[6] They're haunting words when one thinks of Jesse Kilgore and the end that he found to his search for arguments.

"I have been debating since I was in 5th Grade, and never looked back," he wrote. "It is a habit I can't let go of."[7]

.·.

We usually think of debating God's existence as a contest between opposites: belief and unbelief, natural and supernatural, theism and atheism, secular and religious, God and godlessness, immanent and transcendent. But the definitions of these words and the motivations of those who have claimed them haven't always been what we might expect.

The atheist in a Greek tragedy was someone whom the gods have abandoned, while for Plato it was one who dared to deny that capital R Reason rules the world; those who suspended their judgment about gods, or who positively denied them, went by names like Skeptic and Epicurean. Half a world away, they might have been called Buddhists or Taoists. The idea of atheism as we tend to think of it now has been, for much of history, more chimerical than actual—a dangerous, illegal, and possibly unthinkable pseudo-option that was spoken against far more than spoken for. Believers pretended they were aiming their proofs at it when, more often than not, they were mainly aiming at each other. Like Gaunilo's defense of the fool against Anselm, and Kant's critique of Anselm too, most refutations came from among those who still believed that a God exists. Their purpose was to trade worse arguments for better ones, or a false God for a true one, and thus to reach closer and more soundly toward the beatific vision.

This situation began to change over the past several centuries in the West, as atheists have begun to declare themselves as such. One need not conclude, though, that the rise of unbelief is due solely to the success of counterarguments. The state-established churches in Europe broke down, new explanations of nature arose, and wars made plain the cruelty that people are capable of, in the name of God or otherwise. Atheism is only part of the result. The United States remains awash in its sea of faith, but it is also a society aware of its own diversity, and of the world's bewildering diversity beyond. As much as Americans are faithful, they are also restless, and polls say that almost half of us today end up leaving the tradition we grew up in.[8] Experiences like mine are more common than ever: mixed marriages and religious shopping sprees. I might feel like an oddity, but oddity is increasingly the norm.

Before, the genre of proof mainly dealt with the matter of what God is, what existence means, and what could be proved and how. But now it became enlisted in a plainer, starker question: whether any God actually exists.

So, which came first, the chicken or the egg? God or no God? With no evidence, revelation, or proof at all, would it be more reasonable to believe in a God or not to? It's a question that takes us back to Ibn Tufayl's island, to a state of nature. Descartes says yes, the idea of God lurks in us, and we have access to it. Locke says no. The British philosopher Antony Flew argued in a 1972 essay, "The Presumption of Atheism," precisely that: God is a nonobvious idea, so nonexistence, like innocence in court, should be presumed until proven otherwise. The burden of proof is on the believer. History, however, only confounds the matter. If any belief is truly native in us, chances are we've forgotten the word for it. That's what this was.

As for myself, I can remember only so far back. But where there is a question of which came first and which is basic for me, I think I know the answer.

Dizzy Gillespie once wrote a tune called "Night in Tunisia": a spree of juxtaposition, exotic and uncomfortable. That's what this was. Specifically, a tiny hotel room on the edge of the old medina in Tunis, where the imposing, regal avenues left behind by the French meet the tiny streets that came before, curling around the buildings and markets like veins. The day had been long and full of traveling up from the holy city of Kairouan. I was in a hard, narrow bed. My uncle, my mother's brother, the same uncle I had met on the road trip in Colorado, was in another. Our bicycles filled all the remaining space.

He was coughing, as he had been for days. His skin was burning hot. The wrinkles that cut through his face, deep enough already from years of cigarettes and sun, had become canyons, running along his jaw and cheekbones. His eyes, when he opened them, had grown dark and seemed ready to disappear into their sockets. His long, graying hair looked like metal fibers. The red light from the square below filled our room. Between coughs he talked, quickly and uninterruptibly.

The whole trip we had been talking about formidable things—he, especially, had been talking. About war and the history of all we were passing through. About his life and the mother of his children, who had grown up in this country. About the machines we were riding on, these bicycles, old buses, and ships. Most of all, as always, he talked about science. He talked wonderfully. About how we had evolved. About nature's coy and ambivalent self-disclosure in rocks, ants, consciousness, and chaos. On the ferry from Genoa, as we watched Tunisian men dance under a disco ball, he spent hours explaining how to sequence a gene. His point for me was this, I couldn't help but think: turn back, you've gone too far.

I was still in college, and it was winter break. I had been baptized less than two years earlier.

In all he had seen, there is no God; he had seen no evidence. Miracles aren't needed to understand the world. Evolution explains life. There is no life after death besides the next generation, for us any more than for animals. That night, in that hotel room, I heard his breathless speech again. I heard it as care and as love. I know I let go a tear, though I don't know if he saw it. The tear was warm. What for Jesse Kilgore was shocking and unbearable, for me felt like home.

And so I said it.

"A part of me has never stopped being an atheist," I whispered, trembling, hardly able to utter the words. He said he knew. It was a relief to know he did. Then, I said a silent prayer before falling asleep.

The next day, riding up along the Mediterranean coast on my own, I came upon the ruins of St. Cyprian's Church, where Monica prayed through the night while her son Augustine sailed to Italy. It overlooked the decrepit, colonial-era resort hotel where we had stayed our first night in the country ten days before, when dark caught us on our bikes with no place else to go.

Though we had been so close, we hadn't bothered then to look up and notice the ruins above.

That's not a metaphor; metaphorically, we had been looking up the whole time, up to nature in its self-sufficient immanence, itself a miracle with no need for the word. But on my own, I found other miracles too—stories, prayers, characters, and inadvertent pilgrimages like this one. Coming upon that church was an explicable mystery. A significant coincidence. I knew my God wasn't quite the one my uncle had been railing against but somehow encompassed us both.

Soon, by way of a ferry and a string of trains, we were in another tiny room, in Barcelona, and my uncle began to recover. We watched people passing by on Las Ramblas. I followed his eye and his expansive talk through Gaudí's wrought iron and Mies van der Rohe's glass pavilion. Days later, I was back in the States, in California, at my grandmother's bedside, watching her disappear, wishing she could speak.

Sharing the wilds of thirteenth-century Paris with Thomas Aquinas was a man called Siger of Brabant. He and his followers were known as Latin Averroists for their devotion to the writings of Ibn Rushd. Among the doctrines attributed to them—and singled out, together with some of Aquinas's, in the Condemnation of 1277—was the tantalizing notion of "double truth." Those words alone have a ring of the familiar to me. Siger allegedly taught that there are two simultaneous and yet opposing kinds of truth: one known to faith through revelation and one known to reason. Something might appear true to reason—say, the eternity of the universe—while its opposite is true to faith, and neither can be denied.

The horribly bifurcated world of double truth, where truth contradicts truth, seemed like the worst kind of confusion that Greek philosophy and its Arabic interpreters had to offer. Try it on in the world, and you'll see why. Try it on your uncle, or your grandmother, or your friend who keeps you up all night, interrogating your justifications with the honest expectation of

consistency. The Condemnation ruined Siger's career in Paris. It probably cost him his life, which is said to have ended with either execution or suicide or being stabbed with a pen by his secretary. Yet Dante, less than a century later, imagined Aquinas in heaven praising Siger's "envied truths," though in life they were opponents.[9] Siger had seen something about the limits of reason, and the cost of faith.

Speaking of Dante: he also describes a punishment for the uncommitted and lukewarm, a vestibule at the gate of hell for those not even worthy of entering, like Pontius Pilate and the ones who took no side in the rebellion of Satan and his angels. These people wouldn't take a stand in life, and now they have no place. He's following Revelation 3:16: "Because you are lukewarm, and neither cold nor hot, I am about to spit you out of my mouth."

I have to think and hope this double truth of mine is not that. I know, at least, in my looking and finding and converting and remaining, I am not lukewarm.

∴

By the middle of the twentieth century, many leading philosophers and scientists seemed to agree that there is no God or gods, no supernatural beyond nature. They brushed off the conventions and habits of the past, premodern world, and especially its world beyond. The whole vocabulary of metaphysics that had been rudiments of the classical proofs—necessity, contingency, perfection, and cause—were casualties of the new order. It all seemed like arbitrary nonsense. Bertrand Russell and Alfred North Whitehead had begun the century by trying to ground all of mathematics in philosophical logic, and nearly succeeded. Meanwhile, the school of logical positivism proposed to limit philosophy to only what can be verified with mathematical precision or scientific observation. Anything unobservable, intangible, and incalculable was no longer allowed, and that included God.

The young A. J. Ayer published in 1936 the book that would bring logical positivism into English: *Language, Truth and Logic.* In it, he meant to stop the question before it could even be asked: "To say that 'God exists,'" Ayer wrote, "is to make a metaphysical utterance which cannot be either true or false." He wouldn't even go so far as to call himself an atheist; the whole idea of a God is, in the most damning verdict a positivist can muster, "unintelligible." Those philosophers who try to explicate and demonstrate it are wasting their time. Far short of any actual proof, they "are merely providing material for the psychoanalyst."[10] Sigmund Freud had already published his scathing psychoanalytic study of religion about a decade earlier, *The Future of an Illusion*. It didn't seem, at the time, like there would be much of one.

This was the kind of thinking in the air when twenty-seven-year-old Antony Flew stood up to deliver a short paper, "Theology and Falsification," before Oxford's Socratic Club in 1950. He asked whether a religious claim can be treated like a scientific one: can it be disproved? If I were to say that this night will never end, and you present me with the dawn, everybody should recognize that I'm wrong. That's how science advances. But, said Flew, the way religious people talk about God admits no falsification. When a prayer for the sun to stand still isn't answered, believers will mince words about how God's inscrutable wisdom decided not to stop it. Such just-so stories lurk behind every conceivable defeater for God's existence, so Flew threw up his hands. If nothing can be denied, nothing is really being asserted. In the end, again, God is dead: "Death," as Flew put it, "by a thousand qualifications."[11]

To just about anyone under the sway of Ayer and Flew, the classical proofs—cosmological, teleological, and ontological—were dead on arrival. As for actual argumentation, there seemed little more to do than repeat the refutations of Hume and Kant. When I was in college, as I sat in the office of one of my professors talking about design arguments, he assured me that the matter was more or less settled centuries ago. And the proofs had been more than just confounded; they had been replaced, supplanted, and exceeded with science.

Cosmology is a branch of physics now, not just a topic of speculation. You can look through telescopes into billions of years of cosmic history, across unimaginable distances. The equations of relativity and quantum mechanics tell the history of our universe. One can devote lifetime upon lifetime to unraveling what happened in those first seconds and milliseconds without ever reaching an end, or a beginning, much less any divine cause. "The more the universe seems comprehensible," the Nobel-winning physicist Steven Weinberg famously wrote, "the more it also seems pointless."[12] No point, no God. That's a sensation, of course, not an argument, but sensations go a long way to persuade.

For those eager to tear off the bonds of traditional religion, the proofs could seem like a poisonous conspiracy, veiling ignorance behind a shroud of patchy reason. During her period as an atheist—before falling under the spell of Theosophy and moving to India—the late-nineteenth-century Englishwoman Annie Besant denounced the proofs one by one and left them to rot astride the dying horse of patriarchy. "If we once begin puffing divine smoke-rings," she wrote, "the only limit to the exercise is our want of occupation and the amount of suitable tobacco our imagination is able to supply." The proofs are dead and their promulgators know it, she's saying, but men in smoking jackets preserve them for amusement and to prop up the religion that secures their dominance. She wanted to expose their secret and their lie. Wrote Besant, "Truth is a thing to be shouted from the housetops, not to be whispered over the walnuts and wine after the ladies have left."[13] Conspiracy or not, it is true that the genre of proof had always been a men's club. And society was changing in ways that, for the first time, could make one wonder if that might be a bad thing.

Bertrand Russell, who would himself marry an eminent feminist, helped ensure that twentieth-century analytic philosophy would be largely wedded to atheism. Although he once had a youthful epiphany of the ontological argument's soundness, the maturer Russell compared the proposition that God exists to the chances that there is a china teapot orbiting the Sun somewhere between Earth and Mars—you can't exactly disprove it, nor do you have any reason to believe it's true. And when asked what he would say if brought before the presence and judgment of God, Russell's response was, reportedly, "Not enough evidence! Not enough evidence!"

More recent philosophers have formalized Russell's complaint in an argument from "divine hiddenness."[14] The existence of atheism *is* evidence, the reasoning goes; a God that hides from rational, well-intentioned people is probably a God that doesn't exist. After all, wouldn't an omnipotent being who wants a relationship with all of us, at the very least, make provision for our belief?

I've had trouble enough learning to believe in a God, trying to practice faith first and then to face the consequences of it later—with my family, with my own skeptical moods, with the doubts that wait to present themselves until nights in foreign hotel rooms. When Pascal made his wager, I wonder how well he knew what it feels like to try believing in what one cannot, when one feels so alone and confused that even being abandoned by God seems like a consolation. What a cruel master this world must have, if by such a hard-to-get belief we are somehow saved. A lack of evidence, anyway, is only the least of what one might expect that a perfectly loving, all-powerful God wouldn't allow.

∴

When I was little, my mother used to sit on the side of my bed at night and read to me from a picture book about the life of the Buddha. We read it over and over, sipping the sweet, warm milk that I hoped would keep me from insomnia. The pictures showed Siddhartha as a beautiful, androgynous boy, a prince who was protected by his father from seeing anything painful or unpleasant. Only when he grew to be a man, with a wife and child, did he finally sneak outside the palace walls and see how his subjects lived. What he saw shocked him. I stared into the pictures. There were bodies broken, helpless with old age. Sickness consumed people from the inside out, marking them with spots and cysts, which warned the healthy to pass on the far side of the road. Finally, he saw death. A lifeless, stinking corpse covered in flies, vacant except for the agony of the last moments still recorded on the face. The next time Siddhartha left the palace, it was for good.

After years of wandering and self-mortification, he finally emerged from under the Bodhi Tree and began his career as the Buddha. The first of the Four Noble Truths he taught is precisely what his father had tried to hide from him. It couldn't be plainer, more obvious, or more tempting to forget: *There is suffering.*

Neither the Buddha nor my mother talked about God. But what if we do? Why would a God allow us to suffer? This is the most ancient, basic, and ineluctable problem for God and for those who would claim there is a God at all. To call suffering a "problem," even, is to put it optimistically, as if there were a solution on hand or in mind. Written around the same time as the Buddha was alive, the Book of Job tells of a man demanding an account from God for his pain; the reply he gets is a whirlwind of mystery and power. The Greek philosopher Epicurus reportedly taught the problem as a paradox: God is either all powerful and not all good or all good but not all powerful, but not both. The God who rules over a world of suffering therefore cannot really be God.

From Epicurus on, thoughtful believers found ways around his dilemma. Leibniz coined a term for such attempts: *theodicy,* a justification of God. "An imperfection in the part," he wrote, "may be required for a greater perfection in the whole."[15] This might have seemed reasonable in the royal courts he frequented, aloof from the general misery. But then came the All Saints' Day earthquake of 1755 that flattened Lisbon and killed tens of thousands, prompting Voltaire to mock Leibniz's "best of all possible worlds":

Come, ye philosophers, who cry, "All's well,"
And contemplate this ruin of a world.[16]

The twentieth century was especially full of evils that would allow no justification, sufferings whose utter, unnecessary horror could be denied by no one. First, a whole generation of Europeans died over petty rivalries in their trenches, and the survivors wound up with a flu epidemic. Then Hitler murdered a third of the world's Jews, and tens of millions more died in the process. Russians and Chinese starved en masse in the name of revolution. The world powers stockpiled weapons whose sole purpose is extermination. Suicide bombers vaporized themselves while uttering religious words. One death of God after another. Elie Wiesel saw it happening at Auschwitz: "He is hanging here on this gallows."[17] If any of the blows that the modern world has thrown at God and the God of proof are fatal, it is evil.

When the Australian philosopher J. L. Mackie published his paper "Evil and Omnipotence" in 1955, he intended not simply another challenge for the classical proofs. (They have already been "fairly thoroughly criticized by philosophers," says the opening sentence.) Instead, he meant this as an outright disproof, a demonstration that the very idea of God is "positively irrational."[18] It essentially restates the Epicurean paradox: God can't be perfectly good and omnipotent and permissive of evil all at once. Wouldn't anybody with the power to prevent suffering, and the goodness to want to, do so? Wouldn't you, in God's position?

The argument is appealing for the same reason as Anselm's ontological proof. It deals almost entirely in pure concepts. If it can establish a genuine logical contradiction between the concept of God and the fact of suffering, it's decisive. For Anselm, a perfect God that doesn't exist is impossible, so God has to exist. For Mackie, you can have God or evil, but not both. It's that simple.

Mackie tried to anticipate the strongest and oldest objection to this kind of argument: free will. He thought he had addressed it. But soon this objection was mounted again with a new level of precision by a confident young Christian philosopher named Alvin Plantinga.[19] Plantinga recognized that, to refute Mackie, you don't need an all-out theodicy to explain exactly how and why God allows evil; all it takes is to show that such an explanation is possible. He called his a "free-will defense." To explain *moral* evil—evil done by moral agents like human beings—free will does the trick.

The crux is in what Plantinga calls "Leibniz's lapse." Leibniz assumed that an all-powerful God can create any possible world, but this isn't exactly so, says Plantinga. If a world is to contain persons who are really free, and therefore capable of moral good as well as moral evil, even an omnipotent God

would be stuck. Free persons suffer from what he calls "transworld depravity"; if they're really free, they are always capable of doing something wrong, no matter what kind of world they find themselves in. The choice is really up to them, not to God. Since free creatures can make wrong choices, God would have to permit evil in order to have the good of creaturely freedom, for even omnipotence can't decree a contradiction. Since this is a plausible enough account of why an all-good, all-powerful God might allow moral evil into the world, it's enough to defeat Mackie's claim that there could be no such thing.

Plantinga goes on to argue that similar reasoning can encompass *natural* evil too—diseases, floods, hurricanes, and the like. He borrows the notion from Augustine that such things could be the work of, say, Satan and his fellow fallen angels, operating by their own free will. Or one could tell the story of Eve and Adam freely choosing to sin in Eden, unleashing death onto the world. It doesn't really matter, and it doesn't even have to be true. As long as in some possible world evil can coexist with God, the logical argument from evil doesn't work.

Plantinga's defense is sometimes hailed as one of the few times that philosophy has really come up with a definitive solution to an ancient problem. Of course, Mackie and others have complained that it relies on a misunderstanding of free will; in 1999 the Christian philosopher Richard Otte pointed out a technical problem with transworld depravity, one serious enough that it compelled Plantinga himself to demote the defense from "proof" to a "fairly compelling" argument.[20] But by then most philosophers had given up on the purely logical approach to the problem of evil anyway. Whether or not one is satisfied—or amused—by Plantinga's fallen angels, the whole enterprise seems simply too vulnerable to that kind of imaginative rejoinder, and too abstract.

Still, logical contradiction or not, evil remains a problem.

∴

Forget about the concept. Turn instead to actual evils, to actual suffering. These are after all what brings us to the problem so inescapably in the first place.

Lightning strikes a dead tree towering above a remote forest. It catches fire and falls, and the fire spreads. There are no people nearby, but there is a fawn that wandered away from his mother. More flaming trees fall, and he is trapped. To escape the inferno, he leaps over a burning trunk, trips, and falls into the fire. A combination of reflex and gravity nudge him out of the flames and he stumbles into a nearby clearing. He is just alive enough to watch the fire burn out and to feel the searing pain of his burns until finally dying from them, noticed by no one, several days later.

New Year's, 1983, Flint, Michigan. A woman and her boyfriend are drunk and fighting, first at a bar, then at a party at a neighbor's house. At the party he attacks her, and her brother knocks him out. He attacks again, and this time she knocks him out herself. Then, at 3:45 A.M., the woman's five-year-old daughter is found dead downstairs in their house. She had been raped, beaten, and strangled by her mother's boyfriend.

The first scenario is hypothetical but surely possible, with no need for human agency; the second, human agency at its worst, was reported in the *Detroit Free Press*.[21] Philosophers have come to call these much-discussed cases "Bambi" and "Sue," or simply E1 and E2. "E" stands for evidence—evidence against God.

William Rowe proposed the first in a 1979 paper that helped put the problem of evil on a new track: not logical, but evidential.[22] Granted, it may be possible for God to allow evil, but does experience really bear this out? Take a particular instance of evil, he says, and see if you can hold on to an all-powerful, all-good God then. Do we really have grounds to think that Bambi's agonizing death served some higher good that an omnipotent being couldn't possibly have achieved without it? Considering E1 head-on, Rowe concludes probably not.

That paper stirred a flurry of criticism, and most believers felt the answer was clear: God's reasons and purposes are far above our ability to fathom them. But Rowe, once a Christian seminarian, wound up an atheist.

This evidential approach continues to be refined by others. Michael Tooley, a philosophy professor at the University of Colorado at Boulder, quantifies the matter.[23] Just look at how widespread and profound suffering is in the world, he argues. If there doesn't *seem* to be a good justification and decent evidence to support it, there probably isn't one.

Tooley lives in a sparsely decorated rambler on a quiet street, under the shadow of the campus football stadium. When I went to visit him there, he recited in his husky, pensive voice some lines from Matthew Arnold's poem "Dover Beach," mourning the loss of a "Sea of Faith" in the modern world:

And we are here as on a darkling plain
Swept with confused alarms of struggle and flight,
Where ignorant armies clash by night.[24]

"That's where I feel we are," he told me. "On a darkling plain."

On top of Rowe's particular cases of gratuitous, unjustifiable evil, Tooley collects more in lists: 18 million poverty-related deaths per year; the 2010 earthquake in Haiti, worse than Lisbon; God's command to massacre the Amalekites in 1 Samuel; carnivorous animals; the deterioration of the human body with aging and disease; the supposed agonies in hell; death itself. The catalog goes on. And on and on.

His reasoning is lengthy and involved, but the result it comes to is simple. By his reckoning, the probability that there is any good to justify apparently needless suffering cancels out in the equations. The chances that all the many inexplicable evils in our world might finally serve justice—and thus the chances that a just God exists—are inversely proportional to the amount of evil. To clarify the point, he turns to Bayes's theorem, a bit of math that allows one to calculate, given what one knows, the likelihood that a given theory is true.[25] With it, Tooley takes the argument out of mere words and into an equation, in a manner more or less like this:

- *G:* God exists.
- *n*: The number of inexplicable evils

$$\Pr(G) = \frac{1}{n+1}$$

Needless to say, $\Pr(G)$ isn't very big.

So if God can't explain the suffering in the world around us, and in us, what can? Paul Draper, who teaches philosophy at Purdue University, tests God against indifference.[26] Imagine two contenders for explaining the whole world and its history. In one corner is the God of proof: omnipotent, omniscient, and perfectly good. In the other, a "Hypothesis of Indifference," which describes a Darwinian universe, with no disembodied person pulling the strings. In the center, between them, are billions of people and animals suffering because of one another and the whims of nature. Start with the evils already listed, and to them add many more—like my cat who, as I write this, is slowly torturing a water bug that came up out of the drain.

Since it's hard to imagine what kind of moral good these things serve, ostensibly, God is in a tough spot. But consider indifference. There, moral good isn't an issue; instead, the indifferent universe measures its denizens by their ability to survive in it. Vestigial limbs and "junk" DNA may not seem like the doing of a perfect being, but they've done their job in evolutionary history. Predatory creatures play an important part in thriving ecosystems. To an indifferent universe, all the suffering actually makes sense. "This very old argument from the existence of suffering against the existence of an intelligent First Cause seems to me a strong one," Charles Darwin himself once wrote. "The presence of much suffering agrees well with the view that all organic beings have been developed through variation and natural selection."[27]

When David Hume proposed a scenario like this centuries earlier, he could answer only with ambivalence. But Draper turns to probabilities and, by his calculation, putting aside other evidence one way or another, indifference wins. You could try other alternatives too. Some philosophers have argued that an omnipotent, perfectly bad demon is at least as reasonable to suppose as a God.[28] From where we stand, it can be hard to tell the difference.

In the months following my grandmother's death, my grandfather started going to synagogue again. It was something he had done mainly sporadically and halfheartedly in the past. But now he was attending services on the weekend and classes during the week. For the first time we could talk about religion together, which we had avoided since my baptism. Now, my apostasy seemed to matter less because we could recognize each other in our need. He told me over the phone, while I was in college across the country, about what he was learning and thinking. We talked about Moses reaching the Promised Land he could never enter. We talked about Grandma.

There was one thing, Grandpa said, that made him able to have faith after the woman he married almost sixty years earlier was taken away: the rabbi told him it was okay to be angry at God. There are times when you have to be, because there is no other way. You don't know any better, and there is no one else to blame. So he was. He was angry.

.·.

These last pages have gone through a lot of horror, pain, and resentment. But that has rarely been what the world without God felt like for me. When I first encountered the war-weary European existentialists in Ken Knisley's philosophy class, so mired in angst, I wanted to cheer them up. I had already read Richard Dawkins's science books like *The Blind Watchmaker* and *Unweaving the Rainbow,* so when I came upon *The God Delusion* at about the same age Jesse Kilgore did, I didn't see a cause for despair. Those earlier ones describe a world of wonder and celebrate our ability to discover its secrets. Full of allusions to great literature, they dwell at the intersection of nature and human imagination. I didn't have to settle for Arnold's "darkling plain"; Carl Sagan's books and TV specials showed me science and reason as "a candle in the dark." My uncle, the scientist and atheist, repeated these lessons as he passed in and out of my childhood.

He and my mother live together now, as brother and sister, in a kind of monasticism without the name. He spends his days programming a forever-unfinished universe on his computer, while upstairs she studies Sanskrit and, with software he created, edits texts about her guru. When I was at their house not long ago, my uncle had just discovered something and wanted to show me. On his old laptop in the basement, he typed something into the command line, and up came the 1987 BBC documentary version of *The Blind Watchmaker,* hosted by a baby-faced Richard Dawkins. Then, in the background, behind the scenes of animals and the primitive computer graphics, my uncle added music—stochastic music, atonal music, sounds that sort of fit the images and sort of didn't. And then, with time, they really did: a sensible accident, a fitting cacophony.

"This is atheist music!" he said. The Mozarts and Tchaikovskys composed for a world of order and life eternal, their cadences resolving every dissonance in bliss. (As an old hymn puts it, "How the heavenly anthem drowns out all music but its own!")[29] But a composer like John Cage wrote for this life and this world, for nontransmigratory souls. Take the time to get used to it, and it's just as beautiful—or more, my uncle says, because it's *true*. This is our universe. I nod and listen and love hearing him talk, as I have since I was little. Another atheist, the writer Kurt Vonnegut, instructed that his epitaph should say: THE ONLY PROOF HE NEEDED FOR THE EXISTENCE OF GOD WAS MUSIC.[30]

With my uncle, pathos always came balanced with grandeur. He would trust in inquiry and be reckless in curiosity. And it was partly what I had learned that—to his dismay, perhaps—brought me to the baptismal font. When a new world opened up to me through the God of Christ, and a new me to me, in I began to go, with eyes open, as far as I could.

Proofs for and against God intermingle in the history of the genre. Aristotle's mover was an answer to the poets' stable of capricious spirits, and fell far short of the LORD of the Bible. The God Spinoza proved made people call him an atheist, but he wouldn't accept the label. Hume's skepticism threatened to undermine secular science as well as theology. Hegel could reconstruct the proofs only by inverting the God they describe. None of these delivers a pro or con, a God or no-God, a theism or atheism, as such. If I'm trying to render that simple question opaque and mostly beside the point—does God exist?—I've got company.

One of my favorite contributions to the genre near the twentieth century's end comes from the Irish, Oxbridge-trained philosopher and novelist Iris Murdoch. In the last decade of her life she published *Metaphysics as a Guide to Morals,* a collection of essays that keep coming back to the ontological proof. I picked it up in a used bookstore during my last spring break in college, when I was weighing the decision of whether to move out to California for graduate school. The margins filled with notes as I traveled.

Murdoch's starting point is the long tradition of attacks against Anselm's proof, from Gaunilo to Kant, up through a 1948 paper by the South African philosopher J. N. Findlay, "Can God's Existence Be Disproved?"

Findlay's answer is yes; his method is the ontological argument itself. "It was indeed an ill day for Anselm when he hit upon his famous proof," writes Findlay. "For on that day he not only laid bare something that is of the essence of an adequate religious object, but also something that entails its necessary nonexistence."[31] Like Spinoza, Findlay found that ontological reasoning brings one somewhere other than the God of orthodox religion. The necessary being it describes would transcend all understanding, revelation, and worship. Murdoch takes his point this way:

> No existing thing could be what we have meant by God. Any existing God would be less than God. An existent God would be an idol or a demon. . . . God does not and cannot exist.[32]

She then takes Findlay's inversion of Anselm and inverts it in her own way, back toward the abstract forms of ancient Platonism. If not God, what? Add an *o* to the word: good. "The goodness of God," she writes, "is sometimes lost to view in logical discussions of the proof."[33] Anselm didn't really give a proof of God, she contends, so much as a proof that goodness is real and sovereign over the world. You can't think it away. You can't think at all without finally recognizing, as she puts it, "the unavoidable nature of morality."[34] We know this unavoidability best in moments of pain, in the face of evil, because it's then that we're sure there must be something better.

Murdoch recognizes that religious proofs are not only thoughts, but ways of thinking. As Anselm makes so clear, proof is an experience, binding together feeling and longing with intellect. Yet the God he thought he was praying to on that early morning in the monastery, for her, is really the goodness and beauty that structure the universe and any attempt to make sense of it. Good—as God was thought to be—is necessity in itself. Like Anselm's God, and Augustine's and al-Farabi's and Leibniz's, her necessary being is the sum of all perfections. The beautiful, the good, and the real converge. The parent who shows us where to look—toward what is pretty and interesting and worthy of attention—is actually teaching us right from wrong. There are morals in all great art. Anselm's proof, in Murdoch's hands, becomes proof for the value of living a good and creative life.

Most philosophy professors today, however, to say nothing of novelists, rarely concern themselves with proofs of God's existence. A 2009 survey found that only 5.6 percent of philosophers it queried count religion among their specialties.[35] Schools upon schools of ethics, epistemology, political theory, and metaphysics are out there that make little or no reference to the divine. Almost 70 percent of philosophers "accept or lean toward" atheism, while just over 16 percent nod to the existence of God. The most commonly cited influence is David Hume. When I asked Michael Tooley why this is, he said, "I think the best explanation is that they follow the arguments where they think they lead"; these figures are almost exactly opposite those of the U.S. public as a whole, so if philosophers are distinctive in this way, mustn't it be due to their philosophizing?[36] Yet, in practice, proofs for God seem more often sidestepped than followed. Together with no small part of the society around it, philosophy has found ways of arguing about the good without need for much reference to a God.

But God never dies for long. In these same philosophy departments, a resurrection has meanwhile been brewing.

EIGHT

Not Dead Yet

THEISM MAKES A COMEBACK IN PHILOSOPHY

Antony Flew, as it turns out, came around. Sort of. At eighty-one years old, in early 2004, the author of some of Anglophone philosophy's seminal atheist texts—"Theology and Falsification," *The Presumption of Atheism, God and Philosophy*—began telling people that he thought God probably exists.

The son of a prominent, absent Methodist minister, Flew lost his faith as a teenager. He served as an intelligence officer in World War II and afterward wound up at Oxford studying philosophy. While still in his twenties, he took a public stand against God and kept it up over the course of a long career. He came to represent philosophical atheism personified: rigorous, confident, moralistic, and dismissive. He mounted the podium in debates against believers. For them, Flew was the ultimate prize.

The change of mind seems to have had its beginnings in a 1985 all-star conference put on by the Catholic businessman and philosophical impresario Roy Abraham Varghese, a marathon four-on-four debate about the existence of God, in which Flew was invited to participate. He began a lasting friendship there with Varghese, as well as with the Liberty University philosopher Gary Habermas, whose specialty is historical evidence that Jesus' resurrection really happened. He kept in steady contact with both men in the years that followed, discussing arguments for God's existence, the claims of Christianity, and conservative politics. (Flew had already undergone another conversion from Marxism to Thatcherite neoliberalism.) Slowly, certain arguments began to impress him. He came to feel that the universe must indeed have had a first cause to design and uphold the natural order.

Rumors began spreading on the Internet by 2001 that Flew was moving toward belief in God, maybe even toward Christianity. In a letter published on the website Internet Infidels he announced, "Sorry to Disappoint, but I'm Still an Atheist!"[1] The clearest view into Flew's state of mind that year, though, is his review of a book by David Conway, a philosopher who, like him, frequented the British right-wing think tank circuit. It was called *The Rediscovery of Wisdom*. Conway, a nominal Jew, argued that philosophy should revive the God of Aristotle, the self-thinking thought: a God of contemplation, of logos and the *philo* (love) of *sophia* (wisdom). While reasserting traditional proofs for God against the critiques of Hume and Kant, Conway saw no need to accept revealed, scriptural religion—to me, he described his view as "a Spinozistic understanding of revelation."

Flew, like most philosophers of his milieu, had thought of Aristotle as a kind of pagan secularist, and *The Rediscovery of Wisdom* left him shaken. "It is a long time since I read a book so illuminating, and so disturbing," the review begins.[2] What Conway offered, and what appealed to Flew, was a God purely of philosophy, a world guided by a reasonable mind.

When the moment of decision arrived, Flew turned to his Christian friends in the United States. In January 2004 he told Gary Habermas he had become a deist, and they began conducting a lengthy interview that was finally published at the end of the year. That December, too, Varghese arranged for the Associated Press to break the story, and Flew's conversion sprang into the news cycle. This was the height of that decade's culture wars, just as George W. Bush had won an election by appealing to religious "values voters." Some rejoiced in the new Flew. But others thought that old age, combined with the manipulation of Varghese and Habermas, had gotten the better of him. "He once was a great philosopher," lamented Richard Dawkins. "It's very sad."[3]

With Varghese's help, the plot thickened to book length. He served as Flew's coauthor, alongside an uncredited ghostwriter, a pastor named Bob Hostetler, for a "last will and testament." *There Is a God: How the World's Most Notorious Atheist Changed His Mind* appeared in 2007, published by the religious imprint HarperOne for a general audience. In addition to penning the preface and an appendix in his own name, Varghese stitched the book together in Flew's first-person. Even while admitting the influence of David Conway's Aristotelianism, the book carries Flew's newfound openness regarding the logical possibility of Christian revelation to the point of awkwardness. While denying that he had become a Christian—he continued to call the biblical God a "cosmic Saddam Hussein"—*There Is a God* makes him seem like he is inching his way to the altar call, drawn by philosophy, plus nostalgia for his father's faith. A second appendix by the Anglican bishop and biblical scholar N. T. Wright gives a quick argument for the historicity of Jesus—a strange thing to include, without counterargument, in a book by someone who doesn't accept it.

When the journalist Mark Oppenheimer visited Flew in Reading, England, to interview him for a *New York Times Magazine* article, he wasn't impressed by the philosopher's state of mind. "With his powers in decline," wrote Oppenheimer, "a conversation with him confuses more than it clarifies."[4] Up close, what warm words Flew had for Christianity seemed to be mainly a foil for the post-9/11 vitriol against Islam that preoccupied him. "If I had printed all the things he said to me, I would have worried for his safety," Oppenheimer recalls.

Habermas and Varghese insist that, aside from a bit of trouble with memory, Flew's faculties were undiminished. They hoped that his deism would be a stop on the road to Christianity. But in his most lucid moments, Aristotle's God seems to have been enough for Flew—a God rapt in contemplation, best enjoyed by a lifetime of philosophy. So far as he changed his mind, he changed it to that.

Flew held out no hope for an afterlife. In his words, he had placed no "Pascalian bets." When he died in April 2010, survived by his wife and two daughters, that was it for him. Yet this change of mind was also the sign of changes larger than himself.

With the same red-letters-over-black-background as *Time*'s famous "IS GOD DEAD?" cover, the cover of *Christianity Today* in July 2008 gave an answer: "GOD IS NOT DEAD YET." The corresponding article was by William Lane Craig, a man who played no small role in what he was describing. Despite the hesitation in its title ("yet"?), Craig's article announced a triumph, one often celebrated in certain academic conferences and church groups but rarely noticed outside them: over the past forty years or so in English-speaking philosophy departments people had begun taking God seriously again.

Craig came of age at a time when believing in God was practically unheard of among philosophers. If you believed, you probably wouldn't say so; the logical positivists had ruled religious language meaningless, after all. Discussions about God might consist of a brief exercise for students in which the old cosmological, teleological, and ontological proofs were presented, along with tidy refutations, as textbook examples of weak arguments. Nobody championed this attitude so much as Antony Flew. "We went to schools of philosophy where reading him was a must," Habermas remembers. For believers who had labored under Flew's shadow, his late-life conversion marked the end of an era, the hard-earned culmination of what they had accomplished: as Craig puts it, "a renaissance of Christian philosophy." It might have been better called a coup.

.·.

Forget for a moment about proving God. Just try to prove a simple and ordinary claim that we take for granted every day of our lives: prove that solipsism isn't true. Prove that your mind isn't the only real thing in the universe, and that the other people you encounter, learn from, and love aren't just imaginary or automatons.

Where would you begin? With whom? What could you trust? Far short of reaching beyond nature to the supernatural, or beyond experience to eternity, all I'm asking for is a bridge from one person to another, sturdy enough to assure me beyond doubt that I'm not the only conscious thing there is. Even Descartes found it easier to prove God's existence than to be sure of this. Alvin Plantinga was a bit humbler about God; the two questions, for him, are about equally hard. But that means they're equally easy too.

This analogy—between God and the people around us—is the pivot of Plantinga's first book, *God and Other Minds,* published in 1967. The renaissance began with it.

Plantinga wasn't the first to draw a connection between knowing God and knowing other people. Anselm borrowed the language in his letters to friends for the terms of his proof for God. And recall when Augustine argued, in "Concerning the Faith of Things Not Seen," that faith in God is like trust in a friend; you have to start trusting someone before you can know for sure that he is worthy of it. Nobody worries about having *-ological* arguments for the existence of acquaintances before believing that they exist. No one can afford to. So why bother demanding that of another person—of God? "I no more believe in God on the basis of such an argument than I do in the existence of my wife," Plantinga told me.

God and Other Minds undertakes, Kant-like, a stepwise critique of the cosmological, ontological, and teleological proofs. None of these can quite do what it purports, Plantinga finds. None can give us God. Next, he turns around and does the same with arguments *against* God: the problem of evil and the logical positivists' claim that the idea is altogether meaningless. He

concludes that neither can really rule out a God entirely. But then he reviews the arguments for the existence of other minds, and they come up short as well; they fail in ways similar to the arguments for God. The followers of Ayer and Flew can't claim that theism is meaningless unless they're willing to say the same about belief in people. Rule out God, and you risk ruling out your wife too.

In the final sentences of the book, Plantinga comes to a "tentative conclusion": "If my belief in other minds is rational, so is my belief in God. But obviously the former is rational; so, therefore, is the latter." Like so many of his arguments to come, it's a modest claim but one well placed to have consequences.

"This book," according to the atheist philosopher Quentin Smith, "displayed that realist theists were not outmatched by naturalists in terms of the most valued standards of analytic philosophy."[5] By 1980 *Time* magazine had already answered its own question of whether God is dead in an article on the nascent renaissance. "Not entirely," the article said. It declared Plantinga, with probably too many qualifications, "America's leading orthodox Protestant philosopher of God."[6]

∴

Philosophers have a way of belying their roots. Aquinas and Anselm fled from Italy to France, Descartes and Locke hid away in Amsterdam, and even Kant, who stayed at home, fixed his mind on the transcendental. Plantinga is at least partly an exception. The gist of his thought is an apologia for where he came from, a description of what his native faith feels like. From birth through his undergraduate years at Calvin College, a Midwestern, Dutch Reformed culture nurtured and saturated him. He told me he learned early on that "religion ought to pervade all of one's life, and it's not just off in one little corner." Tracing their roots back to the sixteenth-century Swiss reformer John Calvin, the churches he grew up attending preached no proofs for God's existence; Calvin had taught that there is an inborn sense of God in each of us, a *sensus divinitatus*.[7] Faith in the God of the Bible justifies itself. Plantinga grew up debating the finer points of doctrine with his father, a philosophy professor. The habit stuck, as has the mustache-less Dutch beard that skirts the edges of his face. When Plantinga developed his "tentative conclusion" into an explicit theory in the decades after *God and Other Minds,* he called it "Reformed epistemology."

A broken theory of knowledge, he argued, runs implicit from Descartes through the Enlightenment and all the way to positivism—that the only justified beliefs come from self-evident truths (say, all circles are round), what presents itself to the senses (the Sun looks like a circle), or what can be inferred from those (the Sun is round). It's on this basis that so many philosophers concluded that there isn't enough evidence to justify believing in God. But, Plantinga asked, why should we accept this? It's an epistemology—a theory of knowledge—that can justify neither so many of the beliefs we depend on in everyday life nor even itself. It isn't self-evident, or apparent to the senses, or inferable from beliefs that are.

Recall the matter of other minds; we're inclined to believe that the people we meet have minds like ours, and that they have real sensations and experiences, even though the evidence is inconclusive. Really, we have to. Beliefs like other minds and the existence of God are, in his terms, "properly basic." Against Antony Flew's "presumption of atheism," Plantinga argued that belief in God is reasonable even before going through the exercise of proof. Faith, by itself, is a perfectly admissible form of knowledge.

That can seem like a pretty low bar for entry. Just think of Gaunilo and his famous objection to Anselm about the perfect island; if Plantinga's claim works for theism, why can't it justify the rationality of any belief? His version of Gaunilo's island is the Great Pumpkin, borrowed from Peanuts Halloween comics: how is believing in the Great Pumpkin any less rational than believing in God? Couldn't this be properly basic just as easily?

Plantinga's answer begins by recognizing that theism happens to present itself convincingly to many people, in life experience and through a community of believers. It does so more or less coherently. The Great Pumpkin doesn't. He argues that these conditions serve as a basis for rational belief in God but not in the Pumpkin. That's an easy case, though. Those who would claim voodoo and atheism as properly basic, for instance, remain unscathed.

To strengthen Christianity's hand, Plantinga spent the 1990s developing a three-volume account of the "warrant" that Christians have in actually knowing their beliefs are true, and competing beliefs are false, from the starting point of properly basic faith. If my mind is functioning properly, and my *sensus divinitatus* senses God, I am warranted in believing that God exists and all else that follows from it. That being the case, atheists and voodooists must have fallen victim to improperly functioning mental faculties, misguided by the "noetic effects of sin."[8]

Taking Plantinga at his word, one might conclude the whole genre of proof is no longer necessary. But just because one doesn't need arguments for God doesn't mean there aren't a few decent ones out there. Some widely circulated lecture notes of his list "two dozen (or so)" of them.[9] He worked on several of his own.

Plantinga's version of the ontological argument, for example, relies on state-of-the-art modal logic—the logic of possibility, probability, and necessity—recoding Anselm's and Leibniz's old proof into modal terms like "maximal greatness" over all "possible worlds." It goes a little something like this:

1. There is a possible world with maximal greatness in it.

2. A being is only maximally great—omniscient, omnipotent, and morally perfect—if it has those qualities in every possible world.

3. A maximally great being exists in every possible world.[10]

For Plantiga, this argument is both a proof and an exercise in the limits of proof. It depends on one's prior acceptance of premise (1)—that a maximally great being is, at least, not contrary to reason. But people are unlikely to accept this who don't believe in God to begin with. If they do, (1) is true, and all else follows, but if they don't, the argument is stuck. There is no neutral ground. Prior beliefs can't help but shape how we use our reason.

Plantinga's theistic arguments in later years have tended to hinge on the very fact that the universe is rational, that we can comprehend it at all. Numbers, sets, abstract truths, physical constants—how could these exist if there is no infinite mind to sustain them? With this passel of arguments and more, Plantinga brought belief in God from a backwater to the cutting edge in analytic philosophy writ large. He was at the forefront of the resurgence of metaphysics that would doom logical positivism for good. Even those who thought him wrong couldn't ignore him.

Plantinga, all along, was showing others how to do Christian philosophy that would live up to the standards of the secular academy. But he also paid accidental homage to the old, politically incorrect aspiration of al-Ghazali that even philosophers should cling to the religion of old women; to Plantinga, an unschooled, unphilosophical faith can be properly basic and warranted by proper function—you're justified in taking it for granted. The Calvin College philosopher Kelly James Clark, his former student and among the best propagators of his ideas, concludes, relieved, "Theistic episte-mology preserves the rationality of my grandmother."[11]

Plantinga's own arguments have been just part of his contribution to the renaissance William Lane Craig's article was celebrating. He has also been its great prophet and exemplar. Tall and sharp-featured, speaking with an unhurried baritone, he exudes a confidence that has warmed with age. It's contagious. His mere presence in the field has cleared the way for also-bright but less self-assured believers to follow. In papers and lectures, Plantinga is straightforward and methodical, as if hiding behind nothing. Propositions are numbered, concepts scrupulously defined. Oppositely, his thought exper-iments and examples are usually outlandish: Alpha Centaurians, unicorns, a camel on the freeway, or expressions of his affection for mountains and Dutch names. (You know you're "in" if you've been rock climbing with him.) Former students, several of whom are now themselves leading philosophers, gush about his life-changing influence.

Alvin Plantinga called Christians in philosophy to task: no more hiding, no more compromising. Be bold, and give your grandmother's faith some credit.

By 1978 the renaissance became an organization. Plantinga cofounded the Society of Christian Philosophers, or SCP, in—but not quite *of*—the mainstream American Philosophical Association, or APA. Soon it was hold-ing its own conferences around the country and publishing a journal, *Faith and Philosophy.* The society was infused with the spirit of Plantinga's work: Christians should be welcome in philosophy *as Christians,* and they should philosophize as Christians too. They can't do this always feeling isolated and wary in the secular establishment. ("Nothing true can be said about God from a posture of defense," says a character in the novel *Gilead,* by Plantinga's fellow Calvinist Marilynne Robinson.)[12] Plantinga taught that Christian philosophers' loyalty is first to the religious community with which they share fundamental commitments and only second to the academy. At SCP meetings, they can discuss their projects and encourage each other with a sense of common purpose. They trust in their faith even as they work on articulating, understanding, and—when called upon—defending it.

∴

Academic conferences rarely give one much to write home about, and a typi-cal meeting of the SCP is no different. It takes over a building or two at the center of a Christian college's campus for a few days during spring break. The campus is otherwise almost empty. A few dozen professors and graduate students drift in on the first afternoon, after leaving their bags back at the on-campus hotel. As they register and affix their name tags, old friends and acquaintances reacquaint. The room is as fluorescent as the southern sky is overcast outside. At the opening plenary, with everyone gathered in one room, the demographics are on display: eight in ten are men, many wearing beards, and almost all are white. Afterward, they break up into smaller groups in separate rooms to hear the papers that interest them.

As a newcomer, I frequently lose my hold on the technical jargon. Old hands say this sometimes happens to them too. The words become only sounds, or fragments, as if etched on stone slabs and found centuries later, broken apart, their original purpose forgotten. *Actually ontologically dependent. Accidentally constitutive. In order to exist, it has to have instances. There are relations. Identity universals, identity tropes. Supervenience. Are essences accessible? Are you your singleton set? Again: Everything depends; $\forall x, depends(x)$.* The riches, the ingredients of proof, are hidden in there somewhere.

They keep talking about a certain somebody: "the theist." He—though some speakers are careful to alternate with "she"—is a believer in theism, an affirmer of the proposition that a worship-worthy person called God exists, just as (or more than) the Empire State Building and a toaster and the force of gravity do. The theist could be a Christian, a Jew, or a Muslim, or some other monotheist, but is technically, for the purposes of this fiction, indifferent. He has no scripture, prophets, commands, rituals, or religion. He is a mannequin, an overlapping consensus, a creature of proof; his only job is to affirm the God of philosophy. The theist's chief enemy is "the naturalist," the equally caricatured nontheist who thinks the universe is all there is and that it neither has nor needs divine nudging. They're stick figures made to oppose each other on a playground of abstraction.

I hear names like Plato and Plotinus, Descartes and Locke, Spinoza and Hegel. Sometimes they'll be claimed as theists, sometimes not. Looking back to the past, and certainly to other groups out there today, the line between theist and naturalist becomes harder to draw. But here the conference-goers set out to make that distinction as plain as they possibly can.

I'm grateful for my first friend at the SCP, Colin—a bit out of place there too. He is a retired professor at Principia, the country's only college for Christian Scientists, where he taught English. His favorite writer is James

Joyce. When I sit with him, we commiserate about the arid papers and try to sort through their meaning. He loves philosophy, and he loves religion, so he comes to as many of these conferences as he can. He strikes up conversations with the graduate students about Mary Baker Eddy and the feminine aspect of God and spiritual healing. Since he's the only Christian Scientist around, this is sure to spark disagreement, though the grin he wears throughout keeps it friendly. He asks questions more than he gives answers. Then he changes the subject to Broadway musicals, or Italian art.

A few weeks after I got home from our first conference together, a letter arrived from Colin. In it was a poem he wrote about Anselm's proof.

> More times
> than a well runs dry in Arizona
> I have tried to corral your proof that God exists,
> but like a wild pony
> it always outruns the rope.

Many people have been coming to these conferences for years, and they're in their element. At the APA conferences, where naturalism dominates, they tend to find themselves on the defensive. But the smaller SCP gatherings, they tell me, feel completely different. It's so much more collegial. Everyone is nicer. (This is true; strangers greet you with a smile while waiting for a panel to begin rather than pretending to be busy with their notes.) Believers don't need to justify their beliefs at every step, so they can challenge the strength of each other's claims without threatening to bring the whole world crashing down in consequence. They pepper these exchanges with theological inside jokes and friendly barbs. Prayer requests might accompany the presentation of a paper.

Some of the discussions are expressly about God, and some of those in turn are about how to argue for God's existence, but others are nothing of the sort. Regular, nuts-and-bolts philosophy is welcome too. Yet all of it is, in some sense, in the service of proof. They know that, as Christian philosophers, they're the ones who carry its burden. In these indistinguishable rooms, under this bland light, the genre has been kept alive and advancing.

∴

Today there are only a handful from the SCP's early days still attending. One by one they've been retiring, or worse. But their names come up again and again in papers and between sessions, in hushed and reverent tones: Alston, Adams, Wolterstorff, Mavrodes, McInerny—though none more than Al Plantinga.

It was William Alston who first approached Plantinga, his onetime student at the University of Michigan, about the idea of starting what would become the SCP. Plantinga resisted at first, not seeing what good it would do, but he soon relented. The first meetings were wildly popular, and Alston became the society's first president.

He had grown up Methodist in Louisiana, discovered philosophy while in uniform during World War II, built an academic career, drifted out of religion, and then returned again in the mid-1970s—"not primarily through philosophical reasoning," he says.[13] Part of what drew him were the offerings of "charismatic" churches: a baptism in the Spirit and speaking in tongues. The music too. From then on, he wanted religion in his philosophizing, and that's when he called up Plantinga again.

Alston focused on an argument from religious experience—perhaps because that's what he had just gone through. It's an argument familiar to mystics and ordinary believers all through history: to *feel* God is to *know* that God exists. He spoke of "perceiving God." While Plantinga argued that religious beliefs could be as basic as other minds, Alston added that perceptions of God shouldn't be any less reliable, in principle, than those of our eyes and ears. He denounced the "epistemic chauvinism" that deems a religious perception false until it's somehow proven otherwise. That's a double standard, he thought, and an unfair one.

The reasoning is parallel to Plantinga's, and so are the objections. If a Christian perceives Jesus and a Hindu perceives Shiva, which one is right? What about someone who perceives neither? But for Alston, this was no dead end; what impressed him more is how consistent people's religious perceptions actually are. Just think of music, for instance. Everyone can hear it, but not everyone has perfect pitch. He was satisfied to leave the differences up to the historical and doctrinal debates that people already use to establish religious orthodoxy and heresy.

Another old, often taken-for-granted proof that turned up again among the SCP's founders was the moral argument. This was mainly thanks to Robert Adams, who taught at UCLA and Yale. It has predecessors in Plato's *Laws* and Kant's second *Critique:* if there is a moral order to the universe, there must be a God to dictate it. And there is an objective moral order, says Adams. Torturing infants for fun is wrong, no matter what, as the popular example goes; there is no circumstance that makes it right. So where would that absolute wrongness come from if not God? How could a universe not guided by a loving God have rightness and wrongness so built in?

Naturalist philosophers have tried to give their own accounts of objective morality, ones in which a God is unnecessary, or even in the way. But for Adams, the best explanation is theism. He is comparing worldviews, again in stick-figure form: theist against naturalist. What better explains the sensation we have that the world is comprehensible—morally, and also mathematically and scientifically—than that it was made by a comprehending God? What better explains our sensation of consciousness, he adds, than a God who is consciousness itself? None of these is quite knockdown on its own, but together, and together with Plantinga's and Alston's explanations, there's a certain coherence in what Adams was getting at. A knockdown proof isn't the point. Alston and Adams, like Plantinga, are as much out to undercut the need for proofs as to revive them.

None of Plantinga's allies, though, goes back longer than Nicholas Wolterstorff. The two met as students at Calvin College and together fell under the spell of the philosopher Harry Jellema, and eventually both went East for graduate school—Plantinga to Yale and Wolterstorff to Harvard. In the 1970s and 1980s Wolterstorff helped develop Reformed epistemology, but his interests branched out from there. He has also written books about art, education, and social justice. What Plantinga did with the question of God, Wolterstorff has continued in theories of politics and the public sphere. No more checking religion at the door, he thought. No more hiding God in church and at home. If you know your religious belief is warranted, says Wolterstorff, you would be dishonest to hide it. Secularists had tricked many among the faithful into thinking that their faith is irrational, and by extension unwelcome in political debates. Plantinga, Alston, Adams, and Wolterstorff, and the many more who would join them, intended to reclaim their rationality.

∴

By the time the Society of Christian Philosophers opened up shop, logical positivism was already headed the way of alchemy. Ancient proofs were finding new champions, and even if they weren't always winning over souls, they were being taken seriously again. But in the minds of many there remained, and remains, no challenge for theists like the challenge of evil. It stews and stinks, appears in ever new guises, and returns every morning with the newspaper. It accuses believers in God not just of irrationality, or of having made some mistake in their proofs, but of being insensitive to cruelty and horror. The fact of evil will accept no solution, yet for the theists again and again, as the exhausted and dying Plato sighed in the *Laws,* an attempt must be made.

Plantinga's free-will defense to the logical problem of evil is one of his most celebrated achievements. As rarely happens in philosophy, a sweeping argument was posed, and then answered, in a satisfying and rigorous way; a loving, omnipotent God and evil can at least potentially coexist. The evidential formulation of the problem—that particular evils in the world dramatically reduce the likelihood of such a God—has been more lingering, though Plantinga's approach has a way of addressing that too.

All things being equal, an instance of terrible, unjustified suffering might be a strike against the probability of God. But if belief in God is properly basic, the calculus changes. God is not just the conclusion, but a premise. Take faith for granted, and explanations readily present themselves: to allow for human freedom, or to call our fallen world and minds back to blessedness. God being God and people being people, we'll probably never know and must be content with that, unsatisfying as it may be. There, philosophy's official business ends; if that's not good enough for you, Plantinga commends you to the purview of "pastoral care."[14] But others think philosophy can do better.

Eleonore Stump, for instance. She came to Catholicism as an adult, but when I asked about it, she wasn't eager to talk about the details of how and why. She referred me instead to an essay of hers, written under the pretense of autobiography but containing almost none of it. Instead, the essay is about evil. "The ghastly vision in the mirror of evil," Stump writes, "becomes a means to finding the goodness of God, and with it peace and joy." For the Christian, evil shouldn't be a stumbling block but a guide: "It shows us our world; it also shows us ourselves."[15]

Stump's work as a philosopher has been a feat of striding between ages. She's an authority on medieval thought, especially that of Thomas Aquinas, but she has always brought that expertise to bear in the idiom of modern analytic philosophy. Maybe that's why there's a timelessness about her—an unfailingly elegant bearing, with a crown of black hair flanked by wings of gray, and a voice that's fervent, then lilting. Her latest book, *Wandering in Darkness,* is the result of a life spent dwelling on evil as a challenge, a question, and a task. Using Plantingian modal lingo, she treats the medieval Thomist view as a "possible world," a theodicy in which a loving God and suffering can coexist. But she also reaches beyond territory familiar to either Plantinga or Aquinas. She borrows insights from neuroscience and autism research. She emphasizes "Franciscan knowledge," a kind of knowing more interior and experiential than analytic philosophers—or Dominicans like Aquinas—would normally notice. And she calls for narrative to be taken more seriously as a mode of doing philosophy, for every theodicy is in some sense a story. Stories, she recognizes, are how people deal with the problem of evil in their own lives. Suffering needs to be understood not just as a fact, a thing, or a quantity to be measured and evaluated; it is what people endure and witness and encounter face-to-face.

There was another question I asked that she didn't want to answer. Among mostly male colleagues, she has always been a rare woman. Though philosophy now has more women in it than when she was in graduate school, they're still few. Outright feminism is hardly more than a rumor. Stump would rather leave unsaid what might make women's contributions to Christian philosophy distinctive. "But," she told me, "if you look at my new book, and you look at any book by a male of my generation, you're not going to have any difficulty figuring out that there's a gender difference here." She added, "It's not an accident."

It may not be an accident either, then, that women like Eleonore Stump and Marilyn McCord Adams—the wife of Robert, and also a philosopher—have chosen to approach the problem of evil less in terms of combat against nontheist critics than constructively, from within the resources of Christian faith, with fellow Christians in mind. Really, this is becoming more and more common in general, and it's what Plantinga has always advocated: the turn from mere philosophical arguments for theism toward a truly Christian philosophy, for Christians.

This wasn't supposed to be possible. Analytic philosophy, as imagined by Bertrand Russell and A. J. Ayer and Antony Flew wouldn't allow it. No small number of others today might say the same. Yet there it is. It is happening.

.˙.

In the pages of *Faith and Philosophy,* and in the meetings, books, and blogs that accompany it, today's SCP has turned the founders' pidgin into a language unto itself. *Divine foreknowledge, Molinism, divine-command theory. Open theism. Skeptical theism. Bare theism and hiddenness. Horrendous, trivial evils; inscrutable evils. Transworld depravity.* Christian philosophers' shared commitments have far-reaching consequences. As a bloc, they tend to depart from the philosophical mainstream in affirming a series of concomitant doctrines: mind-body dualism, libertarian free will, and the "A-theory" of time.[16] Each, in its way, has some bearing on their proofs.

The movement's influence now extends well beyond its particular subculture. Not only have Plantinga, Alston, Wolterstorff, and Stump served as presidents of the Society of Christian Philosophers, but they've been division presidents of the American Philosophical Association as well. With its membership hovering around a thousand since the late 1980s, the SCP is among the APA's largest affiliates. The Reformed publisher William B. Eerdmans, based just a few miles from Calvin College in Grand Rapids, publishes SCP members' books, but so does Oxford University Press. Even as Christians declare their independence, in part, from the concerns of mainstream philosophy, they've become a force that the mainstream can't ignore.

"It has just been astonishing, there's no doubt about it," Eleonore Stump told me. In a celebratory lecture at Calvin Seminary in 2001, Nicholas Wolterstorff made more exalted claims. "I think this is an act of God," he said, and—so there would be no mistaking—added, "in the sense that I think it is miraculous."[17] I've heard younger philosophers deliver conference papers trying to pinpoint exactly what was miraculous about this, and how.

Since its founding, the Protestant-heavy SCP has broadened its scope. Early on, members were convening meetings with Catholic philosophers at Notre Dame, whose faculty tended to be associated with the older, more insular American Catholic Philosophical Association. Plantinga himself took a job at Notre Dame in 1982, making its department the renaissance's unofficial headquarters. Catholic influence on the society's thinking grew stronger as a result. In his later work on warrant, Plantinga came to claim Thomas Aquinas as an ally rather than a foil as before; ecumenically enough, he dubbed the core of that project the "extended Aquinas/Calvin model." Meanwhile, SCP members have gone on trips to meet with non-Christian philosophers in Iran and China. The society's open membership requirements—"anyone interested in philosophy who considers himself or herself a Christian"—mean that members of fringe traditions can join, including Mormons and Christian Scientists like my friend Colin.

Openness hasn't pleased everyone. By the late 1990s the growing influence of Mormons in the society began to trouble some members—including William Lane Craig, who by then sat on the executive committee. He didn't think Mormons belonged in Christian philosophy's flagship organization. "The Mormon sect is really a crass form of polytheism," he told me. "This strange cult has been trying now to pass itself off as just another legitimate Christian denomination." But Craig was constructive with this displeasure. He redirected his considerable energy toward another organization, one that drew its boundaries the way he liked: the Evangelical Philosophical Society, or EPS. Though it had been around since 1974, the EPS largely fell off the map when the SCP appeared, its influence confined to conservative seminaries. Craig led the charge to change that. "I thought, let's kick this organization into high gear," he recalls.

The EPS's journal, *Philosophia Christi,* got an overhaul. Now it has almost twice the circulation of the SCP's *Faith and Philosophy,* as well as a slick, up-to-date website—unusual for a scholarly journal. Nor is the EPS the ordinary scholarly society. Its annual meetings happen jointly with an "apologetics conference," where EPS luminaries give practical talks to evangelical laypeople by the hundreds, or thousands. The talks are then collected into books for general readers with argumentative titles like *Contending with Christianity's Critics* and *Set Forth Your Case.*

"We feel a responsibility to be equipping people in the pews so that they're ready to defend their faith in the marketplace of ideas," says Paul Copan, who has been the EPS's president since Craig stepped down in 2006. "We don't just want to be an academic community, without regard for our brothers and sisters who are slogging it out day to day."

In its new incarnation, the EPS formed especially close ties with the Talbot School of Theology at Biola University, which provides it with office space and institutional support. A few years earlier, in 1993, Talbot made its entrance on the Christian philosophy scene with the founding of a philosophy of religion master's program. William Lane Craig joined as a research professor three years later. Now the program has more students than any other philosophy graduate school in the world, and more than a hundred of them have gone on to do PhD's elsewhere. That's the goal: to prepare a new generation, grounded in biblical religion, for doctoral study and teaching careers at the top secular schools. In just a few years, Biola has made itself a new seat of the theistic renaissance. After Antony Flew's conversion, for instance, the university presented him with its Philip E. Johnson Liberty and Truth Award, named after the mastermind of intelligent design. "It's very intentional and very strategic," says Craig. And it's working.

About 70 percent of philosophers today still don't believe in God. But among those who specialize in philosophy of religion, 70 percent do believe.[18] Philosophy graduate students in general are 5 percent more likely to be theists than their teachers, and the next generation of teachers will reflect that.

The genre of proof is no longer the work of solitaries in dim rooms; today it's done by professionals, people who do this as their jobs. They may sometimes resemble the genre's earlier characters but often not. They have families and children and mortgages. They go to church. Could Descartes, or Spinoza, or Hume, or Leibniz, or Kant have been so courageous in their heresies if they had families to support and pious spouses at home? Would Anselm have so craved his proof? Could William Lane Craig be quite so settled and certain in his ideas were it not for his wife Jan's constant presence, preparing three meals a day and typing for him his every written word?

I once asked him about that, and he said to my rather impolite question, politely enough, "You know, it's not anything I've ever given any thought to."

Craig's *Christianity Today* article is a proud report-back to the faithful that the battle has been mostly won, Christianity's intellectual respectability assuredly gained. "The very presence of the debate in academia," he writes, "is itself a sign of how healthy and vibrant a theistic worldview is today." But some have begun to feel that "debate" doesn't quite describe what is happening, that philosophy is becoming confused with simply asserting one's faith, and that honest argument suffers as a result. The SCP and EPS are organizations defined around certain commitments, responsible to certain religious communities. Is that any way to do philosophy? And in a world of so many different religions and beliefs, the Christian renaissance threatens to drown out the rest.

"Their basic strategy," says Wes Morriston, himself a Christian who teaches philosophy at the University of Colorado, "is to circle the wagons and shoot down whoever tries to penetrate the interior."

Nontheist philosophers of religion are feeling beleaguered in much the same way that theists did a few decades ago, during the reign of Antony Flew and company. In September 2010, Keith Parsons of the University of Houston announced on his blog, "No more. I've had it."[19] Explaining that he would withdraw from the philosophy of religion to focus on other topics, he continued, "I have to confess that I now regard 'the case for theism' as a fraud and I can no longer take it seriously enough to present it to a class as a respectable philosophical position." One man's proof is another's farce.

Or perhaps, as has been whispered to me by triumphant Christian philosophers, nontheists like Parsons are simply falling back and crying foul. They realize, but won't admit, that the argument really has been won for God.

∴

Late in May 2010 I took an overnight train from New York, up the Hudson, and westward to South Bend, Indiana, just shy of Chicago. There, at Notre Dame, Alvin Plantinga was celebrating his retirement. For lifelong academics, retirement tends to be a relative term, begging qualification; many take the break from teaching as a chance to write more than ever, or to reach a new audience, or simply to keep on haunting the corridors of their departments. And it's not enough to celebrate the occasion with just a party. Those scholars who really leave a mark, who've earned the highest honors their colleagues can possibly muster—they get a conference.

Plantinga's tribute came in three days of lecture after lecture by friends, colleagues, and former students. Wolterstorff was there, along with Stump and other heroes of the SCP. Dutch names and Dutch beards were common, with even a yarmulke or two in between. Plantinga's family, from fellow elders to teenage girls, sat through spells of it. At the end of most papers, he would rise to the microphone and offer a comment or a question. Graduate students in the back held up their digital cameras and cell phones to record him. The room turned especially quiet and still but for his remarks.

Two propositions were taken for granted in those sessions and during coffee breaks in the atrium just outside. First: theism is not only defensible, but has been positively defended—even if the exact details of how best to do so are still up for debate. Second: Christian philosophy, guided by the Promethean touch of Plantinga, has undergone a sweeping and glorious revival. Victory has been won, though not so completely as to preclude a bright and creative future for Christian philosophers, and for the genre of proof.

One would be mistaken to look for objectivity at a retirement party. Neither should I have expected it at the dive bar across town where I found myself afterward, with a pack of Notre Dame graduate students: a liberation theologian, a Foucauldian, and a poet. The theologian and I arrived there early, but he got a call from a waitress he had been chasing, so he left me at a booth with his friend Scotty, who was working on his PhD in philosophy. "You two should talk," we were told.

Scotty wasn't very eager to do that. He told me to wait while he finished working. He had a laptop out on the table before him, his head bent toward it. In his right hand was a cigarette—and then another and another—and at his left, a pitcher of cheap beer. His face was soft and a bit chubby, with a goatee and a mustache. His ears held his long, stringy blond hair in place. Then I realized that he's the guy whom the poet had mentioned to me earlier. She said he was an atheist who had once been a very serious Christian.

When I finally got him talking, we started by sizing each other up, trading big words and comparing notes. The balance established in his favor, I asked him to explain some of the things said at the conference that I didn't understand. It was good banter. He said you could drive a camel through the holes in most of the arguments we had heard that day. Plantinga is over the hill and hasn't done important work in decades. The SCP is just a blip on the philosophical radar. Being a member can still hurt a person's career.

Raised an Episcopalian, Scotty had grown frustrated by what seemed to him the vacuous sermons and half-held beliefs of habitual religion. Only when he was sent to a Pentecostal camp one summer did he discover a faith that felt real. As he told me this—hastily yet exactingly—I could tell this was somebody who wants nothing more than to believe what is true and banish ambiguity. As a teenager he immersed himself in books to support his new convictions. He became enamored with the Reformed theologian Cornelius Van Til's transcendental arguments, ones contending that rationality itself depends on the existence of God.

But over the years, his proofs came apart. The more he read philosophy, he found reasons for things like ethics, science, and logic that don't depend on a divine ordainer. Philosophy was an escape from the religious universe, and ultimately he rejected the whole thing. Most of his fellow graduate students and most of the contemporary thinkers they study aren't theists either. There's a lot left to do when God is out of the picture.

Even in its latest triumph, the search for proof of God's existence is the activity of a minority, of holdouts—a torch to be carried for the sake of a world that would just as soon let it go out.

NINE

God, Hypothesis

PROOF SNEAKS INTO THE LATEST SCIENCE

Another young man with a gun to his head; another beginning with nearly another end.

The night of his twentieth birthday, John Clayton held a .22-caliber rifle between his legs, pointed upward. "I was finding pleasure," he says, "but I was not finding happiness."[1] Even more troubling, though, was that his way of seeing the world had been falling apart. As a follower of the atheist provocateur Madalyn Murray O'Hair, he was the founder and self-appointed president of the Indiana Atheist Association, which made good money organizing lawsuits against churches' tax exemptions. His father, an atheist philosophy professor, was proud. Clayton schemed to write a book called *All the Stupidity of the Bible,* so he stole a Bible from a hotel room and read it three times through, looking for contradictions and scientific inaccuracies. But he came up empty; by his lights, at least, there weren't any. Falsehoods he thought he knew about—the six-thousand-year-old universe and the special creation of species, for instance—weren't really in there. Every kind of living thing appears in something like the order that the fossils suggest. The Bible, given the chance and interpreted rightly, seemed to sit so well with modern science that he actually started to believe its occasional miracle stories. Discovering this made John Clayton miserable.

Meanwhile, he was dating a woman named Phyllis—a woman who stood for something with even more conviction than O'Hair. She stood for being a Christian. Instead of pulling the trigger on that gun, he married Phyllis and became a Christian too.

Together, by the late 1960s, they started running a ministry called *Does God Exist?* in the garage of a local church. Phyllis died in 2008, but

Clayton continues to publish a newsletter, produce videos, host websites, give lectures, and lead tour groups through canyons out West each year. All proclaim Paley-esque examples of "Dandy Designs" in nature: the wings of bees, the tails of squirrels, and helicopter maple seeds. Now he has a mailing list twenty thousand subscribers strong, invitations to speak around the country, and letters coming in every day with tirades from all sides, along with gratitude from people who have been helped by hearing him years or decades before.

Silver-haired and heavyset, Clayton is retired after forty-one years as a science teacher in Indiana public schools. When Alvin Plantinga's retirement conference brought me to South Bend, I made sure to look Clayton up, and we met at a café just down the road from the University of Notre Dame. He had taken a friend to the hospital for treatment that morning, as he often does, and because of a misunderstanding he spent an hour driving back and forth across town trying to find me. At first he was gruff from all that time in the car, until the conversation calmed him down. His crescent-shaped smile made it hard to believe his stories of a reckless youth, but the occasional PG potty language lent a hint.

"My fundamental message," he explained, "is science and faith are not enemies; they're friends. If you've got a conflict, you've either got bad science, or bad theology, or both." He cares most about reaching young people, particularly bright Christians who think they should stay away from science to keep their faith.

I asked if God's existence can be proved. "If you're talking absolute proof, of course not," he said. We were sitting at a patio table, and Clayton looked out, past the parking lot, at the cars charging through the busy intersection nearby. All along we had been talking over their noise and breathing their exhaust. "If I'm going to get in my car and drive down the road, how do I know some idiot won't cross the line and hit me head-on? I don't have proof of that. But that doesn't prevent me from driving my car."

This is also how he understands science. You won't get the absolute, logical certainty that philosophy aspires to, but a well-substantiated theory is proof enough. "Whatever we're talking about, I want to talk about evidence," he said. "I think there is strong evidence for the existence of God." Big bang cosmology describes a beginning, just as Genesis 1:1 does. "God created everything. Duh. It doesn't tell us how." The details will have to come from science.

On these intimations, John Clayton could fashion a reason to live, a proof, and a ministry for his spare time. During the day, he could teach science in public school and know that God is lurking in there all the while, the ultimate hypothesis.

.·.

Some months after South Bend, I was at it again in Oxford, England. There was another conference, again honoring an elder. The excuse this time was the eightieth birthday of John Polkinghorne, a physicist and Anglican theologian who has written a passel of books treating theology as a matter of scientific inquiry. The conference's theme was, straightforwardly enough, "God and Physics." A somewhat older crowd gathered this time, with fewer graduate student groupies but a similar amount of mutual congratulation among the generation that had built the field of science-and-religion practically ex nihilo.

The morning before things got going, I walked along the Thames, past boathouses and houseboats. It took me to the center of town, which was crammed with packs of foreign high schoolers there for the summer session, gabbing in their native languages. Following Woodstock Road north, I stopped at a university apartment complex in the kind of dull modernist style that makes the future feel like a mistake of the past. That's where I found Richard Swinburne—or, rather, he found me, waiting in the courtyard and flipping through his book *Faith and Reason* one last time before our appointment.

Swinburne led me inside and up the stairs to his cramped study. Its walls, such as they were, were entirely books. There is a shyness about his manner, though I learned at the Plantinga conference that there's a sharp tongue in him too. He lives alone. Some years earlier, he had undergone a divorce from his wife, then one from the Anglican Communion. "The Church of England has lost its conviction that it is the vehicle of revealed truth," he says. Through a solitary journey of "book-learning," he ended up becoming Eastern Orthodox. Part of what drove him there, he told me, was what could be the refrain for the whole genre of proof if it were a song: "I have no wish to worship a God who does not exist."[2]

As Plantinga and company were conquering American philosophy for theism, Swinburne was doing his part in Britain. But whereas Plantinga tried to show that faith could justify itself as such, Swinburne was busy mounting up the evidence.

When he came to Oxford as a student in the 1950s, and for some time afterward, Swinburne was careful not to say too much about religion. His Christian convictions stayed in the back of his mind, as they had been when he was a child growing up in an unreligious home. Strategically, he chose to focus on philosophy of science. "I needed to establish my credentials in this area," he would later explain, "in order that those who respect such work might listen to what I had to say when I began to write about religion."[3]

Swinburne came to philosophy just in time to watch logical positivism come undone. Positivism's requirements for what makes a claim meaningful—whether it can be verified by observation—didn't fit with the latest and most exciting scientific discoveries. Practically everything of interest to physicists, from swirling electrons to quarks, wasn't directly observable except through the most abstract theories and oblique experiments. Yet there was no question but that the theories worked. Just ask the atomic bomb.

Swinburne paid close attention. "I thought that if we took this seriously, then we would take religion seriously," he remembers. "It too can be supported by evidence and be opposed by evidence."

In 1968 he published a book, innocently enough, titled *Space and Time*. Then, two years later, he began dipping into religious waters with another, *The Concept of Miracle*. But not until he had settled into a professorship at the University of Keele in the early 1970s did he begin working on God in earnest. He took what he had learned studying science and turned to theology. "At this time," Swinburne would write, "I discovered that someone else had attempted to use the best science and philosophy of his day rigorously to establish Christian theology"; he had discovered Thomas Aquinas.[4] The Five Ways, starting from the evidence of experience and working their way to God, became a model for what he set out to accomplish.

This was a lonely time to be doing philosophy of religion. There was still no Society of Christian Philosophers, and even when it finally got going, its centers of gravity would be an ocean away. But that suited Swinburne just fine. "I like controversy," he says. "If everybody had agreed with me, I wouldn't have gone into philosophy." A decade later, the project he had been planning all along was finished, in the form of a trilogy: *The Coherence of Theism* appeared in 1977, then *The Existence of God* in 1979, and *Faith and Reason* in 1981. Together, they amounted to a case for God's possibility, probability, and intelligibility.[5] Their success paved Swinburne a road back to Oxford, where he became Nolloth Professor of the Philosophy of the Christian Religion.

What makes a metaphysic any good, he argued, is the same as for a scientific theory. First, it has to fit with what we already know and with what we observe. That's relatively easy, given a bit of imagination. But what he especially stressed is simplicity. A simpler theory is intrinsically more likely than a complicated one. Complexity ratchets down the chances that it is true in reality. When nature seems more complex than we might expect, there had better be a good reason. This is how science works, he figured, so it should work for theology.

Take Leibniz's question, which Martin Heidegger later dubbed "the fundamental question of metaphysics": *Why is there something rather than nothing?* There could have been nothing, Swinburne suggests. Nothing would have been simpler than something. It certainly would have been simpler than a world so full of stuff as the one we've got. So the fact that there is anything at all cries out to be explained.

And explained with what? Again, it would have to be something simple. Godless naturalism describes a universe full of separate things operating according to a whole array of laws, so Swinburne reasoned that any explanation for order among them, and solely in terms of them, would have to be incredibly complex. But not if an infinitely intelligent, immaterial God were involved. That, to Swinburne, is the simpler and thus more probable alternative.

It might sound like too easy a way out. (Alfred North Whitehead: "Seek simplicity but distrust it.") After all—and J. L. Mackie raised this point— what basis do we have for believing in a person without a body? Without a brain? In our experience, persons and bodies seem awfully intertwined. Take a certain chemical pill, and it can upend your sense of self. Unplug parts of the brain, and parts of the mind disappear with them. Besides, being a person hardly feels very simple; modern psychology only underscores how multifaceted we are.

Swinburne's answer, though, is that you *do* know persons without bodies. You are one, even if the person you are happens to have a special relationship with a certain body. You must be, for personhood to mean anything. How could you make choices if you were just a machine made of flesh, determined by physical laws? A choice that's already determined isn't really a choice.

If you are a person apart from a body, God can be one too. What's more, such a God is also the best explanation for where you—a disembodied and conscious person—came from. Where else but from a disembodied, personal God?

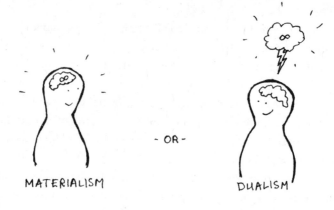

MATERIALISM   - OR -   DUALISM

For each addition to Swinburne's sprawling argument, God is the best and simplest explanation: that there are natural laws at all, that those laws could produce complex life, that people have relatively consistent religious experiences, and more. Each has some force on its own, but as a whole they're even stronger. Against the problem of evil he mounts an especially complicated theodicy—as usual, with free will as its centerpiece—but all in service of simplicity.

The whole structure fits together in a calculus of Bayesian probability, like Tooley's argument against God from evil. By formalizing his reasoning like this, Swinburne carries it even closer to the scientific ideal. The medium is part of his message.

- E: The evidence—the universe, its laws, the evolution of life, consciousness, religious experience
- G: God exists
- $\Pr(G|E)$: The likelihood of G, given E (and suitable background information)

$$\Pr(G|E) = \frac{\Pr(G) \times \Pr(E|G)}{\Pr(E)}$$

To offer a fair starting point, he sets the chances that God exists at fifty-fifty, initially. E, however, is quite a bit lower; he multiplies the probability of every improbable fact about the universe with the others, which makes E progressively smaller as one little fraction multiplies another and then another. So when you put in these approximate values—they're called "prior probabilities"—Bayes' theorem does its magic, and out comes something of an answer:

$$Pr(G|E) > 0.5$$

It's more likely than not, that is, that God exists, given the evidence. The more probable God is and the less probable our universe is, the greater the probability becomes that God exists.

Others have even more boldly plugged God into an equation like this, making Swinburne look comparatively restrained. In 2003 a risk analyst named Stephen Unwin published a book with his own best guess of the Bayesian probability for God: 67 percent, precisely. But then an atheist reviewer of Unwin's book adjusted some of his parameters, did his own calculation, and got 2 percent. A Christian reviewer came up with 98 percent.[6] This gross discrepancy leads back to the Achilles' heel of Bayesian reasoning: prior probabilities. Whatever you choose to use for them determines everything, and it isn't at all obvious what to choose. Is God's existence likely or unlikely, before the evidence comes in? Compared to what other universe can one conclude that ours is so unlikely? Using a formula—and even actual numbers—can give the appearance of an exact science, even if the reality is anything but.

After leaving Swinburne's study and saying good-bye, I made my way back to Woodstock Road and headed south, toward the center of town. The university's buildings and colleges became larger, more frequent, and older. It wasn't long before I reached St. Anne's College, where the "God and Physics" conference would soon begin. With an hour to spare, I stopped by the Oxford Oratory church, which has become something of a shrine to John Henry Newman, the nineteenth-century Catholic convert who drifted toward Rome while living in Oxford. Pope Benedict XVI would come to England a few months after I was there to beatify him. Without rejecting science by any means, Newman's *Grammar of Assent* was a defense of the imaginative character of religion, against the encroachment of narrower, more scientistic urges. It described not a hypothesis for the mind but a pilgrimage of the whole person. I knelt beside Newman's portrait—with respect for this argumentative man, if not exactly fondness.

Over the next few days at the conference, I heard papers about the beginning and end of the universe, the laws of nature, chaos theory, how God might experience time, and a new experiment in gravitational wave astronomy. A theologian from Korea sketched Gödel's ontological proof. John Polkinghorne delivered a reflection, to which a retired bishop added a coda, warning us not to be too confident about seeing God in our equations.

Each time I passed St. Anne's, I couldn't help but look across Woodstock Road and see the entrance to Green Templeton College. The name Templeton was very much on my mind. It's hard to think of one Sir John without the other; John Polkinghorne and John Templeton were friends and allies. Polkinghorne once won a Templeton Prize, and the John Templeton Foundation was funding the conference, just as it had funded Plantinga's send-off. The handful of other journalists there covering it had all been on Templeton-Cambridge Journalism Fellowships. Many of the presenters had been getting Templeton grants for decades. Thinkers' thoughts are their own, but the money has to come, and was definitely coming, from somewhere.

∴

John Marks Templeton knew well the conventional wisdom that Richard Swinburne spent his career fighting, the idea that history is supposed to go like this: science advances, modernity follows, God retreats—repeat until religion is gone. It's a story credited to those Enlightenment thinkers, from Descartes to Kant, who challenged the religion of their day in the name of reason (even if they thought true religion was what they were saving). For those who want religion to have a future, this story is at best a fallacy, at worst a tragedy. But for Templeton it was an opportunity.

"To get a bargain price," he was liable to say, "you've got to look for where the public is most frightened and pessimistic."[7] When potential value far exceeds the asking price, a lot can be done with a little. This was a maxim that served him well, making him one of the most successful investors of the twentieth century. In his second career as a philanthropist—through his annual, bigger-than-the-Nobel Templeton Prize and the multibillion-dollar John Templeton Foundation—he used it in an attempt to hijack how we think about the meaning of life.

Templeton's life was a paragon of the American dream. He was born in 1912 in Winchester, Tennessee, less than a hundred miles from the scene of the Scopes trial, to a family fairly well-off for a poor corner of the world. The upbuilding aphorisms of Benjamin Franklin instilled in him the value of single-minded hard work, thrift, and tireless enthusiasm. From his mother, meanwhile, he acquired an eclectic spirituality, particularly through the then-fashionable Unity School movement, which emphasized positive thinking and healing through prayer. Unity considered itself progressive and even, loosely speaking, scientific: a practical application of Christianity to modern life. Officially, though, Templeton was and would always remain a loyal Presbyterian. Calvinist industriousness and habitual optimism proved a mighty combination; beyond any expectations thinkable in Winchester, he made his way to Yale and, from there, to Oxford as a Rhodes Scholar.

Success wasn't long in coming. His first big play as a stock picker is now legendary; in the fall of 1939, as Germany was invading Poland, Templeton bought $100 of stock in every company on the market selling for no more than a dollar per share. He knew that war would have the biggest effect on those at the bottom of the barrel, and it did. A few years later, the military economy had quadrupled his investment. Templeton moved on from war profiteering to become an architect of globalization, with a string of firms bearing his name, expanding corporate ownership through mutual funds and pioneering the hunt for investment bargains abroad.

Those who knew Templeton as a businessman talk about his eccentricities fondly, in hallowed tones. Board meetings always began with a prayer. He was famously frugal with his time, keeping a tireless, to-the-minute schedule and streamlining every task and appointment. Later in life he became a prodigious faxer, though he never took to email. A woman who had been his receptionist at the Templeton Foundation once whispered to me, "He loved everyone."

In 1968 a Cartesian urge for solitude—and surely, though he denied this, the tax benefits—drew him to the Lyford Cay Club, an exclusive enclave in the Bahamas. Though the Tennessee drawl stuck, he became a British citizen. Naturalization enabled him to be knighted by Queen Elizabeth II for his philanthropy in 1987, not least for bankrolling what is now Green Templeton College at Oxford. Thereafter, people always referred to him as "Sir John." And, that same year, he opened the John Templeton Foundation.

Growing older and wealth ever multiplying, Templeton began to turn his attention away from business. "All my life I was trying to help people get wealthy, and with a little success. But I never noticed it made them any happier," he told Charlie Rose in a 1997 interview. "Real wealth is not in money, it's in spiritual growth."[8]

Just as thorough research always guided his investment decisions, Templeton believed that religion should follow where the evidence leads. He liked to rhapsodize about science's amazing progress in virtually every area of knowledge over the past century—except religion, he would say, which remained stagnant. "It is no small wonder, then, that some people believe religion is gradually becoming obsolete," Templeton wrote in his manifesto, *The Humble Approach: Scientists Discover God.*[9] For him, this made religion the perfect investment. He bought in with his foundation, hoping to "discover over 100 fold more about realities which can be called spiritual," as its charter says,[10] in the bombast that is typical of his prose. What he envisioned wasn't simply a louder, timelier enunciation of familiar doctrines but a posture called "humility theology," emphasizing how little believers know about the divine and how much they need to question and test their beliefs, as scientists do. He thought that science could get religions out of their rut.

Throughout his mostly self-published writings, Templeton developed an idiosyncratic vocabulary to describe the quest for "spiritual information" and for God as "Unlimited Creative Spirit." He loved repeating the sayings of far-flung sages, from the Buddha to Norman Vincent Peale, from Socrates to Mary Baker Eddy. Spirituality, in Templeton's usage, is not so much properly theological, or even especially Christian, than it is well-meaning self-help with a metaphysical bent. Uneasy with conventional meanings for "God" and "religion," he speculated in a 1990 document, "Maybe God is providing new revelations in ways which go beyond any religion." He even seems to have thought that if religion were more sophisticated, the line between belief and unbelief might disappear. In a Spinozist turn, he once mused, "Could even atheists, who deny the reality of a personal God, begin to worship fundamental reality or unlimited mind or unlimited love?"[11]

John Templeton died in 2008 at the age of ninety-five. By then, in just over two decades, his foundation had already transformed the ways and means of religion-related research. The number of medical schools with spirituality in their curriculums went from a tiny minority to a solid majority. Researchers who before could expect little more than paltry grants for a sabbatical started overseeing multimillion-dollar projects that brought together physicists, philosophers, neuroscientists, and theologians to study such topics as "Godly love" and "eschatology from a cosmic perspective." The National Science Foundation won't fund a cosmologist to think about what the structure of the universe tells us about God, or a biologist to study traces of divine purpose in evolution, but Templeton will. The foundation shows off its roster of eminent grantees with full-page ads in major magazines about "Big Questions," like *Does the universe have a purpose?* and *Does science make belief in God obsolete?* Templeton money is convincing people in and out of the academy that the existence of God can be a respectable question for science after all.

Those in the money's way can hardly believe their luck. "It's such a privilege to be alive and working in this field during this era," said William Lane Craig when I asked him about Templeton. "I saw the founding of the SCP, the founding of the EPS, the beginning of the renaissance of Christian philosophy, and then this incredible renaissance of work between science and religion that Sir John Templeton spearheaded." And Craig is only one of many eager to show how science, properly construed and Templeton funded, can do the genre's bidding.

∴

Mathematics, which is mainly what we have to go on in these matters, says that the universe started in an explosion—an explosion unlike any other we use the word for. Don't mistake it for the work of a brute. People use explosions to destroy, to reshape the land or obliterate each other. The big bang was an entirely different kind of explosion: one armed with the recipe for creation.

The idea of a universe born this way, first proposed by the Belgian priest-physicist Georges Lemaître, seemed to Fred Hoyle like an affront to proper science, too much like a Bible story. Hoyle, an astronomer, actually coined the term *big bang* during a 1949 BBC radio interview to ridicule it. He and others were trying to develop a "steady state" theory—a universe without beginning or end, like Aristotle's. But then Hoyle found something he wasn't expecting. In his words, the cosmos began to look like a "put-up job."[12]

You've probably been told, with fairly appropriate whimsy, that you're made of stardust. It's true; the only way to account for the heavy elements in living cells—carbon, crucially—is that they were fused together in the furnaces of stars, then blasted out in supernovas to form the clumps that could become life-supporting planets. But even in those stars it isn't immediately clear that this would be possible. Hoyle studied the problem and, in the early 1950s, found a solution. Carbon, he discovered, has a nuclear resonance that makes it easier to produce in a star than it might otherwise be. From there, heavier elements can be formed in sequence. The resonance in carbon, however, must be exactly what it is for this to work. The conditions are just right—*too right,* thought Hoyle. They're hugely improbable. But otherwise, the universe would be just a mush of hydrogen and helium. He became convinced that some kind of higher intelligence must have prepared the way for our arrival. He didn't become a churchgoer of any sort, but he did write some well-received science fiction.

During the subsequent decades, new observations ensured that the big bang would win out over the steady state. Everyone had to accept that the universe started with something of that sort: a miniscule, pyrotechnic beginning that is still expanding into the place where we find ourselves today.

With the big bang came many more examples of so-called fine-tuning in the laws of nature. If the ratio between the strength of the electromagnetic force and gravity were other than it is, no stars like the Sun would be possible. Same with the ratio between the mass of a proton and an electron. If the strong nuclear force were just a little different, supernovas would never happen, so even if heavy elements were to form, they would be stuck in the cores of dead stars. The list goes on. In each of these cases, the differences in question are extremely tiny. It is customary to give at least one unfathomably small number to drive this point home: if the cosmological constant—a number from Einstein's relativity equations related to the expansion of the universe—were just one part in 10^{120} off its mark, galaxies would fly apart, and the possibility of life would disappear with them. I shouldn't have to write out the 1 with 120 zeroes at the end of it to convey how fantastically more likely it seems that an unguided universe would have come about without any provision for us.

Fine-tuning gives the teleological proof a whole new kind of power. Design arguments in biology, like Behe's intelligent design or Paley's natural theology, depend on a designer who tampers in and around, or even against, the ordinary laws of nature. But fine-tuning is different; it's about the laws

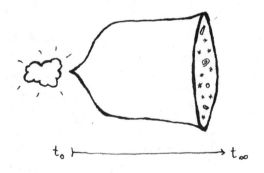

$$t_0 \longmapsto\!\!\!\longrightarrow t_\infty$$

themselves, the constants in them, and the initial conditions. When I asked Alvin Plantinga what he thinks are the most promising arguments for God's existence today, fine-tuning was the first that came to mind. When I asked the same of Richard Swinburne, he mentioned Robin Collins, a younger philosopher whose dissertation on fine-tuning Plantinga supervised at Notre Dame in the early 1990s.

Collins had already done two years of graduate work in physics at the University of Texas before beginning his PhD under Plantinga. Unlike most philosophers trying to tease out the consequences of fine-tuning, he can parse the actual equations in which they occur, making him the argument's top advocate on the Christian philosophy scene. (The domain fine-tuning.org, fittingly, redirects to Collins's website at Messiah College, where he teaches.) With the help of Templeton Foundation grants, he has been honing fine-tuning from a rather general sense of amazement into a rigorous philosophical argument. His approach hinges on the "likelihood principle," a probabilistic method for judging competing hypotheses. Collins thereby concludes that fine-tuning—together with the beauty of physical laws and the intelligibility of the universe—leaves the God hypothesis with an upper hand:

1. Given fine-tuning, a life-permitting universe is very unlikely under naturalism.

2. Given fine-tuning, a life-permitting universe is not unlikely under theism.

3. The theistic hypothesis predates the discovery of fine-tuning and has independent motivation.

4. Given (1)–(2), and buttressed by (3), a life-permitting universe makes the likelihood of theism much greater than that of naturalism.[13]

The most outspoken critic of fine-tuning arguments is Victor Stenger, a physicist now retired from the University of Hawaii. He lives just east of Boulder, where he has an adjunct position at the University of Colorado philosophy department and his wife is a literature professor. (They met at a church during college, though both were already unbelievers by then.) When I visited him at home, he came to the door wearing khakis, thick white socks, and a polo shirt over his paunch. A white beard matched his full head of hair. Stenger devotes himself now to what he sees as the misuses of physics in popular culture, and is a regular on the atheist and "skeptic" lecture circuit. In the 1990s he took on the claims about "quantum consciousness" and "quantum healing" being promoted in New Age circles. More recently, in books like *The Comprehensible Cosmos* and *God: The Failed Hypothesis,* he has turned to those who steer science toward theism—and especially those who do it with the help of fine-tuning. "These fine-tuning claims are ridiculous," he told me as we talked in his sun-drenched living room. "There's no basis in the physics."

Regarding step (1) of Collins's argument, Stenger has done his own math; he wrote a computer program, "MonkeyGod," which shows that a very wide range of randomly selected constants could allow for life-permitting stars, despite the claims of fine-tuning proponents. (Collins replies that the program is far too simplistic to be significant.) Like so much else in the history of science, Stenger believes that fine-tuning can and will one day be explained—so we shouldn't give up and jump to theological conclusions. (For Collins, this is question begging, for it assumes atheism when a better theistic explanation is already available.) And if the universe is so finely tuned for human life on Earth, Stenger continues, what's the use of all the countless galaxies and huge, lifeless expanses of space and time? Couldn't omnipotence have made fine-tuning a whole lot finer? (Collins has some theories about what God's reasons might be.)

An analogy often used to explain away fine-tuning is one that Arthur Eddington proposed in the 1930s, for other purposes. Imagine an ichthyologist whose net has two-inch gaps in it. After a day spent catching fish in a lake, naturally, he reports that all its fish are more than two inches long. It's a selection effect; we see a world well suited for life because we *are* life, and we couldn't see it any other way. Some argue that this is explanation enough.

But, others respond, fine-tuning is different.[14] It's more like having a net that can only catch fish that are exactly 23.2576 inches long—and then actually catching one. Or consider a firing squad: twelve sharpshooters, each with twelve rounds, fire at you 144 times, and you're still alive. Are you really going to chalk that up to good luck, combined with the selection effect of still being alive? Considering what you know about a firing squad, probably not. The trouble is, though, we know a lot less about the universe.

If only analogies were more useful. It's easy to recall David Hume's suspicion of them here. This isn't a fishing trip or an execution; this is the universe, and the rules governing its rules are beyond what our intuition knows how to handle. But the analogies and the data do at least say something. They say that fine-tuning is a problem in need of a solution. The solution might be God, but even that would be a God whose proof is vulnerable to new discoveries. Science might learn that our universe can't be any different from what it is, and why. Or else, something more outlandish: that ours isn't the only universe.

·.·

In March 2003 the Templeton Foundation sponsored a meeting at Stanford University called "Universe or Multiverse?" It was a scientific event but one that was sure to weigh heavy with theological consequences. Chairing the discussion was Paul Davies, winner of the 1995 Templeton Prize and author of books like *God and the New Physics* and *The Mind of God*. True to Templetonian form, the thirteen other participants were a distinguished and varying bunch. Robin Collins was there, as was the physicist Don Page, another evangelical Christian. In from Britain were Martin Rees, the Astronomer Royal who would go on to win the 2011 Templeton Prize, and the Oxford philosopher Nick Bostrom—both atheists. With them were the minds behind some of the leading multiverse proposals.

Stanford's Andrei Linde, for instance, developed the idea of an "inflationary multiverse," in which our universe is just one of many stable bubbles, each with its own laws of physics, floating in an ever-churning, chaotic sea. There was also Leonard Susskind, who helped invent string theory decades earlier. He had come to believe that it predicts a "landscape" of universes in which the appearance of fine-tuning would be a matter of course. Max Tegmark of MIT had just published a paper suggesting—dizzyingly—that we may live in as many as four different kinds of multiverses at once. Each of these theories is viciously speculative, built from mathematics that may or may not correspond to reality. Reaching beyond ordinary time and space, they're still impossible to confirm or deny by observation. But, for the moment, at the very edge of human knowledge, they're at least a possibility.

You might think a multiverse would make things a whole lot more complex than just a single universe, but in some respects it's actually simpler. If there is only one universe, the finely tuned constants that we observe seem like they would have been nearly impossible to nail without intelligent help. But if, as recent string theory suggests, there are in the neighborhood of 10^{500} kinds of universes to choose from, dumb luck has better odds. The whole cosmos would have to be much bigger, but our universe wouldn't be so obviously the miraculous fodder for a teleological proof. Bernard Carr, one of the scientists at the 2003 Templeton meeting, states the dilemma baldly: "If you don't want God, you'd better have a multiverse."[15]

Multiverse theories can look immediately suspect to believers eager to collect on the promise of fine-tuning. Christoph Schönborn, the Catholic archbishop of Vienna, has accused scientists of concocting the idea of a multiverse specifically "to avoid the overwhelming evidence for purpose and design found in modern science."[16] William Lane Craig agrees. "The very fact that skeptics have to come up with such an outlandish theory," he says, "is because the fine-tuning of the universe points powerfully toward an intelligent designer." He thinks it's a sign of desperation: "Some people will hypothesize anything to avoid reaching that conclusion."[17]

At the cluttered offices of the (again, Templeton-funded) World Science Festival in a Times Square high-rise, I asked the Columbia University string theorist Brian Greene whether physicists invented multiverse theory to sidestep God. He started laughing. "That's so ludicrous I don't know how to respond," he said. "Absolutely not. The math leads us to ever more possible universes, as opposed to what we'd hoped." What they hoped for—and what many still hope for—is a single, cohesive theory that explains the universe as we know it. Greene told me, "I've not yet given that up."

In case multiverse theory turns out to be true, though, the professional theists are getting ready for it. Robin Collins argues that any "universe generator"—whatever drives the multiverse—would still have to be well designed for life to be possible in *any* of its universes. Fine-tuning remains. Collins also thinks that a vast and varying multiverse may be an even more worship-worthy expression of God's creativity than just one. For his part, William

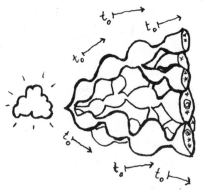

Lane Craig often touts the 2003 Borde-Guth-Vilenkin theorem, which shows that even an inflationary multiverse must have had some kind of beginning. This ensures that the first-cause logic of his signature cosmological argument would still hold.

The metaphysics of multiverses, unfortunately, isn't much more conclusive than the physics. That's sure to disappoint those eager to wrap up, settle God's accounts, and be done. "Expanding this area of positive knowledge doesn't remove the question of God," Andrei Linde once reminded me. "It just pushes it further away."

∴

The undecidability in these things means there's generous room for interpretation. What scraps of knowledge scientists produce, and then attempt to popularize, become the ink blots in a Rorschach test taken up by any and all contenders for ultimate truth. It should be clear already that the latest physics seems amenably bendable by both Christian theists and atheist naturalists; even if they aren't equally right, each can come up with a plausible enough case. And it gets messier still. However much some would like to pose the matter in terms of a contest solely between Christianity and its atheist opposite, there are other contenders in the running as well.

The Dalai Lama—Templeton Prize winner, 2012—has been organizing science conferences of his own, declaring Buddhism's amity with the scientific method, no matter what it uncovers. And the spooky world of quantum mechanics seems almost entirely up for grabs to whomever can claim it most loudly. The Hebrew University physicist Gerald Schroeder has been doing so for decades—interpreting it, together with recent findings in neuroscience and cosmology, in light of the Torah and medieval Jewish Kabbalah. The physicist and New Age teacher Fred Alan Wolf (aka Dr. Quantum, a cartoon superhero with a yellow cape) has meanwhile been showing people how the latest quantum discoveries are really aids to self-confidence and empowerment.

More mystical and adaptable spiritualities like these have a special affinity to new science, which is so alien to anything the authors of old Scriptures or the Scholastic philosophers might have imagined. For New Agers, it's native territory. Their magazines and websites are full of articles delighting in the latest discovery, though often stretching it to the point of abuse. Traditional religions tend to be cautious, in contrast, vetting new scientific ideas that are potential threats before being willing to accept them. Maybe that's just a matter of discretion, or maybe it's a sign that the traditional doctrines are showing their obsolescence. "These ideas were perfectly valid in the fourteenth century," Dr. Quantum told me. "They're not valid in the twenty-first."

On September 10, 2010, the physicist Stephen Hawking appeared via satellite on CNN's *Larry King Live,* putting the inkblot test on display. No scientist in the world has more cachet than Hawking; due in no small part to his crippling amyotrophic lateral sclerosis, he's the archetype and carica-ture of what people expect a scientist to be. Speaking from his wheelchair through the voice of a computer, his face remains expressionless—objec-tivity incarnate. CNN played some of Hawking's digital utterances over a starscape backdrop, as if the universe itself had found the wherewithal to speak. Speak he did, and bluntly: "The scientific account is complete; theol-ogy is unnecessary."

Hawking had just published a new book, *The Grand Design*, which, despite its teleological title, went further than he ever had before to announce the superfluity of the God hypothesis. He was ready to cast his lot with M-theory, a promising version of string theory that provides for ex nihilo quantum fluctuations and a multiverse to explain fine-tuning. Philosophy is dead, he declared; science has killed it. Culture wars pundits went into an uproar.

Larry King convened a colorful panel of commentators to unpack what Hawking was saying from on high—first, Hawking's coauthor, the Caltech physicist Leonard Mlodinow. Next to him in the studio was Robert Spitzer, a bespectacled and collared Jesuit priest who had just published a new book of his own, *New Proofs for the Existence of God: Contributions of Contemporary Physics and Philosophy*. King seemed to have Spitzer picked out for a stooge defending conventional pieties. But a glance through Spitzer's book shows it is a work that reaches for all the most vaulted ambitions of its genre.

With bullet-point clarity, *New Proofs* summarizes the scientific evidence for a universe with a finely tuned beginning.[18] Spitzer then launches into 110 pages of stepwise proofs for a creator, a "one unconditioned reality": Aquinas's Ways retold in the idiom of a meticulous, science-wise philosophy. These lead him upward, to love, the good, the beautiful, and so forth, gesturing toward a proof from degrees to their perfection. The book concludes with five practical questions people can ask themselves as they strive to live in the image of the God just proved. Hardly any of this got on *Larry King*, though at one point Spitzer made the mistake of trying to fit "unconditioned reality" into a sound bite. The most he was finally able to add was an insistence that something really can't come from nothing, even if Stephen Hawking says it can.

Larry King's obvious favorite among the guests, also piped in via satellite, was guru-to-the-stars and quantum-healing apostle Deepak Chopra, wear-ing a pink shirt and jewel-studded glasses. Chopra said he'd read *The Grand Design* three times through. "I found it validating everything I knew from my own experience with wisdom traditions and perennial philosophies," he said. No problems in it for him. He quoted the thirteenth-century Muslim poet Rumi. Nothingness is consciousness, "the formless mind of the infinite being." Chopra continued, "God did not create the universe, God *became* the universe." King had to cut him off for the sake of time.

Mlodinow, who balked at giving his own religious opinions, grinned approvingly at Chopra's enthusiasm. Despite a standoff in the past, here they hinted on-air about plans to write a book together. Hollywood and science seemed to be in agreement: yes to New Age wordplay, no-thank-you to that of the old God of proof.

∴

Near the end of my time in Oxford, I stopped by the Institute of Cognitive & Evolutionary Anthropology, housed in a Victorian mansion near the "God and Physics" sessions. I was there to see Justin Barrett, an American psychologist who studies not the distant beginnings of the universe, or proofs of a God beyond it, but the mechanisms in our minds that allow us to think about either. Immediately wry and self-effacing, he was eager to do away with any formality I brought to the encounter. In a cordoned-off section of his office was Pug, a mini lop-eared rabbit he keeps as company and as a research assistant for his developmental studies on children. While Barrett and I talked, it was hard not to get distracted by Pug going about his business. Barrett's ideas help explain why.

Evolution, he says, has built into our minds a mechanism he calls the HADD—the "hyperactive agent detection device." We're geared to be oversensitive to the presence of agents around us, whether it's a tiger in the bushes or a face on Mars. We assume some*one* is there rather than just some*thing*. The HADD is why teleological proofs have always been so popular: seeing purpose in the world is a matter of instinct. He thinks it's part of why we have religious beliefs in the first place. Behind a rustle in the bush, a tiger; behind the universe, a God.

"Belief in God comes naturally," Barrett says. "Disbelief requires human intervention."[19]

He is one of many scientists over the past few decades who have been proposing that the rudiments of religion are a by-product of the evolutionary process, an unintended bonus from the equipment that allows us to do not especially religious things, like working well in groups and avoiding predators. They've conducted ingenious experiments to show that religious beliefs across cultures are "minimally counterintuitive" in similar ways and that ritual behavior mimics language acquisition. Meanwhile, neuroscientists have linked certain religious experiences to certain parts of the brain, thanks to imaging studies of meditating Buddhist monks and praying Catholic nuns. The Canadian psychologist Michael Persinger claims to have induced mystical experiences in subjects wearing a snowmobile helmet loaded with well-placed electrodes. (Apparently it didn't work on Richard Dawkins.)

Such findings are ripe for polemic's picking. When the anthropologist Pascal Boyer summed up this research in a book called *Religion Explained,* a reviewer summed up Boyer's implication in turn: "What he means, in fact, is that he has explained it away."[20] Showing that religion has roots in evolution could after all be science's ultimate victory; locate God in a tic of the brain, and you can conclude that religion, together with the whole genre of proof, is just a symptom of a glitch in our wiring.

This is an inference with a lot of precedent. David Hume tried to explain religion away with the best natural philosophy he could muster in his *Natural History of Religion*—where he even proposed the idea of the HADD, minus the acronym. Ludwig Feuerbach similarly took all he could glean from Hegel to show, in *The Essence of Christianity,* that the God of religion is really a self-projection of the human mind. Sigmund Freud's science of the unconscious treated religion as a matter of overindulged infantile urges. The new cognitive and neuroscientific theories are not so different from those predecessors in principle, though adorned in more sophisticated science. For Hume, Feuerbach, and Freud, explaining looks an awful lot like explaining away. The truth is, though, it's yet another inkblot test.

Nowadays, it's the New Agers and Western followers of Eastern religions, again, who seem least adverse to the latest cognitive science research; they take the discovery of neural correlates for their spiritual experiences as validating. Several of the neuroscientists doing this work are Buddhists. One of Michael Persinger's associates, Todd Murphy, even has a website where he sells "Shakti" headsets—"Designed for Intense Altered States"—to spiritual healing centers and curious customers.[21] People like him have found it especially easy to align brain research with their beliefs. But more traditional religions are learning to play that game as well.

Take Justin Barrett. He first studied psychology at Calvin College, the fount of Reformed epistemology, and it rubbed off. For him, the naturalness of religious belief is a reason to think that it's true. Wouldn't a God who guided evolution find some way for it to guide us back to our maker? Barrett's speculations on the meaning of his work have always sounded a lot like what John Calvin called the "sensus divinitatus" and what Alvin Plantinga calls "proper function."

Now, those connections are becoming more explicit. In an office across the hall as I spoke with Barrett was Kelly James Clark, who had been his philosophy teacher at Calvin, taking a sabbatical in Oxford to think through the intersections of cognitive science and Reformed epistemology. Also in town that week was the Notre Dame–trained philosopher Michael Murray, a long-time friend of Clark's who had recently become the Templeton Foundation's vice president for philosophy and theology programs, making him Christian philosophy's man on the inside. On arrival he inherited responsibility for Barrett's three-year, $3.9 million cognitive science research grant.

Of course, it should only stand to reason that in a scientific age proof would put on the garb of science. In an age no less industrial, meanwhile, it burgeons into an industry.

TEN

The Proof Industry

OLD PROOFS TURN INTO VIRAL MOVEMENTS

C. S. Lewis heard a recording of himself for the first time in early 1941. "I was unprepared for the total unfamiliarity of the voice," he wrote a few months later; "not a trace, not a hint, of anything one could identify with oneself."[1] A producer from the BBC's religious broadcasting department had come up to have lunch with him at Oxford's Magdalen College, where Lewis taught, and they used the occasion to rehearse. They were getting ready to bring proofs to the masses.

By August of that year, Lewis was commuting down to London on Wednesday evenings to give fifteen-minute talks live on the radio. His purpose was to explain, in ordinary language, how much of Christianity can be arrived at "on our own steam,"[2] without presupposing faith. Lewis himself wasn't much concerned with current events—he claimed a preference for eternity—but his tenor suited them perfectly. The Blitz had only just quieted in London. Those listening were those left at home by the war, under air raid sirens and falling bombs: the elderly, the disabled, children, and women. He called that first series of talks "Right or Wrong: A Clue to the Meaning of the Universe." It appealed to the sense in us that some things are fair and others not, that some are good and others not. He spoke of "Christian morality" as opposed to "Nazi morality"; the difference would have seemed perfectly clear in smoldering London. "Christianity is a fighting religion," he told these people in the middle of a fight.

The proof he relied on this time was a moral argument for the existence of God—or, at least, of a "Somebody." The sense of right and wrong (read: Allies and Axis) is evidence of a moral law inscribed in nature, which must have a moral inscriber. As a scholar, Lewis lived and breathed the literature of the Middle Ages; compared to their medieval counterparts, his fellow Britons seemed to have forgotten that morality reigns over all, even as they felt wronged by their enemies. They believed in their own righteousness but didn't know where it came from. And until they saw the universe-sized contest of right and wrong happening around them, they couldn't see that there was wrongness in themselves.

"The first step is to create, or recover, the sense of guilt," he wrote.[3] The next step, after that, is to show that it leads the way to God, and the Christian God in particular. Once there's guilt, there's need for a redeemer.

This argument came to me, as to so many others, in *Mere Christianity,* a book that collects the radio lectures Lewis gave between 1941 and 1944. The summer before my baptism, when becoming a Christian myself was still only a secret possibility, I brought it with me on a weekend's stay at Gethsemani Abbey, the monastery in Kentucky where Thomas Merton had lived. In my journal I kept describing the argument as *powerful,* even as my head searched for objections.

The radio broadcasts were popular, as *Mere Christianity* continues to be today, but Lewis was never very comfortable lending his voice to the airwaves. He preferred to be a teacher of students and a writer of books. He's best known for *The Chronicles of Narnia,* his children's stories full of barely disguised Christian allegory. Into them he smuggled traces of another proof: the proof that was most beloved to him, the one that brought him over the course of years from atheism to Hegelian idealism, then to pantheism, to theism, and finally—through long conversations with his friend J. R. R. Tolkien—to Christianity. The proof is usually described as an argument from desire, though Lewis would call it, simply, "Joy."

Its roots go back to childhood, to fleeting glimpses he could remember having of pure bliss—"an unsatisfied desire which is itself more desirable than any other satisfaction," he wrote, with an Anselmian cadence.[4] This would come to him at unexpected times: while standing beside a currant bush, or while reading poetry. The sensation, and its transience, seemed to him not an end in itself but the sign of something beyond, something real that we can never quite reach in this life. Other things we naturally long for have their natural satisfaction—food for hunger, sleep for tiredness, sex for wanting it—so it's reasonable to think that this one can be satisfied, too, that this desire should have a real object. Lewis came to realize it must be the God of Christianity (though I've seen his longings for another world quoted in calls for anarchist insurrection also). He felt what Augustine prayed in the first lines of the *Confessions:* "You made us for yourself, and our heart is restless until it rests in you."[5]

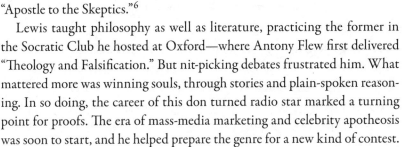

This isn't an argument that Christian philosophers present too often in technical journal articles. But as an *apologetic* argument—as a practical defense of the faith to persuade those who doubt or don't yet accept it—the language of desire speaks to people and opens hearts. Apologetics is the territory where C. S. Lewis was king. A 1946 *Atlantic Monthly* article dubbed him "Apostle to the Skeptics."[6]

Lewis taught philosophy as well as literature, practicing the former in the Socratic Club he hosted at Oxford—where Antony Flew first delivered "Theology and Falsification." But nit-picking debates frustrated him. What mattered more was winning souls, through stories and plain-spoken reasoning. In so doing, the career of this don turned radio star marked a turning point for proofs. The era of mass-media marketing and celebrity apotheosis was soon to start, and he helped prepare the genre for a new kind of contest.

∴

The proof industry's trail led me to California, especially to the concrete sprawl that surrounds Los Angeles—far from the beach, the Sunset Strip, and Skid Row. Californian religion is most famous for its fringes: self-centered therapies, transplanted gurus, boom-and-bust revivals, paparazzi devotion, sci-fi prophets. There's the guru my parents used to take me to when I was little, and the retreat center up in Ojai where my mother goes to study Hindu scriptures. But California is also a kind of R&D department for the religious mainstream. Pentecostalism was born in downtown L.A. a century ago, before spreading across the country and the world. There's the Crystal Cathedral, Philip Johnson's postmodernist glass sanctuary in Garden Grove, which shares its campus with a drive-in church from the early sixties, where people could attend services without leaving their cars. A bit farther down Interstate 5 is Saddleback Church, the twenty-thousand-strong evangelical congregation of Rick Warren, whose *Purpose Driven Life* is one of the

best selling books in history. Megachurches like this have found the perfect solution to the lethargy of suburban life: collective effervescence on Sundays with free child care, tight-knit small groups meeting through the week, and plenty of parking spaces. The Bible Belt may carry the sword of American old-time religion, but suburban California is its cutting edge, more modern than modern.

My first stop was a visit with Ray Comfort at the headquarters of his Living Waters Publications, a two-story white building with columns in front, just off the main drag in Bellflower. I went through the parking lot around back, where an assistant greeted me at the sliding-glass door. She led me inside and sat me down at a long, wooden conference table with chandeliers overhead while she revved up the old-fashioned popcorn maker. Mr. Comfort arrived to greet me as the kernels started popping.

Though his accent betrays him as a New Zealander, Comfort fits in better around Southern California than I do—intensely relaxed, resolutely casual. Yet he has the natural frenzy of someone who could have a successful surfing-supply-and-leather-jacket-making business by the age of twenty, as he did. It has been said, and repeated by Comfort himself, that he looks a bit like the young Albert Einstein, with a bushy mustache and a half-Jewish round nose—even more so back when his hair was wilder. And he's got a friend in Hollywood, as seems requisite around here: Kirk Cameron, the grown-up, born-again teenage star from the sitcom *Growing Pains*. Together, Comfort and Cameron host their own TV show, *The Way of the Master,* promising "100 percent scientific proof that God exists," "without mentioning faith or the Bible."

Given his "ADD on steroids," as he put it, Comfort little better than endured a sit-down interview with me. Only when we got to the tour did he seem to be enjoying himself. About thirty people work at Living Waters, all apparently well prepared for banter as he passes. There's a TV studio, a warehouse, and a call center, where the staff was taking orders for the twenty million or so books, tracts, and DVDs they sell each year. But mostly it's a funhouse, full of the toys and contraptions Comfort has built or accumulated over the years, and which he uses as evangelistic props: a facsimile of the Ten Commandments, a skeleton hanging in a closet, a giant stuffed ape. "I've got a fertile imagination," he confessed. In his office, there was a pair of plastic bananas. Comfort is, after all, the Bananaman.

"Behold, the atheist's nightmare!" the schtick goes, repeated in countless talks and tracts.[7] He holds up a banana. Look, he says, how the ridges are perfectly suited to fit the human hand. There's a tab on the top for easy opening, and there's nourishing fruit inside. He compares these features to those of a soda can—which, obviously, must have been intelligently designed. So the banana must be too. This is the "scientific proof" he was talking about.

He can throw in another proof, just for good measure. If the banana was teleological, try cosmological. It's perfectly clear that, just as a build*ing* must have a build*er,* creat*ion* must have a creat*or.* Simple as that. To be an atheist, you have to claim the ultimate absurdity, says Comfort: that "nothing created everything." *You Can Lead an Atheist to Evidence, but You Can't Make Him Think,* says the title of one of his recent books; if an atheist starts to think, by definition, he's no longer an atheist.

Once Comfort has hooked you with the promise of proofs, whether you like them or not, he turns to what really matters: sin. Go through the Ten Commandments. Have you ever lied? Even once? Well, you're a liar. Stolen anything, ever so small? You're a thief in the eyes of God. Have you ever even thought about committing adultery? By the standard Jesus gave in the Gospels, you're an adulterer, and you're headed for eternal punishment. You've only got one way out, and it's to repent and give your heart, mind, and life to God in Christ.

We can argue about God's existence forever, Comfort knows, but time is short to repent. "There's the legitimate addressing of the intellect," he told me. "But it's up to you whether or not you want to waste your time spending hours arguing with someone, or whether you want to show them God's forgiveness." A proof is only a bait, a placeholder, a recognition of the obvious. It gets the atheists' attention. The Fox News commentator Bill O'Reilly does much the same thing with his own favorite sound-bite proof for God: "Sun goes up, sun goes down. Tide goes in, tide goes out. It always happens. Never a miscommunication." O'Reilly, like Ray Comfort, won't listen to any quibbling about it. He states the case and moves on to something else.

This isn't what I want to hear by now, this far into the book—proof as a joke, a platitude, an insult, or a gimmick. Yet that's what Comfort makes of it. And after talking with him, I started to worry that there's truth in what he's saying. Alvin Plantinga and Richard Swinburne can't claim to have won multitudes to faith by their proofs. Yet Comfort, by his street preaching and pamphleteering, can. He puts thinking in its place and moves on to what will really make a difference. Proof is a trick. It keeps a certain self-styled intellectual type of person in the conversation. Let them have a proof, or two, says Comfort, if that's what will make them pay attention to the fate of their souls. For that, any trick is justified.

At the end of our tour, he introduced me to his wife, hard at work in the warehouse, then saw me off with a couple of his books, a season's worth of DVDs, and a stack of tracts disguised as trillion-dollar bills.

．·．

What if Ray Comfort is right? What if proofs are just a holding pattern for those among the faithful liable to get distracted by their thoughts, a game to keep them busy in their pews, pondering? Maybe they're like Sudoku on a long flight—engrossing enough to keep your attention but probably not enough to keep you from falling asleep.

About twenty-five miles north and east of Comfort, the people at Reasons to Believe are expert at this patient, lulling tinkering. Of course they believe it's more than that; "If you don't remove the intellectual barriers," says their founder, Hugh Ross, "you'll never be able to address the heart issues." Reasons focuses on the first.

Ross is an astrophysicist, originally from Canada, who first moved to California to do a postdoc at Caltech. He and Ray Comfort are about the same age, but besides that they're opposites. Ross is bald, for one. There aren't any toys lying around the Reasons office, only a clutter of scientific journals and magazines, popular books by scientists, academic textbooks, and multivolume editions of philosophical classics. When his wife, Kathy, first met him at a Bible study in Pasadena, she remembers, "He was the typical reticent scientist. Not very outgoing. He would look down instead of look up." But that didn't stop what he said from changing her life.

At the time, Kathy had been questioning the Christianity she'd grown up with, wondering if it could really be reconciled with what she had learned in science classes at college. But Hugh had specific, ready answers for how to understand Genesis in light of science. Then, he was just beginning to develop what would become the Reasons to Believe "creation model," a story of harmony between the scientific universe and the biblical God: billions of years of cosmic history, back to a creation event; divine intervention, evident in finely tuned constants and the complexity of DNA. Hugh Ross studies his Bible as hard as his science, and at every turn he finds ways to make them inform and enrich each other. Our genetic similarity to animals is, to him, God's way of offering them to us for medical testing; God placed the gas giants in the solar system just so to protect Earth from meteor impacts. Hugh's explanations, says Kathy, "gave me so much more joy in my life, and freedom." She isn't the only one. "I've seen grown men stand there at the end of his talks and fight back tears trying to express what it meant to finally see the pieces come together," she says.

Kathy and Hugh became a couple and a team. He developed the ideas, and she helped him communicate them. It started as a ministry at their church, but by the mid-1980s friends were telling them they should start a nonprofit, and backed up the idea with donations. Soon, the imprimatur of culture warrior James Dobson put them in the evangelical limelight. They built a "science-faith think tank," with offices in a small, baby blue–roofed shopping center on a busy street in Glendora. Over the years, Reasons has grown and taken over all the storefronts.

At the center of Reasons today is the team of researchers that helps Hugh Ross develop his model: a biochemist, a younger astrophysicist, and a philosopher. Supporting them, in turn, are a couple dozen people on staff and a few thousand volunteers around the world. Many of them have been trained in online courses through the Reasons Institute, or the Reasons Academy for home-schooled teens. Supporters can join the staff aboard a cruise ship for educational vacations. Ross and his colleagues regularly speak at churches, universities, and the offices of high-tech companies. People keep coming and keep responding and keep donating.

I asked Kathy Ross what kinds of people these are. I had in the back of my mind those who've been part of the genre of proof throughout history—and, without exactly knowing it, so did she.

"We've noticed something about the personality types," she said of those that Reasons to Believe attracts. "Most of us have felt like misfits all our lives." Kathy herself was never comfortable in groups of other women: "They always just wanted to talk about their curtains and their kids." It's mostly men who are drawn to Reasons, but the women she meets tend to be more like her. "They want to know, and they want to know why. They're not satisfied just to live in the subjective, emotional realm," she explained. They ask uncomfortable questions in church, and they want answers. Ray Comfort won't quite do it for them; others might accept the banana, but these people don't. C. S. Lewis can help, but they need the latest science too. They want to keep their faith but only if it's really true.

Nowhere did I find more people like Kathy Ross was describing than at Biola University—back south again, off of the 5. Biola's campus is in La Mirada, at the bottom edge of Los Angeles County, a community founded by the mapmaker Andrew McNally. By the 1950s it was being called "the nation's first completely planned city." But today, with a population of about fifty thousand, La Mirada feels neither so well planned nor especially city-like; the pastiche of suburban streets and cul-de-sacs are broken only by a couple of large strip malls, a pirate-themed water park, a golf course, and Biola itself. The school moved there in 1959 from downtown L.A., where it began as the Bible Institute of Los Angeles. Its campus follows the logic of a gated community, with card-swipe locks and guard stations at the entrances. "Random people from La Mirada can't just walk in," the guide of a tour for prospective students assured me. Yet Biola is the largest employer in town, and outside the gates it shows. Stop in a given strip-mall café to take notes, and you'll hear Christian rock playing in the background. At the next table, a group of teenage girls is having a Bible study.

The Biola application asks students, "Do you know Christ as your personal Savior?" followed by a space to put down the date of conversion. They're asked if they agree with the page-long doctrinal statement, which emphasizes biblical inerrancy, Christ's atonement, and the "conscious, unutterable, endless torment of anguish" awaiting the hard-hearted. Applicants get a few lines to cite points of disagreement, as well as those on which they haven't yet formed an opinion. Such basics matter; Biola was founded in 1908 by Lyman Stewart, the oilman who would soon finance *The Fundamentals*, the biblical-literalist texts that launched modern fundamentalism.

The students I met there—mainly master's students in Biola's philosophy and apologetics programs—wanted to get their fundamentals straight too.

The most determined among them tended to share a common story. They grew up in evangelical homes and, as teenagers, began asking the kinds of tough questions Kathy Ross was talking about. They didn't want to believe what isn't true, and they were ready give up their Christianity if necessary. Mostly, parents and pastors just told them to have more faith, and to be patient, which only made it worse. But somewhere along the line, someone gave them a book like *Reasonable Faith* or *Scaling the Secular City*, whose authors—William Lane Craig and J. P. Moreland, respectively—both teach in the philosophy MA program. Finally, in those pages, someone was taking the nagging questions seriously and putting forth satisfying answers. At Biola, therefore, Craig and Moreland aren't just teachers to their students; in many cases, these men saved their faith.

While Biola's philosophy department takes aim at the secular academy, the apologetics program promulgates Christian philosophy to the culture at large. It's headquartered off campus in an especially drab strip mall, alongside Korean storefront churches, a Christian bookstore, a supply outlet for firefighters, and a Chinese carryout place with suspiciously low prices. The office has no permanent sign, just a torn sheet of paper taped to the glass door that says, BIOLA UNIVERSITY APOLOGETICS. I went there to see Craig Hazen, the program's director, whose office is in the back. I was led past stockpiled issues of the latest *Philosophia Christi*—the Evangelical Philosophical Society's journal that Hazen edits—and past the cubicles of assistants and coordinators. I walked by the office of Clay Jones, whose *Prepared Defense* computer program makes rebuttals to skeptics' arguments only a mouse-click away. Water was coming in from the roof at the time, so tarps had been laid in strategic places. If Hazen kept his office door shut for too long, it would become unbearably hot inside. Fortunately, most apologetics students don't actually see this place; they take their courses on the Biola campus or online.

Hazen makes himself seem born for the job. Having my recorder in front of him switched him on, with a grin that squinted his eyes and never completely left his face. He translates the department's peculiar circumstances, together with the religion it promulgates, into an enthusiasm that's both contagious and a little suspect.

"One reason we're this funny stepchild on campus is we're budgeted so differently from everybody else," he explains. "It's *much* more entrepreneurial." He's expected to recruit his own students, many of whom are mid-career professionals rather than traditional graduate students coming straight out of college. Some are inmates in prisons. They can work toward a master's degree or just a certificate, and they don't have to bother with as many requirements as in the philosophy program. Many students pick up the entrepreneurial bug, too, and start apologetics ministries and websites of their own. More than once around campus, I was asked if I know HTML.

The apologetics program's specialty is putting on high-profile lectures and debates at Biola and at churches around the country. "We're always thinking about how to do things that grab attention," says Hazen. "It's been really fun for us eggheads." They've assembled an all-star cast of faculty, though most are in reality little more than occasional appointments. Their ranks include intelligent design royalty like Phillip E. Johnson and William Dembski, on loan from the Discovery Institute. There's also Lee Strobel—once a reporter, then a pastor at Saddleback Church, now a full-time apologist who has sold millions of copies of books like *The Case for a Creator* and *The Case for Christ*. Kenneth Samples, a Biola graduate and the resident philosopher at Reasons to Believe, is on the list too. These are the kinds of people the program is trying to produce more of: smart, creative Christians ready to go out into the world and stand their ground with proofs.

∴

Hazen probably wouldn't want to hear how much he reminded me of the New Atheists. By the middle of the twenty-first century's first decade, this cadre had hung a very public effigy of God from a string of best-selling books, websites, and related enterprises. Yet they bear no small resemblance to the schemers at Biola: they're sick of faith by faith alone, and they want to believe only what is plainly, evidently, and exactly true. Either religion's most daring claims about the universe are correct or they aren't. The minor difference between the two camps, which makes all the difference, is where they actually come out on the big question. The New Atheists are also better writers.

The New Atheists' first salvo was *The End of Faith,* in 2004, by an unknown author named Sam Harris. He claims to have started writing it on September 12, 2001. True to its timing, *The End of Faith* is an act of war against terrorism and the supernatural religions Harris blames for it. The book includes sixty pages of endnotes, which read like the syllabus of his still-fresh philosophy BA from Stanford, combined with remnants of the preceding eleven-year hiatus of reading, drug experiments, and study with meditation masters in India. By 2005 it was a surprise best-seller.

Then, in 2006, came another. *Breaking the Spell*, by the Tufts University philosopher Daniel Dennett, was a rather redundant call for studying religion "as a natural phenomenon." It served, nevertheless, as an adequate opening act for the book that would appear later that year: Richard Dawkins's *The God Delusion*. With that came the real birth of a movement, complete with the "New Atheist" moniker, coined in a *Wired* magazine article.[8] Backed by the dashing literary agent John Brockman, the book sold more than two million copies in English, making it the movement's biggest seller.

One more British accent finally rounded out the chorus—that of Christopher Hitchens, who was already a renowned essayist and political commentator in the States. His 2007 book, *God Is Not Great,* added a good many more punch lines to the New Atheist arsenal. Hitchens also hosted their first in-person meeting at his home in Washington DC that year. The resulting two-hour, unedited conversation over cocktails and cigarettes appears online in streaming HD video as *The Four Horsemen* (of the apocalypse, implicitly). The viewer gets to feel privy to a conspiracy.

The New Atheists bring up metaphysical proofs when necessary, but they don't tend to rely on any. "There aren't that many people whose faith is based on having been convinced by the cosmological argument," Sam Harris told me over lunch on the roof of a trendy hotel in downtown L.A. "I'm looking for where people are actually placing their weight." The New Atheists seem unfamiliar with the best arguments of contemporary atheist philosophers like Paul Draper and Michael Tooley; the problem of evil in general is largely absent, compared to its centrality in the academic discussion. Nor do they attempt to answer in any detail the arguments of Alvin Plantinga, Eleanore Stump, or William Lane Craig.

"I'm kind of self-taught in religion, with all the benefits and liabilities of that," Harris says. "I've never studied it formally with anyone." None of them have. The literary critic Terry Eagleton, in one of *The God Delusion*'s many unfriendly reviews, wrote, "Imagine someone holding forth on biology whose only knowledge of the subject is the *Book of British Birds,* and you have a rough idea of what it feels like to read Richard Dawkins on theology."[9] Or, perhaps more to the point, *When Animals Attack!*

To the extent that the New Atheists take on the proofs for God's existence, they do so in order to be finished as quickly as possible. In *The God Delusion,* Thomas Aquinas's Five Ways are "exposed as vacuous" in a few paragraphs, and Anselm's ontological argument is "logomachist trickery."[10] Intelligent design theory prompts a lesson in evolution, and fine-tuning raises the prospect of a multiverse. Dawkins turns, also, to the "who made the maker?" gambit, which goes back at least to Hume's *Dialogues:* if you try to explain a design with a designer, you have to explain the designer, too, and it stands to reason that the designer would be at least as complex as anything designed. Invoking God doesn't solve the problem at all, then; it only raises a new one.

Among professional philosophers of religion, even the atheists don't take much stock in any of this. Science, for instance, relies on unexplained explanations all the time; Darwin himself outlined the process of evolution without knowing about the genetics that makes it work. Besides, it's easy enough for the theist to say that the God in question is and always has been, by definition, utterly simple and infinitely smart. The one necessary being *couldn't* have been made by anything else. To that, Dawkins has retorted with yet another explanation-by-definition in the form of a popular Internet "meme" (a word he himself coined in the 1970s): the Flying Spaghetti Monster, which just as easily could have created the world with the aid of His Noodly Appendage. Touché. It doesn't really address the issues, but it's an amusing distraction.

Once the proofs are out of their way, the New Atheists get on to their real zingers. Teaching religion to children is child abuse, they say. Moderate and liberal believers are as dangerous as extremists because they lend credence to the extremists' basic suppositions. Who could even begin to take seriously an invisible God that's reading six and a half billion minds at once, answering their prayers erratically, and damning most of them to eternal fire? Religious faith merely accepts, while naturalistic science questions and discovers. A bumper sticker could be made from any of these—less so, the rarefied tenets of Alvin Plantinga's Reformed epistemology.

At Society of Christian Philosophers and Evangelical Philosophical Society conferences, papers and hallway conversations about one or another New Atheist claim are still a fixture—always with the caveat, of course, that the New Atheists aren't serious philosophers and don't know what they're talking about. Yet they seem to especially obsess the younger scholars, those who came of age debating on the Internet, whose friends and siblings and students are reading this stuff and buying into it.

The thing is, Dawkins and his fellow Horsemen are having a noticeable effect. People who were once afraid to come out of the closet as atheists have begun doing so more. It must be partly thanks to the New Atheists that the portion of Americans who identify themselves as atheists almost doubled between 2001 and 2008.[11] So, over a similar period, did the number of chapters of the Secular Student Alliance. Groups like the Center for Inquiry, American Atheists, and even the Revolutionary Communist Party have jumped on the New Atheist bandwagon. Dawkins and Harris created their own antireligious, pro-science organizations: the Richard Dawkins Foundation for Reason and Science (website banner: Dawkins looking wistfully up and ahead) and Project Reason, respectively. With the Four Horsemen, atheists have their own heroes to rally around. If their books had been on hand when I was making my way toward baptism, I wonder whether my own path would have been different. Maybe. That was just a year before *The End of Faith* appeared.

Shuttling around greater Los Angeles, I caught a glimpse of this burgeoning movement when I went to meet another beneficiary of the New Atheist craze, Michael Shermer. He founded the Skeptics Society and edits its magazine, *Skeptic*. He was once an evangelical Christian with a knack for apologetics; he even took a class on C. S. Lewis while a theology student at Pepperdine. But his faith began to wane during graduate school, and he realized that he felt more comfortable among unbelieving science types than in churches.

I joined Shermer in Pasadena for a typical Sunday afternoon with the Skeptics: a lecture about science in a lecture hall at Caltech, followed by a big dinner—everyone's welcome—at a nearby restaurant. He sat at the head of the table, flanked by some of the volunteers who work with him to keep the Society going. One of them showed off a brand-new iPad, the first that most of us had seen up close. The conversation was that of a community still learning to find its tone and its center. Somebody would make a strident antireligious remark, and then Shermer would step in as the voice of reason to moderate it. Someone else might then feel a bit more comfortable and say something complicated about his past life as a Mormon. Then Shermer would say something strident against religion himself, if a bit more eloquently than the first. It's hard to know where the lines are drawn and what's okay to say.

While I was with the Skeptics Society, I thought back to Reasons to Believe and Hugh Ross, whom Shermer confronts from time to time in debates. Both are vying for influence at Caltech, and both take their members on educational cruises to Alaska. They both say they care about science first and foremost but have been compelled by necessity to talk about God to clear up others' confusion.

"I'm tired of the God question, really," Shermer told me. "Enough already. But Dawkins unleashed the beast." He wants to stop publishing big cover stories about it in the magazine, and to stop his group from being so much associated with atheism. Then again, he added, "The God issues sell well."

∴

The only time William Lane Craig has faced Richard Dawkins in a debate was on November 13, 2010, during La Ciudad de las Ideas, a three-day, all-star conference in Puebla, Mexico. Dawkins had always refused to debate Craig—"I'm busy," he had said—but the event's organizer, the Mexican television personality Andrés Roemer, convinced him to take part. The question at hand: "Does the universe have a purpose?" Its implication: Does God exist? Every year, the conference's big debate has been some variation on this theme. "Nothing gets more enthusiasm than this topic, because everyone has an opinion," Roemer later told me.

The setting in Puebla suited the drama of the occasion; the podium stood at the center of a full-size boxing ring, which the debaters mounted in turn—"*gladiatores mentales,*" as Roemer likes to call them, in "a war of intelligence and arguments." There were three men on each side, including Michael Shermer on Dawkins's team. Three thousand people watched live in the audience, and as many as ten million saw it on TV, especially when it was rebroadcast after the boxing match the following night between Manny Pacquiao and Antonio Margarito. In the ring, each gave his usual stump speech, as he had countless times before. Dawkins called questions of ultimate meaning "silly," and Craig pleaded for the thought leaders present not to be infected by Dawkins's "self-defeating scientism and antireligious bigotry." At last, they and the other gladiatores gathered for a photo-op.

The boxing ring in Puebla was only an especially caricatured version of what has become commonplace on college campuses and in churches all over: a formal debate about the existence of God, or some topic that implies it. Debates like these are almost guaranteed to draw crowds, usually much larger than the debaters could attract on their own with a lecture. It brings in the ambivalent, the undecided, the apathetic, and the true believers alike. If nothing else, it's a good show. A debate at a college catches students when they're open and vulnerable to new ideas, away from home for the first time and freer to think on their own. Both religious and antireligious student groups sponsor them; each side goes in assuming that the other will come out of it looking the worse. It's a gamble. But for an apologist, debate is the ultimate test.

In these debates there can be only two sides, with nothing in between. The way to win is to take a strong, steady position and stick with it. Unlike doing actual philosophy, debating is no time to try to learn from the person you're up against, or to be forthright about the weaknesses of your own position. Those who hope to sway the audience by making graceful concessions, or by finding common ground in the middle, are only asking to get clobbered. One side must be right, and the other must be wrong. I love/hate it.

For the evangelical philosophers, the apologetics industry, and the hobbyists who carry on endless arguments in online forums, Craig is the knight, champion, and gladiator. He never loses his cool. At the podium, his face alternates between a beaming smile and an earnest, brow-furled, thinking man's focus. He has an answer to every challenge and a quotation to support it in his notes. He stands before a fortress of seemingly incorruptible orthodoxy, and he looks good defending it.

Craig started debating in high school, even before he was born again a Christian. The neuromuscular disease he suffers from meant that he couldn't be much of an athlete, but he realized that he could make a name for himself on the debate team. Competitions took him all over Illinois. When he went to college, he continued debating there—four years in high school, four years in college. But it wasn't until finishing his PhD in philosophy that he realized what the training had been preparing him for. That was when Christian clubs on college campuses began inviting him to debate atheists.

"It was wonderful," he says. "I was thrilled to be able to do it again as a means of sharing the gospel." In Craig's mind, this is the purpose of his life and of all history: to ratchet up the tally of souls who've made a decision for Christ, trading an eternity of punishment for everlasting happiness and enjoyment of God. To this end, he debates.

Past opponents accuse him of being a charlatan or a sophist. Some of them have told me he's an outright liar. They say he uses tricks. But really, he does just about the same thing every time. "Boo hoo! Poor atheists!" Craig once wrote on his website. "Big, bad Bill Craig has debate training, and that's why they can't even mount a decent response to the same five arguments I've been putting out there for 20 years!"[12]

For the most part, that's true. The arguments he uses for God's existence are almost always a variation of the following, his own set of Five Ways:

1. The kalam cosmological argument
2. Fine-tuning
3. The objectivity of morality
4. The historicity of Jesus's life and resurrection
5. Personal experience

He knows these as well as anyone else, and has heard just about anything one can throw at them. He even got a second PhD in biblical studies at the University of Munich in the 1980s, so as to better hold his own on historical matters.

It isn't hard to see why he wins. A big part of it is that he knows how to use the clock—to present a lot of arguments quickly and not get sidetracked. Typically, the opponent only manages to respond to two or three of the five and runs out of time for the rest, or bumbles them. Then Craig gives his recap, reviewing the arguments he gave and listing how many remain unaddressed. Some try to beat him with ridicule, or with bombast, or with one particular knockdown argument. These don't really work. He's unshaken. He turns the opponent's remarks into a self-refutation. He presses his case, the same case you can find again and again in the many other debates on YouTube. You don't have to think he's right to know he has won. Sam Harris remarked, while debating him at Notre Dame in 2011, that Craig is "the one Christian apologist who seems to have put the fear of God into many of my fellow atheists."

It's a sensitive subject. When I once told Richard Dawkins that I had been spending time with William Lane Craig, he grew irritable. A few months earlier, Craig had spoken at Oxford's Sheldonian Theatre and kept an empty chair onstage reserved for Dawkins. "Why are you publicizing him? Why are you publicizing him?" Dawkins demanded of me. "*Whose* side are you *on?*"

What I keep noticing among these combatants in either camp, however, is more their similarity than their difference, in almost all respects evident to a superficial observer, compared to the general population—William Lane Craig with Richard Dawkins, Hugh Ross with Michael Shermer, Ray Comfort with, say, the Flying Spaghetti Monster. I can't help wishing, when I'm with either group of gladiatores, that they're both wrong, that there's some sort of heaven they can enjoy together, apart from the rabble. For now, the closest thing is a God debate.

∴

Periodically during the Evangelical Philosophical Society's 2010 conference in downtown Atlanta, a small, comfy shuttle bus would arrive to pick up some of the leading philosophers. I hitched a ride. It took us out of the city, through rush-hour highway traffic and into the far suburbs, among wide roads, McMansions, and what's left of farms. Forty-five minutes later we were pulling into the gigantic parking lot of Johnson Ferry Baptist Church in Marietta, the place where William Lane Craig has been spending his Sundays for the past decade. Johnson Ferry is a sprawling consequence of the last boom in the housing market, newly built in the old style, with drab, fluorescent corridors that open onto stately halls and opulent meeting rooms. The sanctuary is a country Baptist church made huge, with balcony seating and neon blue lights illuminating the stage. An enormous screen hangs down overhead. At dinner, together with Alvin Plantinga, Craig, and his wife, Jan, I met the pastor, Bryant Wright, who had been elected president of the powerful Southern Baptist Convention just a few months before.

Back and forth we went between Atlanta and Marietta, for two nights and a morning of keynote talks and breakout sessions. More than fifteen hundred men, women, and teenagers were there for the annual "Apologetics Conference," this year with the theme "Set Forth Your Case." The proceedings in the sanctuary were emceed by Craig himself, wearing a starched white shirt with cufflinks, bright red suspenders, and a darker red tie. There was an American flag pin on the lapel of his navy blue blazer.

He's at his best in front of a big crowd like this. Whether at the pulpit or sitting in the front pew next to Jan, he wore his usual wire-thin headset mic, which carried his voice to the loudspeakers and, eventually, to the recordings that would be on sale downstairs. With his image projected on the screen behind him, Craig warmed up the audience with his mastery of public hyperbole—enthusiasm without trading any earnestness. He praised the church ladies who helped organize the event in Anselmian terms: "A greater cannot be conceived!" Later, Craig told me how thrilled he had been by the turnout; half the people there weren't Johnson Ferry regulars, and some came from as far away as Switzerland and New Zealand.

Alvin Plantinga delivered the first keynote. More than once it was said that here stood the greatest Christian philosopher alive today, and the audience plied him with applause. By the end of his talk, as he got into the numbered propositions and symbols, people became noticeably restless, and later I heard couples laughing about it to each other, gesturing that it had gone over their heads. But all the more could they appreciate that there was a giant in their midst.

As I searched for various breakout sessions through the church complex's labyrinthine halls, I passed by a basketball team, a women's group, and a karate lesson. One of the breakout tracks was for teens, one was about "culture," and one was about the existence of God. The overriding message every speaker harped on, again and again, was that there are reasons for this faith. There is evidence. No "blind-leaping," as Craig Hazen—who was also one of the conference's chief organizers—puts it. And tell your friends! Answer their questions, refute their errors, and let the truths in the latest and best Christian philosophy be known. Anyone can do it, and everyone must. On the stage of a black-box theater in the basement, Hazen assured his audience, "You don't have to be an Alvin Plantinga to make a nuisance of yourself in a public space!" He told jokes about his graduate work at a godless, secular university—in the same department where I had studied, actually, with some of the same teachers. People burst out laughing at every beat. Hazen the entrepreneur is also a gifted performer.

During dinners and shuttle bus rides, I got to know some of the other speakers. There were several from Biola, a pair from Jerry Falwell's Liberty University, and a bioethicist from a line of civil rights royalty. The sole woman among them, besides Craig's wife, was Mary Jo Sharp. She has an apologetics degree from Biola and a ministry called Confident Christianity. Sharp told me that she had always been a tomboy, and always demanded reasons. She became a Christian only as an adult. "My background leads me to disbelieve rather than to believe," she said. But in Christianity she found "a great knowledge tradition." Now she tries to get other women interested in apologetics by connecting it to their practical concerns, like holding together marriages and families and raising kids. Put that way, they see the point immediately. Doubts can tear apart relationships, they recognize, and reasons can quell doubts. Sharp also specializes in debating against Muslims.

After each module of sessions, I followed the crowd down to the bookstore, spread out across two crowded reception rooms. The speakers stood behind tables with books they had written and recommended, and people were buying them up by the armload. I've never been in a room with so many professors who have theirname.com websites. "The academic business just doesn't pay that much, and anything you can do to sell a book here or there is really helpful," Hazen told me. Plus, "Various modes of communication just help to further the cause." He made sure to use his time onstage, for example, to mention his own latest book, an apologetic novel. Snaking around the bookstore was a long, slow line that ended where Plantinga sat as he signed copies of *God, Freedom, and Evil* and *Warranted Christian Belief.* A teenage boy said to the girl next to him in line, "You can have your face signed. Or your butt."

I stood for a while by the table for the local chapter of the C. S. Lewis Institute, an offshoot of a secretive Christian political network called "the Family," best known for hosting presidents, legislators, and dignitaries at the annual National Prayer Breakfast.[13] There, I spoke with a man who had come with his son—maybe ten years old—all the way from New York, like me. He works at a bank downtown and lives in Queens. He said I look like "that Christian actor"—then paused, turned downward to think about it, and looked back up with a grin. "Kirk Cameron!"

Out on the sidewalk, as I stepped out to leave one of these sessions, I was joined by a trim and cheerful man in glasses, with bits of gray showing through in his hair. Having seen my name tag, and that it identified me as a journalist, he addressed me by name and started asking questions about what I was writing. I did my best to explain and then began asking questions of him. He was a freelance apologist up in Canada. He'd undergone a training program in England, and he and his wife sold "everything" they owned. But now he was having difficulty paying the bills.

The questions turned back to me again. What do my parents think about what I do, about this book I'm writing? Do they share my faith? What does my mother think? I told him about the tolerance that's so central to her kind of faith. He asked what I pray about for her—for her salvation? "I pray for all our salvation," I said.

"What about *you?*" he said, stopping where he stood, eyes to eyes. "*You* don't *know* with *certainty* you're *saved?*" He sounded like he had just heard an especially shocking piece of gossip. He had his in. He had me cornered.

From there his friendliness got far more aggressive. He asked me to look into his eyes while he informed me of God's love. We can all use the reminder, I know, but somehow there and then I wasn't feeling it. He said, in backbeat staccato, "Don't you think God in his perfect love wants you to know of your salvation?" And, by implication, the cursedness of others?

My experience of that love is imperfect, I tried to say. Just like my logic, just like my reason. I tried to say thank you and wished him well in his—I almost said "business." But for minutes more, he wouldn't let me go, trying to catch me in biblical and philosophical traps, trying to assure me of my mother's damnation and my own salvation, all with furious, blue-eyed love and more backbeat spoken word. When I finally broke it off and thanked him and left, I felt angry, and angry for feeling angry. Maybe it was the shame of being wrong about something, or maybe the horror of witnessing an abomination: the prospect that God is really so small, so petty, and so particular, having seen in apparently flawless steps that human reason inclines toward a God who is so pathetically like ourselves.

.·.

Rather than an entire complex like Johnson Ferry, the Washington DC outpost of the Center for Inquiry, or CFI, took up only a storefront on a block of stores and restaurants in the Eastern Market neighborhood, less than a mile from the Capitol along Pennsylvania Avenue. I arrived there for the Apologetics Conference's atheist counterpart, where the other side was training its own citizen army for the cosmic warfare of debate. The room was much, much smaller than Johnson Ferry's sanctuary, though it was also packed. Thirty or forty people filed in, and their chairs took up all the space from the podium to the window in back, which faced the street. Most of them were older men, though not all. On the wall behind the podium was a bookshelf whose holdings included a volume of Harun Yahya's *Atlas of Creation* lying on its side. Next to the bookshelf, behind the loudspeaker, hung a portrait of the CFI's octogenarian founder, Paul Kurtz.

This, like the EPS Apologetics Conference, was a chance for laypeople to spend three days stocking up on the best arguments they can get to defend their creed (for $129 per nonstudent, compared to $20 at Johnson Ferry). The theme here: "Religion under Examination." Its organizer and lead speaker was John Shook, the CFI's education director. He's tall, with a head of curly black hair, a knoblike chin, and dark, insistent eyes. He talks rapidly, in short and quotable salvos loaded with deadpan one-liners. Shook has the confidence in his bearing to match Craig and Hazen, and becomes just as flippant and condescending toward the opposition when he's wound up. As others asked questions, he listened, drumming beats with his fingers on the podium.

I saw later that one of the young women present noted her "♥" for him in a comment on Facebook.

Shook doesn't come with the de-conversion story that's common in these circles. "I was born an atheist," he says, eyebrow cleverly raised. "Right from the cradle, I didn't believe in God." Religion doesn't make sense to him, and he has to strain to imagine why it could for anyone else. He adjures believers to grow up out of their beliefs, to do "what adults are supposed to do," and adopt "the kind of reasoning we expect from an eight-year-old." The CFI denies that it's an evangelizing organization, but Shook makes clear that he's out to win converts for his worldview, secular humanism. "I would love to get a lot of agnostics off the fence," he says.

Before becoming a philosopher-in-residence at the CFI, he had a tenured position at Oklahoma State, specializing in pragmatist thought. His new job puts him in a different kind of role, one that he thinks has actually made him a better philosopher. He can't rely on academic jargon anymore, he says. "You have to explain it to someone with a tenth-grade vocabulary who hasn't been to college in thirty years." The apologetic task makes it harder to get away with sloppy thinking. Or subtlety.

The job has also forced Shook to learn things he had no need of before. "I've had to study the ways of the enemy, so to speak," he told me. "I've studied a *ton* of theology." In the process, he wrote a book called *The God Debates,* a summa of popular religious arguments and their rejoinders. His talks over the course of the seminar bore the fruit of this, as he presented counters to theistic arguments from creation, design, revelation, and morality. To him, all of theology amounts to an occasionally interesting but mainly pointless attempt to "put a smiley face on a mystery."

The specter of William Lane Craig hung all along over the CFI seminar's little room. John Shook has debated him, as have Victor Stenger and the biblical scholar (and H. P. Lovecraft expert) Robert Price, who were also there. A fourth Craig-debater participant, the Los Angeles lawyer Eddie Tabash, kept asking the others for advice on answering this or that particular claim Craig likes to make. Tabash thinks that beating the top theists in debates is one of the most important things atheists can do to further their cause. He has also run for state legislature, in part under the singularly unpopular banner of being an atheist.

They're ambivalent when they talk about Craig. "He's a very friendly guy," Shook told me. But then he'll go the other way. "In the end, I don't think he's actually debating. In the end, he thinks his mission is witnessing. I don't think he really cares about the arguments." Later, Shook on Craig again: "His theology is about as powerful as it gets."

The crowds I found at the EPS and the CFI sessions each had their share of unusually argumentative people—in a good way. The Q&A periods were always lively, and people seemed to be itching in their chairs through the lecture until it began. Questioners pushed, and speakers pushed back. This was especially so at the CFI, not least because of the intimacy of the space. There was lots of friendly heckling. The people in both crowds talked reverently about their speakers during breaks. Both crowds asked questions that reflected their experience having these kinds of discussions with peers, at the water cooler or at school or wherever—"My Christian friend said to me the other day . . . ," and the like. These proofs aren't just for experts. Ordinary people need them too; there's a market for this, and an opportunity. It might not be enough to make you rich—although Craig earns five-figure debating fees—but at least you have a decent shot at getting famous on the Internet.

.·.

When I first encountered William Lane Craig, I didn't know what I was up against. Remember that "God Is Not Dead Yet" cover story he did for *Christianity Today* in 2008? I dashed off a hasty critique that was published in an online magazine and expected that to be the end of it. But then comments started appearing on my website against what I had written, mainly exposing how little I knew at the time about the extent of the Christian philosophy renaissance. This was true; I had been caught off guard. Soon, a whole legion of bloggers was replying to my article. They were led by Tom Gilson, a strategic planner for Campus Crusade for Christ in Virginia who has a blog called *Thinking Christian* (tag line: "Do we hold the truth? No, the Truth holds us . . . "). Gilson and the others were standing up for their man, Craig. A few days later I came home to find that Craig himself had posted a podcast lambasting me. That, anyway, was my introduction to the Internet fray.

If the genre of proof through history has generally been the job of loners taking part in an invisible communion, now they can do it in real time, online. This is where a lot of the Christian philosophy students I've met at Biola, and at SCP and EPS conferences, cut their teeth. Blogs like *Prosblogion*— dominated by the academic SCP crowd—give philosophers a chance to test their ideas on their peers. But the real action is elsewhere. It's on the blogs of people like Gilson, people who have day jobs and an obsession with arguments. Or take Adam Lee, a software engineer in his twenties, an "interested amateur" whose *Daylight Atheism* and *Ebon Musings* have some of the most well regarded atheist writings on the Internet, even earning him a cameo in Dawkins's *The God Delusion*. A given blog post can garner from a handful to dozens to hundreds of reader comments, ranging from the obscene to the Talmudic to the actually constructive. Some bloggers adopt the trappings of technical philosophy—numbered propositions, detailed arguments, and the like—and so do their commenters. Mixed in with these are more personal observations on unrelated interests, gossip, politics, and logistical housekeeping. Readerships become communities. The blog *Pharnygula*, for one, has made its author, the biology professor PZ Myers, into a New Atheist superstar alongside the Four Horsemen. His antireligious snark has convened a pack of thousands, ready to flood online polls and comment threads at his command.

If text isn't good enough, there's always YouTube. Its crowd is even younger, more confessional, and sometimes much too eager to overshare with the everlasting Internet—on the fly, to an up-close webcam under poor lighting—their pronouncements about things that excite in them more self-assurance than reflection. One will post a video, and dozens of others will respond in videos of their own, subverting, remixing, or just remarking on the original. Richard Dawkins might refuse to debate Ray Comfort in real life, but that doesn't stop YouTubers from splicing a debate together from things they've each said in other contexts. It gets addictive.

TheoreticalBullshit is a popular atheist channel by Scott Clifton, a twenty-something who works as a soap star on shows like *The Bold and the Beautiful* and *General Hospital*. His philosophical monologues on God and morality, with wide eyes and spartan rooms behind him, have garnered tens of thousands of subscribers and millions of views. Among other claims to fame, he scored a (rather dismissive) response from William Lane Craig to his "Kalam Cosmological Argument AGAINST God." That's a distinction so far not won, say, by skydivephil's twenty-eight-minute-long epic, "Debunking the Cosmological Argument," complete with footage stitched together from various science documentaries and her dining-room-table commentaries in front of a backlit starscape.

On the theist side of the YouTube philosopher-kids, few are thought of more highly—or were—than the young, baseball-capped Noah Congelliere, known as Veritas48. In 2010 his YouTube and Blogger accounts were shut down by a hacker, and atheists and believers alike eulogized him as "civil and intelligent" and "one of the kindest, and most congenial, most knowledge-able Christians that you could ever find on YouTube." They began awaiting his sometime return. And then there's also theowarner—real name, Theo Warner—a teacher and a churchgoing Catholic in Manhattan. His videos are often polished, branded, high-toned, and literate, with references rang-ing from Anselm to the singer Rufus Wainwright. But he also spends a lot of time denouncing the Internet's most argued about Christian apologist. Warner started a "William Lane Craig Is Not A" playlist, which includes short videos by him and others about why "William Lane Craig is not a philosopher," "William Lane Craig is not a crashing bore," and "William Lane Craig is not gay."

"It's kind of like pamphleteering," Warner told me. "I like that I can reach out to people I've never met before." Off of YouTube, though, he says he tends to keep to himself.

Like old-fashioned pamphleteering, too, the video scene can be brutal—as Veritas48 discovered. With tens of thousands of followers in tow, YouTubers pose pointed barbs at each other, and challenges and questions. When things really get out of hand, they've even been known to serve DMCA (Digital Millennium Copyright Act) notices and counter-notices against each other, which can wind up getting a person banned from YouTube entirely. A DMCA war between the Christian creationist green-screen master VenomFangX and Thunderfoot ("Science and Education for the win!") ended in public humiliation for the former and nearly a nasty lawsuit.

The Internet makes whole new proofs and prooflike things possible while helping old ones spread more wildly than ever, intermingling and reinventing themselves in new guises. Evangelicals are reading Thomas Aquinas, Hindu yogis are explaining new meanings in Anselm's proof, and Muslim preachers are name-dropping Plantinga. Websites that claim irrefutable proof fill my Google Alert for "existence of God" every week.

Proofthatgodexists.com, for instance, takes you to a site by a "just an aver-age guy" named Sye Ten Bruggencate and his "Sinner Ministries," with four large, gray boxes, each with a statement about Absolute Truth: Does it exist? Or not? Do you know? Do you care? If you don't care, it takes you to the Disney website. Pick anything else, and it will lead you, through a further sequence of boxes to choose from, toward a momentous conclusion: "The

Proof that God exists is that without Him you couldn't prove anything." Accept it, and you're invited to become a Christian, or a better one. If, along the way, you make the wrong move again, back to Disney you go.

The other side has them too. Godisimaginary.com gives "50 simple proofs" that you can test yourself, like "Try praying," "Understand ambiguity," and "Ask Jesus to appear." Godlessgeeks.com, the site of the Atheists of Silicon Valley, hosts a list of 666 proofs of God's existence. In simple, syllogistic form, it includes everything from the familiar cosmological, teleological, and ontological arguments to an "ARGUMENT FROM BEER," two versions of the "ARGUMENT FROM LITTLE BABIES," and the recursive "ARGUMENT FROM MULTIPLICITY":

1. There exists a web page (http://www.godlessgeeks.com/LINKS/ GodProof.htm)
2. That page has hundreds of purported proofs of the existence of God.
3. They can't all be wrong.
4. Therefore, God exists.[14]

Thechurchofgoogle.org, a site devoted to the satirical religion Googlism, gives nine proofs that Google is God: it's pretty close to omniscient, it's virtually omnipresent, and it answers prayers, for instance. Another search tool, WolframAlpha, replies to "Does God exist?" with an apology: "I'm sorry, but a poor computational knowledge engine, no matter how powerful, is not capable of providing a simple answer to that question." That's a pretty pitiful cop-out, considering WolframAlpha's answer to "What is the meaning of life?"—a reference to Douglas Adams's *Hitchhiker's Guide to the Galaxy:* 42.

∴

While I was in Los Angeles attending William Lane Craig's classes at Biola, I got in touch with Luke Muehlhauser, the author of one of my favorite proof blogs, *Common Sense Atheism.* He suggested that we meet at Peet's Coffee in the food court of the Glendale Galleria, a gaudy shopping mall. A few minutes ahead of schedule, I got a text message: *I have arrived. I'm the only 6'6" guy with spiky black hair. -Luke.* It was true; I had no problem finding him. He was wearing jeans and a black T-shirt decorated with a florid graphic, like you'd buy on a boardwalk. We got our coffees and sat down at a table to talk.

Luke and I were the same age—twenty-six—and, without ever having studied it formally, he knew way more philosophy. He grew up in small-town Minnesota, a devoted Christian and the son of a pastor, always pushing himself toward as much holiness as he could manage. In college he studied counseling psychology but became disenchanted with it and dropped out of school before graduating. That was when his faith began to slip. He started learning about the historical Jesus in order to know his savior better, but what he found had the opposite effect. In came doubts, and they wouldn't go away. He turned to the apologetics industry in order to buttress his belief in God, but discovering the arguments of David Hume helped clinch it. The blog he kept then, *What God Taught Me Today*, is still online as a record of his last days as a Christian. He says he finally became an atheist on January 11, 2007. "I feel like I've been born again, again," he wrote a few days later.[15] But it wasn't easy. There was a big task ahead of him.

Luke left Minnesota and moved to L.A., where, when we met, he was making a living setting up computer networks for businesses. But he did that as little as possible—around thirty-five hours a week, and less if he could manage. His real work was the self-education-in-public that was happening on his website. Day to day, Luke was building a worldview. The big priorities at first were answering, in detail, the best theistic arguments he could find. He also needed to develop a compelling moral theory consistent with his atheism. Since launching Common Sense Atheism in late 2008, Luke has posted podcast interviews with philosophers, extended book reviews, and bibliographies of academic articles, linked to PDFs when possible. His readership became large and loyal; it's not uncommon for more than a hundred comments to appear on a post. Many of the readers are philosophy graduate students and professors, and lots more are apologetic hobbyists on either side of the big divide.

What he does best is explicate arguments clearly, fairly, and respectfully. Sometimes he deals with the familiar ones of Plantinga and Craig, and sometimes he helps promote lesser-known thinkers. He's willing to criticize atheists as much as theists. "Irrationality and nonrationality are not religious conditions," Luke told me. "They're part of the human condition." They're also what he wants to minimize as much as possible in himself. He's intent on being wrong as little as possible. It would be trite but true to say that reason is his new religion. Thinking with Luke feels like an act of devotion.

We talked for two breathless hours over our coffees—shop talk about philosophy of religion, mostly—and by then I thought that out of politeness

I should let him go. I thanked him for the conversation and began to gather my things. But as I got up to leave, he said, "I wouldn't mind talking more if you want."

I thought about it for a second, looked at him, saw he was serious, and took off my jacket. I only stipulated that we walk while we talked. And so we did, for five more hours after that, about exalted things, among the mall's chain stores and loiterers, stopping only for a snack of jalapeño-covered Wetzel's pretzels and iced tea. We talked and talked through one proof after another—their strengths and weaknesses, what they mean, and what we know about the people who thought of them. We talked about Plato's concept of friendship, the consummation of all his philosophy.

Something occurred to me on an escalator, and I didn't keep it to myself: this was a new Spinoza. See what I mean? Luke's day job couldn't have been more perfect. What is networking computers but the lens grinding of our day, the delicate and inglorious task supporting the technology that's transforming how we see the world? Luke, like Spinoza, has few in-person friends and many correspondents. The idea of a girlfriend or a wife didn't interest him particularly, though he said he would occasionally go to a party to get laid. Besides that he seems liable, like Ibn Tufayl's Hayy, to shed his body in exchange for truth.

As the "virtuous atheist" of The Hague was said to be, Luke is earnest, gracious, and curious. He listens hard and well, then asks generous questions that make one want to open up and tell all. They're questions through and through, but they feel like compliments. His eyes squint as he thinks.

Now that he had found a purpose in philosophy, he regretted having dropped out of college, because it meant he couldn't apply to graduate school and become a professor. But he said he could just as easily move to some cheap, faraway basement in the desert and keep on doing his research over the Internet. Already, anyway, he had accomplished what not many PhD's can claim; he had the attention and respect of some top people in his field. He was having long, in-depth conversations with them on his podcasts. William Lane Craig has even used Luke's material in class. Yet the more Luke was getting settled in his new worldview, the less interested he was in religion. He was writing and thinking more and more about things like artificial intelligence, meta-ethics, and neuroscience. Rather than the Second Coming, what was starting to concern him most was the Singularity—the prophesied time when machines finally become smarter than their human creators.

After the sun had set in the skylights overhead, the last two hours of our conversation turned a little torturous. We had been talking about these ideas and proofs and consequences in the abstract, and we had agreed on most things. But now he wanted to know more about what I believe, and where I stand, and what conclusions I had come to. What was the *content* of my Catholicism? This was what I dreaded. I could talk about God as love, as community, or as a presence beyond being. I could tell him about the nun I know with the secret ministry to transgender folks, or teach him the tune to a hymn I like to sing before bed—these are the content of my faith. But he would only ask what that means in terms of proofs. I could defer to unknowing and mystery, but he kept pushing me for clarity—gently, but pushing. I tried one tack, and my wind would die, and I'd try again. And the wind would die. That was the best I could do. He stood several inches taller than me to begin with, but I was starting to feel especially small.

Finally, seven hours after we began, night long since fallen and the mall nearly deserted, we made our way to the parking structure and said good-bye. I sat for a while in the car I was borrowing from a friend, a new and newly cleaned Civic, and I wrote down as much as I could remember of what had gone between us. As I wrote I couldn't escape a feeling of being a living contradiction, and of sadness. If there is language to describe this, I hadn't found it. And I think lots of us are like that; in the big tête-à-tête debates about the existence of God, what side we're on isn't always so clear.

At least Luke—and the whole genre of proof that he, ghostlike, represented—had helped hold down the winged words I might otherwise get away with, before the wax they're made of could melt in the sun. The unexamined life is not worth living, nor the unexamined God worth believing. I remain, thank God, no less than ever a question to myself, and God remains a question for me.

God, Alone

The plan, originally, was to build a monastery of stone. Monks first arrived at Berryville, Virginia, in 1950, after Our Lady of the Valley in Rhode Island burned down, but the community never grew big enough for stone. Holy Cross Abbey consists mostly of cinder-block buildings painted sky blue, which surround a mansion constructed in 1784 by a man named William Wormeley. His father, Ralph Wormeley, had bought the land before the Revolutionary War, apparently on the advice of George Washington. Even the mansion's stone walls are hidden under blue paint. Cistercian monasteries have never been grand, but their simplicity typically coincides with a sense of permanence. Not so much at Holy Cross.

Grassy hills roll under clear air, thick with the moist fragrance of whatever is growing or decaying or grazing that season. There's a graveyard of white, wooden crosses in rows and, past it, along the Shenandoah River, a new guest house sits just about where the Engagement at Cool Spring was fought on July 18, 1864. And then there are the stately, crumbling concrete benches, each next to a tree and facing the Blue Ridge Mountains.

During the decade that has passed since my first stay, I've made the pilgrimage back at least once a year. I always arrange to see Brother Benedict, and bring some sandwiches, and we talk for an hour or so about books and the doings of his many friends. These visits turned into a habit, and then a necessity; when things become somehow tough, wherever I am, I want to go back to the monastery.

The time I finally told Benedict that I was writing a book about proofs for the existence of God, he burst out laughing. His eyes rolled up to the ceiling, and he cried, "Haven't I taught you *anything?*" But when I had finished with my traveling and interviewing and note gathering, he and Father Robert welcomed me back there to write. Like I had that first time, years before, they let me stay two weeks inside the cloister, sharing the life they live there, all over again. I would repeat the same exercise that got me started in this, going back to the source.

My first day there I noticed, out for perusal in the chapter room, a photocopy of the annual "House Report": a one-page, rather dour document describing the state of things at the abbey. It said that there were "twenty (20)" members, of whom only "eight (8)" were able to live the full monastic life. No one was in formation. There were no new vocations. They had commissioned a major plan for environmental sustainability, but someone would have to be around to implement it. The report ended by declaring their total dependence on God, their determination to live out God's call, and the intimation that nothing short of a miracle could keep this place going for much longer.

I thought back to Thomas Merton's Gethsemani Abbey in Kentucky. There, along the wall between inside and outside, is a large inscription: "GOD ALONE," it says. This isn't just a saying or platitude; it's the design of the place. These monasteries are societies built around God and, as far as possible, nothing else.

.˙.

I'm not much for describing medical situations. I should do my best, though, to report what I saw when I would go to visit Benedict in his room in the infirmary wing during that two-week stay. It was usually after Vespers, just as Brother Efrain came to dispense Benedict's medication and recite a line of Shakespeare. The medicine was causing him to retain fluids, returning this once-tiny man to the fleshier look he has in pictures from his years in New York. He wore a pajama suit under a flannel bathrobe. There were clear tubes running overtop his ears, alongside his glasses, feeding oxygen to his nostrils. The oxygen machine hummed, or groaned, in the background.

His kidneys were failing. He had been off dialysis for years, shuttling back and forth from the edge of death, yet, inexplicably, remaining on our side of it. When I was still in college I once received a package with a few books in it and a note saying that Benedict wouldn't remain long and wanted me to have them. Year after year, though, I would keep going back to see him. Every visit could have been the last, but it wasn't. At seventy-one years old, he was now well practiced in the art of dying.

His room was full—full of books and papers and things. He had literary quotations about life and death on the wall next to his bed. There was a picture of Thomas Merton, and another of Father Flavian, who had been a friend to both Merton and Benedict. There were papers relating to a book he was trying to finish writing. There were hundreds of letters from friends.

Some days he had energy for conversation, and others he didn't. But there were things he wanted to tell me, things I knew I needed to hear. We fumbled our way toward them. Sometimes, we just rehearsed conversations I could've sworn we had had years before.

The season of Lent had just begun, and the monks are supposed to pick a penitential text to study during that time. Benedict said that he had asked Father Robert if he could choose Plato's dialogue *Phaedo* as his Lenten reading. He told me he wanted a meditation on death "not bound by Christian ropes."

I asked what support, what consolation, he had found in "Christian ropes." I hadn't asked him about this before—maybe because I suspected the answer.

He came close to me and whispered, with half a smile, *"Not much."*

In one of our talks a few days later, he put it another way: he no longer has that "structure of belief."

Structure of belief. He doesn't buy this stuff anymore, basically—the God, and all that follows, on which everything at the monastery is supposed to depend.

But Benedict of all people—I depended on him. He was the sponsor for my baptism and my guide, before and since. He had never pushed me toward any of this, though I pushed myself, trusting him, trusting that if he could do it—believe, or whatever—then I could too.

A cover of silence hangs over the monastery. It's the silence by which one can walk away from conversations without finishing them, by which one doesn't know what the others are actually thinking, by which the monastery's God comes and goes. It's the same silence that made it possible at first for me to even be there, to come and, in time, ease into a faith. It's the silence I returned to after I left Benedict's room that day, to have supper in the empty refectory, feeling sorry for neither of us—actually, relieved.

This structurelessness doesn't bother him now, he said. His doubts used to send him into depressive fits that nearly took his life. Not anymore. Nor does he regret the decision to enter the monastery. This is where he belongs. He told me what he once overheard Father Flavian say to a younger monk who had been complaining about one of his brothers: "There are many different ways to be a monk."

In the middle of my stay, I left for a night to be at my father's sixtieth birthday party—a happy party, full of his old friends telling me stories about him from before I was born. Passing between the house where he lives with his wife and the one where my mother lives with her brother, and the fathers and brothers of the monastery, it occurred to me that there are also many different ways to be a family.

When I returned to Berryville, spring had arrived, a perfect spring. The only thing missing in the monastery was enough exultation. There were birds everywhere; they felt it, even if the monks had to maintain their penitence. On that land, as I chanted and prayed and ate with its caretakers, my religion, and the structure of its universe, seemed to settle into place. I went for a walk around the property trying to learn the lay of it better: to see where the stone abbey was to have been built, where the conservation cemetery might be, and where a garden had once been along the river. When I got back, I found Father Robert and asked him some questions about the geography. He took me to his dark, cluttered office and showed me the map on its wall, pointing out everything. And then he said something rapturous—if, as ever, subdued—about what magnificent land it is.

When I went to see Benedict that day, he was in an especially cheerful mood. He had just written two paragraphs—paragraphs he had been trying to write for years. I told him about the progress of his butterfly garden, and about a passage by Thomas Merton I had just read on something Maximus the Confessor had said about love.

Benedict was also glad because there had been good news about the environmental sustainability plan. A couple turned up who were interested in starting an organic farm at the distant farmhouse. The conservation cemetery had hit a hitch, but that would be worked out before long. He said he thought that this could save the monastery. If it became a model for living close to the land, people would want to come to experience it. Some of them would stay.

But even if the land can't save the monastery, he said, maybe the monastery can save the land. It's surrounded by developers who want to make it another golf course or subdivision. Holy Cross can last long enough, at least, to finish establishing an easement and prevent that. Even if there were no more monks, he said, their sixty years' presence would be a good investment. An afterlife, of sorts.

∴

With the spring, surrounded by the monks, the proofs that I had been writing and worrying about came to life. During dinner, Walter Isaacson's biography of Albert Einstein was being read out loud, and, afterward, as we washed dishes, one of the old monks told me what had struck him in the day's selection. "Isn't it amazing," he said, "that the more we learn about the universe, the more we see signs of God?"

I started thinking again about that old proof of mine, the one I mentioned at the very start of this book, the one that dawned on me so suddenly in college a few months before my baptism. I still don't understand it even now, nor am I convinced it's any kind of proof.

It started, I think, from a sense of longing for the conviction I saw among the people I had been coming to know: Father Bodah, the monks and, among them, Benedict. Now, we can add so many more to that company: Pythagoras to Plato, Aristotle to Augustine, Ibn Tufayl to Maimonides, Anselm to Aquinas, to Descartes, to Spinoza, to Hegel, to the various professors and concerned citizens I've encountered over the years, along with their proofs. Can I say that they're wrong? If I tried to tell them I don't believe in God, they could answer that I don't get what they mean by God yet—that I'm missing something. And I would be. They could keep on saying so, and keep trying to show me why, with proofs if they like, until I finally realize that God is such that God is real. When I do, I have to believe too.

None of their proofs seems to be exactly it—enough to settle the question forever—yet still they carry me together toward that to which they're pointing. In this company, with time and practice, comes my proof, and my trap: I do believe in God.

The idea of God, after it first became lodged in me, and once I even partly entertained it, began to take on a life of its own. This process started through other people, but the idea transcended even them. As Anselm replied to Gaunilo, there's something special about the one most perfect idea, something that applies to no other. You might be able to grasp a humbler notion enough to refute it. But this necessary and infinite being is more elusive, while being also more fully present, than anything else we know. No refutation can suffice. It's too big. Its possibilities never stop exceeding what we

I'D LIKE TO LEARN FROM YOU

I AM MY DESIRE FOR GOD

THEN LET'S DESIRE TOGETHER

might happen to rule out. This God exceeds what we think about it, and what we think we know about it. It even exceeds those of us who can't believe in it anymore, and those who never did.

I used to lie in bed at night and try, maybe by squeezing some dormant muscle in my brain, to see a vision, a confirming signal, even a schizophrenic voice. For all the waking hours I would spend thinking about God in uncountable forms, to my disappointment, none of them ever appeared in my dreams—no savior, no incandescent dove, not even a ghost. Lying in the monastery bed during my first stay there a decade ago, I figured that would have been as good a place as any for it to happen, but no such luck.

Years later and still basically visionless, I would now dare to nominate this genre of proof, which I've toured so much and at least peripherally experienced, for consideration as itself a special kind of sight. Like visions, the genre is a gift (or a burden) not given to everyone, one whose recipients share a common bond. We're tempted to consider some instances of it more legitimate or valid than others, or even more clinically sound—but good luck assigning which to which. The proofs can be explained and taught and respected from a distance, yet still there remains the fact that you either grok it or you don't, and that's that.

To my head these proofs have come to seem much more than a mere domain of inquiry: they represent a blessed community, a subcommunion of saints, an academy. Like Raphael's *School of Athens,* we can imagine these thinkers all present at once, speaking with one another in hushed tones, their echoes carrying across the marble floor. And then we also find each proof in its peculiarity, its incarnation, its moment, with the flesh that gave it life and urgency and meaning. In any case, these proofs are never answers to be over and done with. They're sometimes a comfort, sometimes a wrenching anxiety, and yet all I'm really saying is that they are, quite astonishingly, exactly what they claim to be: a way of knowing something about what it is we mean by God. Whatever good that does anybody lies in the details.

ACKNOWLEDGEMENTS

A book, like a proof, disguises itself as a solitary invention. And while in so many respects both genuinely are, what their authors bring to their solitude is a whole ensemble of voices and friendships and support, including among them debts so great that they can never be paid back, least of all here.

Nobody has shared this task with me more than Krista Ingebretson, my friend and agent, whose generosity of time and consideration and advice over the course of years not only made this book happen in the first place, but shaped it into something far better than it might otherwise have been. I'm grateful also to Anne Edelstein, Krista's boss, and Reed Malcolm at the University of California Press for not thinking the idea was crazy, even if perhaps it was, and for helping it become less so.

Friends and advisers waded through drafts of the book in part or in whole, giving me much-needed corrections and insight. There's no counting the hours and care in this regard of Kelly James Clark, Paul Draper, William Grassie, Patrick Lee Miller, John Mullin, David Plante, Stephen Prothero, Muhammad Rustom, Mitchell Schneider, Adam Shapiro, Jeff Sharlet, Meera Subramanian, Mary Valle, Mark Vernon, and Theo Warner. Richard Amesbury, Wes Morriston, and Mark C. Taylor provided helpful commentaries on the full manuscript, and Sheila Berg's expert copyediting saved pounds of ink in unnecessary commas and more. Quince Mountain helped save me from myself, where he could, with painstaking marginalia. Barbara Croissant and Claire Kelley each marked up the whole thing with palpable love.

I received generous support in the course of this project from the Nation Institute and the Knight Grants for Reporting on Religion and American Public Life at the University of Southern California. Isabelle and Jasmine

Albuquerque, Steven Battin, Kelly Clark, Bill Dailey, David Plante, and Genevieve Yue lent me shelter while I was traveling and working. In a very special way, so did Robert Barnes and Benedict Simmonds at Holy Cross Abbey.

I've been sustained throughout by the communities I've found as a coeditor of both *Killing the Buddha* and *Waging Nonviolence*. Who knew websites could lead us to some of our best friends? Both communities sacrificed to allow me to finish this book and inspired me to want to go through with it.

Finally, I must thank most of all my very first community, my family, beginning with my parents who have given me my first of these experiments, and on to aunts, uncles, cousins, and grandparents, living and gone, and my little goddaughters. Wherever I have gone, it was in order to return.

NOTES

SKETCHES OF BABEL

1. Laurence Cossé, *A Corner of the Veil*, trans. Linda Asher (New York: Scribner, 1999), 31–32.

2. One marvelous exception that has influenced my approach is John Clayton, *Religions, Reasons and Gods: Essays in Cross-Cultural Philosophy of Religion*, ed. Anne M. Blackburn and Thomas D. Carroll (Cambridge: Cambridge University Press, 2006).

CHAPTER 1: FIRST CAUSES

1. Zora Neale Hurston, *Their Eyes Were Watching God* (Champaign: University of Illinois Press, 1991), 27.

2. Giulia Sissa and Marcel Detienne, *The Daily Life of the Greek Gods*, trans. Janet Lloyd (Palo Alto, CA: Stanford University Press, 2000), 167–76; Walter Burkert, *Greek Religion*, trans. John Raffan (Cambridge, MA: Harvard University Press, 1985), 216–75.

3. Iamblichus's *Pythagorean Life*, quoted in Robin Waterfield, trans. and ed., *The First Philosophers: The Presocratics and the Sophists* (Oxford: Oxford University Press, 2000), 98. See also Carl A. Huffman, "The Pythagorean Tradition," in *The Cambridge Companion to Early Greek Philosophy*, ed. A. A. Long (Cambridge: Cambridge University Press, 1999); Walter Burkert, *Lore and Science in Ancient Pythagoreanism*, trans. Edwin L. Minar (Cambridge, MA: Harvard University Press, 1972); and Patrick Lee Miller, *Becoming God: Pure Reason in Early Greek Philosophy* (London: Continuum, 2011).

4. Quoted in Burkert, *Lore and Science in Ancient Pythagoreanism*, 447–48. Translation revised for readability.

5. Edward J. Larson and Larry Witham, "Leading Scientists Still Reject God," *Nature* 394, no. 6691 (1998): 313.

6. Eudemus, as quoted in Simplicius's *Commentary on Aristotle's* Physics, from Waterfield, *The First Philosophers*, 56.

7. Plato, *Timaeus* §28c, in *Timaeus and Critias*, trans. and ed. Desmond Lee (London: Penguin, 1977).

8. Plato, *Republic* §516, in *The Dialogues of Plato*, trans. Benjamin Jowett (Oxford: Oxford University Press, 1892). The Jowett translation ends with a question mark.

9. This is from a blog that Ken Knisley started only two weeks before his death: "No Abstraction," *A Well Lit Room,* September 16, 2005, http://nodogs.blogspot.com/2005/09/no-abstraction.html.

10. See Miller, *Becoming God*; and Andrea Wilson Nightingale, *Spectacles of Truth in Classical Greek Philosophy: Theoria in Its Cultural Context* (Cambridge: Cambridge University Press, 2004).

11. Plato, *Laws* §885, in *The Dialogues of Plato*. "Gods" is capitalized in the original.

12. Ibid., §887–88.

13. Ibid., §886.

14. Ibid., §898.

15. Frederick Copleston, *A History of Philosophy,* vol. 1, *Greece and Rome: From the Pre-Socratics to Plotinus* (New York: Image, 1993), 191.

16. Aristotle, *The Metaphysics,* trans. Hugh Lawson-Tancred (London: Penguin, 1998), §1076a.

17. Ibid., §1072b.

18. Ibid., §1074b. Parentheses in the original removed.

19. John 1:1 and 1:29, King James Version.

20. 1 Corinthians 1:22–23. Biblical quotations are from the New Revised Standard Version, unless otherwise noted. Michael D. Coogan, ed., *The New Oxford Annotated Bible* (New York: Oxford University Press, 2001).

21. 1 Corinthians 2:16.

22. From Augustine's book *On the Usefulness of Believing,* quoted in Robert Louis Wilken, *The Spirit of Early Christian Thought: Seeking the Face of God* (New Haven: Yale University Press, 2003), 162.

23. Augustine of Hippo, "Concerning Faith of Things Not Seen," in *Nicene and Post-Nicene Fathers,* 1st ser., vol. 3, trans. C. L. Cornish and ed. Philip Schaff (Buffalo, NY: Christian Literature Publishing Co., 1887), http://www.newadvent.org/fathers/1305.htm.

24. Augustine of Hippo, *The Free Choice of the Will,* trans. Robert P. Russell, in *The Fathers of the Church: A New Translation,* vol. 59 (Indianapolis, IN: Catholic University of America Press, 1968), §2.3–15.

25. Augustine of Hippo, *Confessions,* trans. Henry Chadwick (Oxford: Oxford University Press, 1991), §10.33. The Latin *quaestio* is translated as "problem" here; "question" is another common translation.

1. See John Kronen, "The Nyaya Argument for God's Existence," http://personal.stthomas.edu/jdkronen/leciii13.html; John Vattanky, *Development of Nyaya Theism* (New Delhi: Intercultural Publications, 1993).

2. See chapter 9 of Herbert A. Davidson, *Proofs for Eternity, Creation and the Existence of God in Medieval Islamic and Jewish Philosophy* (New York: Oxford University Press, 1987).

3. Ibn Tufayl, Ibn Tufayl's *Hayy Ibn Yaqzan: A Philosophical Tale,* ed. and trans. Lenn Evan Goodman (Chicago: University of Chicago Press, 2009), 4–5. The quoted passages that follow are also found on these pages.

4. See Herbert A. Davidson, "John Philoponus as a Source of Medieval Islamic and Jewish Proofs of Creation," *Journal of the American Oriental Society* 89, no. 2 (April–June 1969): 357–91.

5. Aristotle, *The Metaphysics,* trans. Hugh Lawson-Tancred (London: Penguin, 1998), §1072a.

6. Al-Ghazali, *The Rescuer from Error,* in *Medieval Islamic Philosophical Writings,* ed. Muhammad Ali Khalidi (Cambridge: Cambridge University Press, 2005), 89.

7. According to a count by Quentin Smith, reported in his contribution to Michael Martin, ed., *The Cambridge Companion to Atheism* (Cambridge: Cambridge University Press, 2007), 183.

8. William Lane Craig, *The Kalam Cosmological Argument* (New York: Barnes & Noble, 1979), 149.

9. Ibn Tufayl, *Hayy Ibn Yaqzan,* 135.

10. From the *Enneads,* quoted in Frederick Copleston, *A History of Philosophy,* vol. 1, *Greece and Rome: From the Pre-Socratics to Plotinus* (New York: Image, 1993), 471.

11. Ibn Tufayl, *Hayy Ibn Yaqzan,* 96.

12. Ibid., 156.

13. Saba Mahmood, "Rehearsed Spontaneity and the Conventionality of Ritual: Disciplines of Salat," *American Ethologist* 28, no. 4 (2001): 827–53.

14. Ibn Tufayl, *Hayy Ibn Yaqzan,* 164.

15. See W. Montgomery Watt, *Al-Ghazali: The Muslim Intellectual* (Chicago: Kazi Publications, 2002).

16. Ibn Tufayl, *Hayy Ibn Yaqzan,* 166.

17. Moses Maimonides, *The Guide for the Perplexed,* trans. M. Friedländer (New York: Dover, 1956), 3.

18. Ibid., §1.76, 144. This translation actually says "Prime Motor," but I want to avoid the perception of difference between Maimonides' and Aristotle's terms.

19. Ibid. §2.1, 151.

20. Al-Kindi, for instance, attributed a version of this to Aristotle (see Sarah Stroumsa, *Maimonides in His World: Portrait of a Mediterranean Thinker* [Princeton: Princeton University Press, 2009], 12), while al-Ghazali attributed it to the

Caliph 'Ali, the son-in-law of Muhammad (al-Ghazali, *The Rescuer from Error*, 74). Maimonides uses it as well.

21. My approach to masculinity and the lineage of proof is influenced by Nancy Jay, *Throughout Your Generations Forever: Sacrifice, Religion, Paternity* (Chicago: University of Chicago Press, 1992).

22. Quoted in J. Hillis Miller, *For Derrida* (New York: Fordham University Press, 2009), 121.

CHAPTER 3: GRAMMARS OF ASSENT

1. Anselm, *Proslogion* §1, in *Anselm of Canterbury: The Major Works,* ed. Brian Davies and G. R. Evans (New York: Oxford University Press, 1998). Exclamation mark borrowed from a different translation.

2. Ibid., preface.

3. Eadmer, *Vita Sancti Anselmi,* quoted in R. W. Southern, *Saint Anselm: A Portrait in a Landscape* (Cambridge: Cambridge University Press, 1990), 117.

4. Benedict, known to the world as Harvey Simmonds, is the subject of a documentary film called *He Who Is Blessed.*

5. Benedict of Nursia, *The Rule of St. Benedict* (Collegeville, MN: Liturgical Press, 1981), prologue, 45, 49, 165.

6. Anselm, *Proslogion* §2. This translation uses "thought" here instead of "conceived"; I go with the latter, which is more common.

7. Exodus 3:14.

8. See Alvin Plantinga, ed., *The Ontological Argument: From St. Anselm to Contemporary Philosophers* (Garden City, NY: Anchor, 1965), 123–59.

9. Anselm, *Proslogion* §3.

10. Quoted in Majid Fakhry, "The Ontological Argument in the Arabic Tradition: The Case of al-Farabi," *Studia Islamica* 64 (1986): 12, 14. The first passage comes from al-Farabi's *The Enumeration of the Sciences;* the second, from *Aphorisms of the Statesman.*

11. See Jean Leclercq, *The Love of Learning and the Desire for God: A Study of Monastic Culture,* trans. Catharine Misrahi (New York: Fordham University Press, 1982), 176–79.

12. See Sally Vaughn, *St Anselm and the Handmaidens of God: A Study of Anselm's Correspondence with Women* (Turnhout: Brepols, 2002).

13. Southern, *Saint Anselm,* 148.

14. Quoted in Southern, *Saint Anselm,* 144.

15. From *Notebooks,* quoted in Iris Murdoch, *Metaphysics as a Guide to Morals* (London: Penguin, 1992), 401.

16. Anselm, *Proslogion* §1. See also Karl Barth, *Anselm: Fides Quaerens Intellectum,* trans. Ian Robertson (Richmond, VA: John Knox Press, 1960).

17. Dante, *The Divine Comedy of Dante Alighieri,* trans. and ed. Robert M. Durl-

ing, ed. Ronald L. Martinez, vol. 1, *Inferno* (New York: Oxford University Press, 2004–11), §3.130.

18. James A. Weisheipl, *Friar Aquinas d'Aquino: His Life, Thought, and Work* (Garden City, NY: Doubleday, 1974), 322. The preceding anecdotes are drawn from this work as well.

19. Thomas Merton, *The Seven Storey Mountain* (New York: Harcourt, 1999), 188–89.

20. *Summa Theologica* §1.2.3, in Thomas Aquinas, *Introduction to St. Thomas Aquinas,* ed. Anton C. Pegis (New York: Modern Library, 1948).

21. Aquinas, *Summa Contra Gentiles* §3.37–39, in *Introduction.*

22. 1 Corinthians 13:12.

23. See Scott Matthews, "Anselm's Argument and the Friars," *Medieval Philosophy and Theology* 8 (1999): 83–104.

24. Merton, *The Seven Storey Mountain,* 103–4.

CHAPTER 4: ON CERTAINTY

1. Ludwig Wittgenstein, *On Certainty* (New York: Harper & Row, 1972), §467.

2. Ibid., §457.

3. *Meditations on First Philosophy* §3, in René Descartes, *Philosophical Essays and Correspondence,* trans. and ed. Roger Ariew (Indianapolis: Hackett, 2000).

4. *Discourse on Method* §3, in Descartes, *Philosophical Essays.*

5. Ibid., §4.

6. Wittgenstein, *On Certainty* §341.

7. This discussion synthesizes the arguments given in both *Discourse on Method* and *Meditations on First Philosophy.*

8. *Discourse on Method* §4, in Descartes, *Philosophical Essays.*

9. To Marin Marsenne, the La Flèche–educated priest and philosopher, on May 6, 1630, in Descartes, *Philosophical Essays,* 28.

10. Wittgenstein, *On Certainty* §625.

11. Ibid., §625.

12. Quoted in Rebecca Newberger Goldstein, *Betraying Spinoza: The Renegade Jew Who Gave Us Modernity* (New York: Schocken, 2006), 17–18.

13. Benedict de Spinoza, *Spinoza's Short Treatise on God, Man, and His Well-Being,* ed. A. Wolf (New York: Russell & Russell, 1963), 15.

14. Spinoza, *Ethics* §5.P23. Translation quoted in Goldstein, *Betraying Spinoza,* 185.

15. Benedict de Spinoza, *A Spinoza Reader: The* Ethics *and Other Works,* ed. Edwin Curley (Princeton: Princeton University Press, 1994), 91.

16. Spinoza, *Ethics* §1.P14, in Spinoza, *Reader.*

17. Ibid., §1.P15.

18. Ibid., §4 preface.

19. Wittgenstein, *On Certainty* §505.

20. Spinoza, *Ethics* §5.P35.

21. From *Treatise on the Emendation of the Intellect* §10, in Spinoza, *Reader.*

22. Wittgenstein, *On Certainty* §457.

23. Ibid.

24. Dorothy Day, *The Long Loneliness: The Autobiography of Dorothy Day* (New York: HarperCollins, 1997), 286.

25. See Matthew Stewart, *The Courtier and the Heretic: Leibniz, Spinoza, and the Fate of God in the Modern World* (New York: W. W. Norton, 2006).

26. Gottfried Wilhelm Leibniz, "That the Most Perfect Being Exists," in *New Essays Concerning Human Understanding,* trans. Alfred Gideon Langley (Chicago: Open Court, 1916), 714–15.

27. See David P. Goldman, "The God of the Mathematicians," *First Things* (August–September 2010): 45–50. For primary documents (and illustration source), see "Texts Relating to the Ontological Proof," which is Appendix B in Kurt Gödel, *Collected Works,* vol. 3, *Unpublished Essays and Lectures,* ed. Solomon Feferman et al. (Oxford: Oxford University Press, 1995), 429–37.

28. Quoted in Stewart, *The Courtier and the Heretic,* 225.

29. Blaise Pascal, *Pascal's Pensées or, Thoughts on Religion,* trans. and ed. Gertrude Burfurd Rawlings (Mount Vernon, NY: Peter Pauper Press, 1946), 82.

30. Wittgenstein, *On Certainty* §657.

31. Pascal, *Pensées,* 9–11.

32. Ibid., 12–13.

33. Émile Durkheim, *The Elementary Forms of Religious Life,* trans. Karen E. Fields (New York: Free Press, 1995), 427, 447.

34. Wittgenstein, *On Certainty* §625.

CHAPTER 5: COMING OF AGE

1. Dated March 10, 1751, in David Hume, *Dialogues and Natural History of Religion,* ed. J. C. A. Gaskin (Oxford: Oxford University Press, 1993), 25.

2. Confucius, *Analects, with Selections from Traditional Commentaries,* trans. Edward Slingerland (Indianapolis: Hackett, 2003), §2.4.

3. Joseph H. Hertz, trans., *Sayings of the Fathers or Pirke Aboth* (New York: Behrman House, 1945), §5.24.

4. Plato, *Republic* §540, in *The Dialogues of Plato,* trans. Benjamin Jowett (Oxford: Oxford University Press, 1892).

5. David Hume, *Enquiry Concerning Human Understanding* §10, in *Enquiries Concerning Human Understanding and Concerning the Principles of Morals,* ed. P. H. Nidditch (Oxford: Oxford University Press, 1975), 110.

6. John Locke, *An Essay Concerning Human Understanding,* ed. Roger Woolhouse (London: Penguin, 2004), 3–4.

7. From John Locke, *Works* §4.48, quoted in the introduction to *Essay Concerning Human Understanding,* xxii.

8. Locke, *Essay Concerning Human Understanding* §4.10, 547.

9. Richard Blackmore, *Creation: A Philosophical Poem* (Philadelphia: Robert Johnson, 1806), xli, 57.

10. Letter to Henry Home from December 1737, quoted in Paul Russell, *The Riddle of Hume's* Treatise: *Skepticism, Naturalism, and Irreligion* (New York: Oxford University Press, 2008), 131.

11. Dated August 15, 1776, in Ernest C. Mossner, "The Enigma of Hume," *Mind* 45, no. 179 (July 1936): 335.

12. Hume, *Dialogues* §2, in *Dialogues and Natural History.*

13. Ibid., §9, 91.

14. Ibid., §1, 37.

15. Ibid., §2, 49.

16. Ibid., §12, 121 and 130.

17. Hume, *Dialogues,* "Pamphilus to Hermippus," in *Dialogues and Natural History,* 30. On reason and persuasion in Hume's *Dialogues,* see Colin Jager, *The Book of God: Secularization and Design in the Romantic Era* (Philadelphia: University of Pennsylvania Press, 2007).

18. "Preliminary Report," in Moses Mendelssohn, *Morning Hours: Lectures on God's Existence,* trans. Daniel O. Dahlstrom and Corey Dyck (New York: Springer, 2011). This is the more traditional translation, not the one Dahlstrom and Dyck use.

19. Immanuel Kant, *Critique of Pure Reason,* ed. Marcus Weigelt (London: Penguin, 2007), 10.

20. Ibid., 499.

21. Dated April 8, 1766, in Sebastian Gardner, *Kant and the Critique of Pure Reason* (London: Routledge, 1999), 17.

22. Kant, *Critique of Pure Reason,* 499.

23. Ibid., 504. Changed "being" to "existence," as is common in other translations.

24. Ibid., 523.

25. Ibid., 25. Changed "belief" to "faith," as is common in other translations.

26. From Immanuel Kant, *Critique of Practical Reason,* trans. Lewis White Beck (Indianapolis: Bobbs-Merrill, 1956), excerpted in *Classical and Contemporary Readings in the Philosophy of Religion,* ed. John Hick (Englewood Cliffs, NJ: Prentice-Hall, 1964), 172.

27. Immanuel Kant, *Religion within the Limits of Reason Alone,* trans. Theodore M. Greene and Hoyt H. Hudson (New York: Harper & Row, 1960), 5.

28. G. W. F. Hegel, *Lectures on the Philosophy of Religion,* trans. and ed. Peter C. Hodgson (Berkeley: University of California Press, 1988), 164.

29. Ryszard Kapuściński, *Travels with Herodotus,* trans. Klara Glowczewska (New York: Vintage, 2007), 92; G. W. F. Hegel, *Reason in History,* trans. Robert S. Hartman (Englewood Cliffs, NJ: Prentice Hall, 1953), 13.

30. G. W. F. Hegel, *Lectures on the Proofs of the Existence of God,* in *Lectures on*

the Philosophy of Religion, vol. 3, trans. and ed. E.B. Speirs (New York: Humanities Press, 1962), 188. My reading of Hegel's proofs is heavily influenced by Mark C. Taylor, "*Itinerarium Mentis in Deum:* Hegel's Proofs of God's Existence," *Journal of Religion* 57, no. 3 (July 1977): 211–31.

31. Hegel, *Lectures on the Philosophy of Religion,* 105.

32. Hegel, *Lectures on the Proofs,* 359.

33. G.W.F. Hegel, *The Logic of Hegel,* trans. William Wallace (Oxford: Clarendon Press, 1892), 63.

CHAPTER 6: GRANDEUR IN THIS VIEW OF LIFE

1. Immanuel Kant, *Critique of Pure Reason,* ed. Marcus Weigelt (London: Penguin, 2007), 520.

2. Xenophon, *Memorabilia: Recollections of Socrates,* trans. H.G. Dakyns (Project Gutenberg, 1998), §1.4 and §4.3, http://www.gutenberg.org/etext/1173.

3. Aristotle, *The Metaphysics,* trans. Hugh Lawson-Tancred (London: Penguin, 1998), §1075a.

4. Marcus Tullius Cicero, *The Nature of the Gods* §2.5, in *The Nature of the Gods and On Divination,* trans. C.D. Yonge (Amherst, NY: Prometheus Books, 1997).

5. Romans 1:20.

6. H. Freedman and Maurice Simon, eds., *Midrash Rabbah,* vol. 1 (London: Soncino Press, 1939), Genesis 39.1, 313.

7. Qur'an 16:10–12, quoted in Muhammad al-Ghazali, *A Thematic Commentary on the Qur'an,* trans. Ashur A. Shamis (Herndon, VA: International Institute of Islamic Thought, 2000), 279.

8. William Paley, *Natural Theology* (Boston: Gould and Lincoln, 1860), 5–6.

9. Ibid., 294. See also Niall O'Flaherty, "The Rhetorical Strategy of William Paley's *Natural Theology* (1802): Part 1, William Paley's *Natural Theology* in Context," *Studies in History and Philosophy of Science* 41, no. 1 (2010): 19–25.

10. Adam R. Shapiro, "Rewinding Paley's Watchmaker," unpublished manuscript.

11. Charles Darwin, *The Origin of Species* (New York: Gramercy, 1979), 459–60.

12. Charles Darwin, *The Autobiography of Charles Darwin,* ed. Nora Barlow (London: Collins, 1958), 87.

13. Richard Dawkins, *The Blind Watchmaker* (New York: W.W. Norton, 1986), 6.

14. Adam R. Shapiro, "William Paley's Lost 'Intelligent Design,' " *History and Philosophy of the Life Sciences* 31 (2009): 55–78.

15. E.g., Charles Darwin, *On the Origin of Species* (London: John Murray, 1861), 514.

16. Adrian Desmond, *Huxley: From Devil's Disciple to Evolution's High Priest* (Reading, MA: Addison-Wesley, 1997), 279.

17. Jeffrey P. Moran, *The Scopes Trial: A Brief History with Documents* (New York: Palgrave, 2002), 157.

18. Ronald L. Numbers, *The Creationists* (Cambridge, MA: Harvard University Press, 2006), 217.

19. Henry Morris, *Creation and the Second Coming* (Green Forest, AR: Master Books, 1991).

20. Kenneth R. Miller, *Finding Darwin's God: A Scientist's Search for Common Ground between God and Evolution* (New York: Cliff Street Books, 1999), 173.

21. From the July–August issue of *Touchstone,* quoted in Barbara Forrest and Paul R. Gross, *Creationism's Trojan Horse: The Wedge of Intelligent Design* (Oxford: Oxford University Press, 2004), 261.

22. Discovery Institute, "The Wedge," Seattle, 1998, 2. Appeared online 1999.

23. http://web.archive.org/web/20051214055748/www.lehigh.edu/~inbios/news/evolution.htm. The same statement remains on the department's site.

24. Laurie Lebo, *The Devil in Dover: An Insider's Story of Dogma v. Darwin in Small Town America* (New York: New Press, 2008), 62. Lebo covered the trial extensively for the *York Daily Record.*

25. Matt Taibbi, "Darwinian Warfare," in *Smells Like Dead Elephants: Dispatches from a Rotting Empire* (New York: Black Cat, 2007), 92.

26. Christina Kauffman, "Robertson: 'Don't Turn to God,'" *York Dispatch,* November 16, 2005.

27. Guy Lengagne, "The Dangers of Creationism in Education," Council of Europe Parliamentary Assembly report, June 8, 2007, http://assembly.coe.int/Main.asp?link=/Documents/WorkingDocs/Doc07/EDOC11297.htm; Harun Yahya, "Darwinism Has Been Annihilated across the World," *HarunYayha.com,* September 29, 2008, http://us1.harunyahya.com/Detail/T/EDCRFV/productId/9544/DARWINISM_HAS_BEEN_ANNIHILATED_ACROSS_THE_WORLD.

28. See Halil Arda, "Sex, Flies and Videotape: The Secret Lives of Harun Yahya," *New Humanist* (September–October 2009), http://newhumanist.org.uk/2131/sex-flies-and-videotape-the-secret-lives-of-harun-yahya.

29. Arda, "Sex, Flies and Videotape," corroborates the Mahdi beliefs, as have my conversations with former members of Oktar's circle.

30. Walt Whitman, *Complete Poetry and Collected Prose* (New York: Library of America, 1982), 244.

31. Exodus 3:14.

CHAPTER 7: THE DEATHS OF GOD

1. Account based on interviews with Jesse's family; Bob Unruh, "Dad Links Son's Suicide to *The God Delusion,*" *WorldNetDaily,* November 20, 2008, http://www.wnd.com/?pageId = 81459; and Discovery Institute, "The Story of Jesse Kilgore and the Consequences of Teaching One Side," *Intelligent Design the Future*

(podcast), December 17, 2008, http://intelligentdesign.podomatic.com/player/web/2008–12–17T09_37_30–08_00.

2. Jesse Kilgore, *What Say You?* (blog), formerly located at http://users.newblog.com/Jkrapture/.

3. Jesse Kilgore, "Evangelical Atheist," *Jesse's Blog,* August 21, 2007, http://www.myspace.com/jesse_underdog/blog/301720529.

4. G. W. F. Hegel, *Lectures on the Philosophy of Religion,* trans. and ed. Peter C. Hodgson (Berkeley: University of California Press, 1988), 468.

5. Friedrich Nietzsche, *The Gay Science,* ed. Bernard Williams (Cambridge: Cambridge University Press, 2001), §125, 120.

6. Søren Kierkegaard, *Philosophical Fragments,* trans. David S. Swenson (Princeton: Princeton University Press, 1936), excerpted in *Classical and Contemporary Readings in the Philosophy of Religion,* ed. John Hick (Englewood Cliffs, NJ: Prentice-Hall, 1964), 192, 191.

7. Kilgore, *What Say You?*

8. Pew Forum, "Faith in Flux: Changes in Religious Affiliation in the U.S.," April 27, 2009 (revised February 2011), http://www.pewforum.org/Faith-in-Flux.aspx.

9. Dante, *The Divine Comedy of Dante Alighieri,* trans. and ed. Robert M. Durling, ed. Ronald L. Martinez, vol. 3, *Paradiso* (New York: Oxford University Press, 2004–11), §10.138.

10. A. J. Ayer, *Language, Truth and Logic,* 2nd ed. (New York: Dover, 1946), excerpted in Hick, *Classical and Contemporary Readings in the Philosophy of Religion,* 218, 224.

11. Antony Flew, "Theology and Falsification," in *The Existence of God,* ed. John Hick (New York: Macmillan, 1964), 226.

12. Steven Weinberg, *The First Three Minutes* (New York: Basic Books, 1993), 154.

13. Annie Besant, "Why I Do Not Believe in God," in *An Anthology of Atheism and Rationalism,* ed. Gordon Stein (Amherst, NY: Prometheus, 1980), 37, 30.

14. See J. L. Schellenberg, *Divine Hiddenness and Human Reason* (Ithaca: Cornell University Press, 2006).

15. Gottfried Wilhelm Leibniz, *Theodicy,* excerpted in Hick, *Classical and Contemporary Readings in the Philosophy of Religion,* 69.

16. Voltaire, "Poem on the Lisbon Disaster," in *Selected Works of Voltaire,* ed. Joseph McCabe (London: Watts and Co., 1911), 1.

17. Elie Wiesel, *Night* (New York: Bantam, 1960), 62.

18. J. L. Mackie, "Evil and Omnipotence" *Mind* 64 (1955): 200.

19. See Alvin Plantinga, *God, Freedom, and Evil* (New York: Harper and Row, 1974).

20. Alvin Plantinga, "Transworld Depravity, Transworld Sanctity, and Uncooperative Essences," *Philosophy and Phenomenological Research* 78, no. 1 (January 2009): 191.

21. William L. Rowe, "The Problem of Evil and Some Varieties of Atheism,"

American Philosophical Quarterly 16 (1979): 337; Bruce Russell, "The Persistent Problem of Evil," *Faith and Philosophy* 6 (1989): 123.

22. Rowe, "The Problem of Evil."

23. See Alvin Plantinga and Michael Tooley, *Knowledge of God* (Malden, MA: Blackwell, 2008); and Michael Tooley, "The Problem of Evil," *Stanford Encyclopedia of Philosophy*, August 21, 2009, http://www.plato.stanford.edu/entries/evil/.

24. Matthew Arnold, *Dover Beach and Other Poems* (Mineola, NY: Dover, 1994), 87.

25. William L. Rowe, "The Evidential Argument from Evil: A Second Look," in *The Improbability of God*, ed. Michael Martin and Ricki Monnier (Ithaca, NY: Prometheus, 2006), 275–301.

26. Paul Draper, "Pain and Pleasure: An Evidential Problem for Theists," *Noûs* 23 (1989): 331–50.

27. Charles Darwin, *The Life and Letters of Charles Darwin,* ed. Francis Darwin (London: John Murray, 1888), in *Atheism: A Reader,* ed. S. T. Joshi (Amherst, NY: Prometheus, 2000), 196.

28. See, e.g., Wes Morriston, "The Evidential Argument from Goodness," *Southern Journal of Philosophy* 42 (2004): 87–101.

29. "Crown Him with Many Crowns" (1851), by Matthew Bridges, an English convert to Catholicism.

30. Kurt Vonnegut, "Vonnegut's Blues for America," *Sunday Herald,* January 7, 2006.

31. J. N. Findlay, "Can God's Existence Be Disproved?" *Mind* 57, no. 226 (April 1948): 182.

32. Iris Murdoch, *Metaphysics as a Guide to Morals* (London: Penguin, 1992), 508.

33. Ibid., 414. The *p* in "proof" is capitalized in the original.

34. Ibid., 418.

35. David Bourget and David Chalmers, "The PhilPapers Surveys," PhilPapers, conducted November 2009, http://www.philpapers.org/surveys. Numbers cited include only PhD's or faculty.

36. According to Barry A. Kosmin and Ariela Keysar, "American Religious Identification Survey (ARIS 2008): Summary Report," Program on Public Values, Hartford, 2009, http://www.americanreligionsurvey-aris.org, about 70 percent of Americans believe in a personal God.

CHAPTER 8: NOT DEAD YET

1. Antony Flew, "Sorry to Disappoint, but I'm Still an Atheist!" *Secular Web,* August 31, 2001, http://secweb.infidels.org/?kiosk=articles&id=138.

2. Antony Flew, review of *The Rediscovery of Wisdom* by David Conway, *Philosophy* 76, no. 295 (January 2001): 164–67.

3. Richard Dawkins, lecture at Randolph-Macon Woman's College, October 23, 2006, http://www.youtube.com/watch?v = bEPUn__hYso.

4. Mark Oppenheimer, "The Turning of an Atheist," *New York Times Magazine,* November 4, 2007.

5. Quentin Smith, "Metaphilosophy of Naturalism," *Philo* 4, no. 2 (2001): 195–215.

6. "Modernizing the Case for God," *Time,* April 7, 1980.

7. See Alvin Plantinga, "A Christian Life Partly Lived," in *Philosophers Who Believe: The Spiritual Journeys of 11 Leading Thinkers,* ed. Kelly James Clark (Downers Grove, IL: InterVarsity Press, 1993).

8. See, e.g., Alvin Plantinga, *Warranted Christian Belief* (New York: Oxford University Press, 2000), 213.

9. Collected in chapter 8 of Kelly James Clark, ed., *Readings in the Philosophy of Religion,* 2nd ed. (Peterborough, ON: Broadview Press, 2008).

10. Adapted from Alvin Plantinga, *God, Freedom, and Evil* (New York: Harper and Row, 1974), 111.

11. Kelly James Clark, *Return to Reason* (Grand Rapids, MI: Eerdmans, 1990), 158.

12. Marilynne Robinson, *Gilead* (New York: Picador, 2004), 177.

13. William Alston, "A Philosopher's Way Back to the Faith," in *God and the Philosophers: The Reconciliation of Faith and Reason,* ed. Thomas V. Morris (New York: Oxford University Press, 1994), 29.

14. Plantinga, *God, Freedom, and Evil,* 64.

15. Eleanore Stump, "The Mirror of Evil," in Morris, *God and the Philosophers,* 244, 236.

16. Based on the correlation data in David Bourget and David Chalmers, "The PhilPapers Surveys," PhilPapers, conducted November 2009, http://www.philpapers.org/surveys.

17. Nicholas Wolterstorff, "How Calvin Fathered a Renaissance in Christian Philosophy," lecture at Calvin Theological Seminary, February 2, 2001, http://www.calvin.edu/125th/wolterst.

18. Bourget and Chalmers, "The PhilPapers Surveys."

19. Keith Parsons, "Goodbye to All That," *Secular Outpost,* September 1, 2010, http://secularoutpost.infidels.org/2010/09/goodbye-to-all-that.html.

CHAPTER 9: GOD, HYPOTHESIS

1. From text and videos on http://www.doesgodexist.org.

2. Richard Swinburne, "The Vocation of a Natural Theologian," in *Philosophers Who Believe: The Spiritual Journeys of 11 Leading Thinkers,* ed. Kelly James Clark (Downers Grove, IL: InterVarsity Press, 1993), 199.

3. Ibid., 187.

4. Ibid., 186.

5. For the ensuing discussion, see especially Richard Swinburne, *The Existence of God*, 2nd ed. (Oxford: Oxford University Press, 2004), and his more accessible *Is There a God?* (Oxford: Oxford University Press, 1996).

6. Stephen D. Unwin, *The Probability of God: A Simple Calculation That Proves the Ultimate Truth* (New York: Three Rivers, 2003), 70; Michael Shermer, "God's Number Is Up," *Scientific American*, July 2004; Joe Carter, "The Probability of God," *First Thoughts*, August 18, 2010, http://www.firstthings.com/blogs/firstthoughts/2010/08/18/the-probability-of-god.

7. Robert L. Herrmann, *Sir John Templeton: Supporting Scientific Research for Spiritual Discoveries* (Philadelphia: Templeton Foundation Press, 2004), 137. For an overview of the Templeton Foundation, see Nathan Schneider, "God, Science and Philanthropy," *The Nation*, June 21, 2010.

8. *Charlie Rose*, "An Interview with Sir John Templeton," May 14, 1997, http://www.charlierose.com/view/interview/5555.

9. John Templeton, *The Humble Approach: Scientists Discover God* (Philadelphia: Templeton Foundation Press, 1998), 65.

10. John Templeton Foundation charter (2004), 88.

11. John Templeton, *Possibilities for over One Hundredfold More Spiritual Information* (Philadelphia: Templeton Foundation Press, 2000), 178.

12. Quoted in Paul Davies, *Cosmic Jackpot: Why Our Universe Is Just Right for Life* (New York: Houghton Mifflin Harcourt, 2007), 2.

13. Robin Collins, "The Teleological Argument: An Exploration of the Fine-Tuning of the Universe," in *The Blackwell Companion to Natural Theology*, ed. William Lane Craig and J. P. Moreland (Malden, MA: Blackwell, 2009), 202–81.

14. These next two examples come from John Leslie, *Universes* (London: Routledge, 1989). A recent defense of selection-effect reasoning is Elliott Sober, "The Design Argument," in *The Blackwell Guide to the Philosophy of Religion*, ed. William E. Mann (Malden, MA: Blackwell, 2004), 117–47.

15. Tim Folger, "Science's Alternative to an Intelligent Creator: The Multiverse Theory," *Discover*, December 2008.

16. Christoph Schönborn, "Finding Design in Nature," *New York Times*, July 7, 2005.

17. Lee Strobel, *The Case for a Creator* (Grand Rapids, MI: Zondervan, 2004), 140.

18. Robert J. Spitzer, *New Proofs for the Existence of God: Contributions of Contemporary Physics and Philosophy* (Grand Rapids, MI: Eerdmans, 2010).

19. Justin L. Barrett, *Why Would Anyone Believe in God?* (Lanham, MD: AltaMira Press, 2004), 123.

20. Paul J. Griffiths, review of *Religion Explained: The Evolutionary Origins of Religious Thought*, by Pascal Boyer, *First Things*, January 2002.

21. Todd Murphy, "Spirituality & the Brain," http://www.shaktitechnology.com.

1. Letter to Arthur Greeves, May 25, 1941, quoted in Walter Hooper, *C. S. Lewis: A Companion and Guide* (New York: HarperCollins, 1996), 304.

2. C. S. Lewis, *Mere Christianity* (New York: HarperCollins, 2001), 29.

3. Letter to J. W. Welch of the BBC, February 10, 1941, quoted in Hooper, *C. S. Lewis,* 304.

4. C. S. Lewis, *Surprised by Joy: The Shape of My Early Life* (New York: Harcourt, Brace, 1955), 15.

5. Augustine of Hippo, *Confessions,* trans. Henry Chadwick (Oxford: Oxford University Press, 1991), §1.1. Translation slightly modified for readability.

6. Chad Walsh, "C. S. Lewis, Apostle to the Skeptics," *Atlantic Monthly* (September 1946).

7. See *The Way of the Master,* "The Beauty of a Broken Spirit—Atheism," 2003, episode no. 7, produced by Kirk Cameron and Ray Comfort.

8. Gary Wolf, "The Church of the Non-Believers," *Wired,* November 2006.

9. Terry Eagleton, "Lunging, Flailing, Mispunching," *London Review of Books,* October 19, 2006.

10. Richard Dawkins, *The God Delusion* (New York: Houghton Mifflin, 2006), 77, 81.

11. Barry A. Kosmin and Ariela Keysar, "American Religious Identification Survey (ARIS 2008): Summary Report," Program on Public Values, Hartford, 2009, http://www.americanreligionsurvey-aris.org, 5.

12. William Lane Craig, "Question 155, Subject: Debating," *Reasonable Faith,* http://www.reasonablefaith.org/site/News2?page = NewsArticle&id = 8073.

13. See Jeff Sharlet, *C Street: The Fundamentalist Threat to American Democracy* (New York: Little, Brown, 2010).

14. Atheists of Silicon Valley, "Hundreds of Proofs of God's Existence," http://www.godlessgeeks.com/LINKS/GodProof.htm.

15. Luke Muehlhauser, "Short Story," *What God Taught Me Today* (blog), January 17, 2007, http://godtaughtme.wordpress.com/2007/01/17/short-story/.

TIMELINE OF PROVERS

An incomplete list of people who have proffered proofs about the existence of God with page numbers to locate their names in the text.

John Locke (1632–1704) 38, 89, 131

Gottfried Wilhelm Leibniz (1646–1716) xi, 77–79, 137

Richard Blackmore (1654–1729) 90, 107

Christian Wolff (1679–1754) 95

Joseph Butler (1692–1752) 90–91

Voltaire (1694–1778) 137

David Hume (1711–1776) 85–94, 96, 108, 190

Immanuel Kant (1724–1804) 95–101

Moses Mendelssohn (1729–1786) 94, 98

William Paley (1743–1805) 107–109

Georg Wilhelm Friedrich Hegel (1770–1831) 99–102, 129

John Henry Newman (1801–1890) 14, 52, 177

Charles Darwin (1809–1882) 107–113

Annie Besant (1847–1933) 135–36

Bertrand Russell (1972–1970) 136

Cornelius Van Til (1895–1987) 167

C. S. Lewis (1898–1963) 193–95

J. N. Findlay (1903–1987) 144–45

Kurt Gödel (1906–1978) 78–79

A. J. Ayer (1910–1989) 134–35

Fred Hoyle (1915–2001) 181–82

J. L. Mackie (1917–1981) 138–39, 175

Henry Morris (1918–2006) 113–15

Iris Murdoch (1919–1999) 144–45

Year 2000

William Alston (1921–2009) 159–61

Antony Flew (1923–2010) 131, 135, 149–52, 165

John Polkinghorne (1930–   ) 173, 178

William Rowe (1931–   ) 140–41

Alvin Plantinga (1932–   ) 138–40, 153–56, 161, 163–64, 166–67, 191, 210–11

Richard Swinburne (1934–   ) 173–77

Victor Stenger (1935–   ) 183–84, 213

TABLE OF PROOFS

An incomplete list of proofs for and *against* the existence of God with page numbers to locate proofs in the text.

COSMOLOGICAL	RELATING TO THE EXISTENCE OF THE UNIVERSE
from cause	The cause of the universe must be a God beyond the universe 7, 13, 25, 28, 30, 36, 56, 92, 186, 208
from composition	Since inanimate things cannot combine themselves, there must have been an animate first combiner 23–24, 36
from contingency	There must exist something that is not contingent but exists by its own necessity 26–27, 36, 56, 70, 77, 92, 96–97, 188
from creation	The universe must have been created at some point in time, so it must have a creator 28, 29, 30, 197, 198
from mind	Matter alone cannot produce a mind, and because minds exist, a disembodied divine mind must have existed before matter 10, 89
from motion	The nature of motion in the world points to an unmoved mover 10, 13, 25, 36, 56
from parsimony	*The universe is explainable without God, so it is simpler not to believe in God's existence* 184
from regression	*God is not complete explanation because the question remains of what caused God* 92, 204
from something	A God is the best explanation for why there is something rather than nothing 77, 175, 188, 197

DIALECTICAL	RELATING TO PROCESSES OF REFLECTION
from accumulation	Together, several partially effective arguments add up to assure the reasonableness of God's existence 55–57, 160, 176–77, 227
from completeness	God is the best explanation of the universe available that is essentially complete, so it is most reasonable to believe that God exists 183–84
from consequences	The consequences of not believing could be so drastic that one has no choice but to believe God exists 79–80, 97, 114, 119, 153, 197
from diversity	*There are so many diverse opinions about God and gods that they refute each other* 70–71, 89, 131
from progress	*More and more things that were once explained in terms of God are now understood through science, making God unnecessary* 184
from red herring	*What theistic arguments actually point to is not the traditional God* 92, 144–45, 204, 217
from reductionism	*Religious beliefs are by-products of human psychology, so they are not evidence that God exists* 134–35, 189–90, 203
from refutation	*The traditional arguments for God's existence fail, so God probably does not exist* 93, 135, 136, 138, 217
from synthesis	Together, several kinds proof add up to a single, conclusive proof 59, 100–102

HISTORICAL	RELATING TO THE HISTORICAL RECORD
from correspondence	Modern science confirms accounts of nature in sacred scripture, so scripture must be true, and the God it refers to must exist 113–14, 119–20, 171–72, 187, 199
from evils	*There have been so many unjustified evils in the world, God probably doesn't exist* 92, 137–42, 161–62
from higher criticism	*Religious scriptures are evidently human creations, not divine revelation, so the God they refer to is probably also a human creation* 218
from miracles	Miracles that violate the rules of nature have occurred, so there must have been a transcendent God to enact them 149, 151, 163, 208
from scripture	Sacred scripture points to the existence of God, and scripture is infallible, so God must exist 23, 113

ONTOLOGICAL	RELATING TO THE CONCEPTS OF GOD AND EXISTENCE
from divine imprint	The idea of an infinite God would be thinkable to our minds only if God actually exists and imprinted it there 67, 92
from evil	*The existence of God is incompatible with the evil that exists in the world* 137–40, 161
from incoherence	*The concept of God is incoherent, so it is meaningless to say that God exists* 134–35, 204
from infinity	The nature of the infinite in mathematics implies the existence of an infinite God 13, 70
from necessity	The concept of God is necessary by virtue of itself, and therefore God must exist 49, 78, 145, 155, 227–29
from the mere idea	*The idea of God, in principle, cannot tell us anything about whether a God exists in reality* 48, 92, 96
from perfection	A nonexistent God would be less perfect than an existent one, so if God is perfect, God must exist 47–48, 67, 78, 101–102, 155

PHENOMENOLOGICAL	RELATING TO DIRECT EXPERIENCE
from aesthetics	The concept or revelation of God is beautiful, and what is beautiful must be true 120–22
from conscience	People have an innate moral sense, and there must be a God to implant it 145
from consciousness	Human consciousness implies the existence of a conscious God 89, 98, 175
from desire	People innately feel a desire for the transcendent, so there must be a transcendent God to satisfy that desire 153, 194–95
from divine power	The power of nature is so great and the power of people so small that there must be a powerful God behind nature 90
from experience	People have had direct experience of God, so God must exist 92, 159–60, 176, 208
from free will	People have free will, and the best explanation for it is the existence of God 175
from persons	*Since all the persons we know of have bodies, there is no reason to think there could be a God without a body* 175
from skepticism	*Not enough can possibly be known from experience that would prove the existence of a God* 92, 95, 96, 142

SOCIOLOGICAL	RELATING TO HUMAN SOCIETY
from general consent	Most people in the world throughout history have believed in God, so God must exist 10
from hiddenness	*The reasonable, open-minded people who do not accept God's existence stand as evidence that a good God who wants to be believed in does not exist* 136
from philosophical consent	Philosophers across time and place have developed ideas consistent with God, so reason universally points toward God's existence 23–24, 100, 227

TELEOLOGICAL	RELATING TO THE ORDER AND DESIGN OF NATURE
from fine-tuning	If natural laws were slightly different, life would not be possible, so they must have been designed by a God seeking to create living things 181–86, 199, 203–4, 208
from intelligent design	Organisms in nature appear to have been intelligently designed, so they must have had an intelligent designer 90, 92, 107–109, 116, 117, 119, 197, 199, 203
from language	Humans could never have learned language without a God to teach it to them 23
from providence	The order of nature seems to be orchestrated by a purposeful intelligence, which suggests that such an intelligence exists 10, 57, 90, 91–92, 106, 107–109, 119, 123, 198, 199, 227
from unintelligent design	*Nature is so filled with imperfections and mishaps that it cannot possibly have had an intelligent designer* 117, 142

TRANSCENDENTAL	RELATING TO THE RATIONALITY OF THE WORLD
from degree	The imperfection we notice in things suggests the existence of perfect being against which we compare them 7, 17, 41–42, 56–57, 78, 145, 188
from human reason	*It is possible to build a philosophical system that does not depend on belief in God, so such belief is unnecessary* 108–109, 134, 135, 138, 145–46, 167–68, 184, 188
from moral order	The world is suffused with a moral order, which implies that there must exist a moral God 23, 97, 145, 160, 193–94, 208
from universal reason	There could be no laws discoverable in morality, logic, mathematics, or science without a divine lawgiver, so there must be such a God 17, 68, 98, 155, 160, 167, 176, 217

TEXT
11/14 Garamond Premier Pro

DISPLAY
Univers

DESIGN AND COMPOSITION
Lia Tjandra

PRINTING AND BINDING
Maple Press